IMAGES
of America
YOUNTVILLE

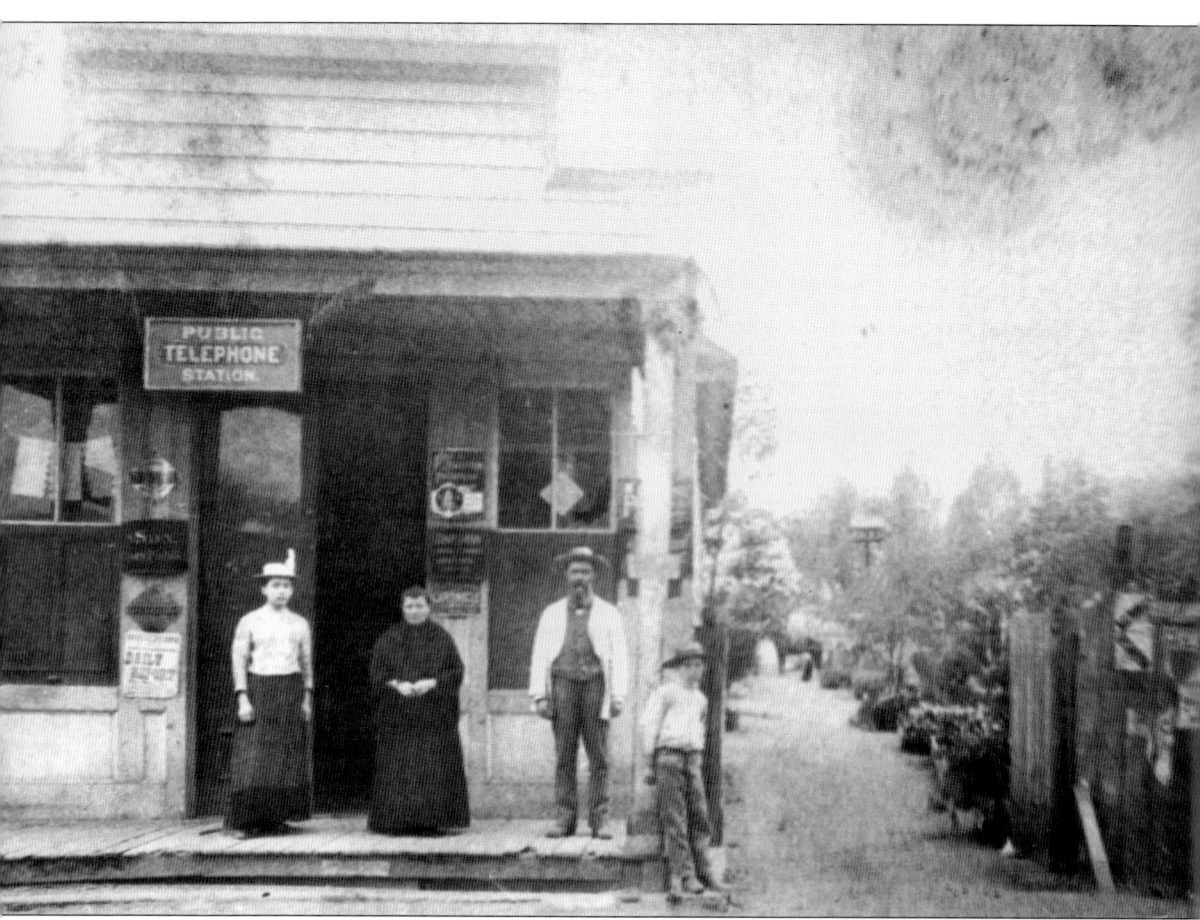

Like many a great town, Yountville had humble beginnings. This photograph shows the location of Yountville's telephone station as it appeared in 1892. Over time, the station moved around to several different businesses throughout Yountville. This photograph shows the storefront of Simon Sax on the west side of Yount Street, approximately 100 feet south of Madison Street. Pictured from left to right are young Anna Sax; her mother, also named Anna Sax; Simon Sax Sr.; and his son, Simon Sax Jr. Later in life, young Anna Sax would marry Johann Wichels and produce a son, John Wichels. Mr. Wichels wrote extensively about the history of both Yountville and Napa. (Courtesy of John Wichels and the Napa Historical Society.)

ON THE COVER: Longtime Yountville residents George "Boots" Dulinsky, his son George "Bud" Dulinsky, and an unidentified gentleman stand on the porch of the Old Depot looking west toward the present-day location of Chandon Winery. Note the absence of Highway 29. (Courtesy of Rick Enos.)

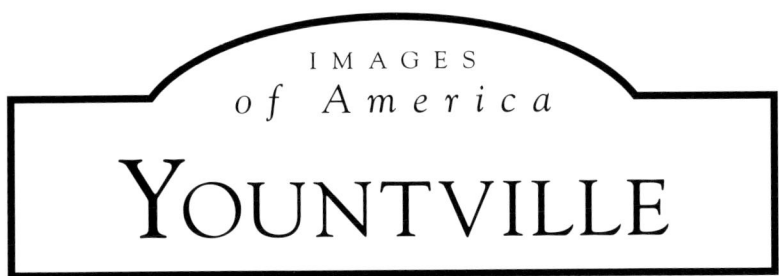

IMAGES
of America
YOUNTVILLE

Pat Alexander and the Napa Valley Museum

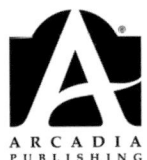

ARCADIA
PUBLISHING

Copyright © 2009 by Pat Alexander and the Napa Valley Museum
ISBN 978-0-7385-6965-9

Published by Arcadia Publishing
Charleston SC, Chicago IL, Portsmouth NH, San Francisco CA

Printed in the United States of America

Library of Congress Control Number: 2008936807

For all general information contact Arcadia Publishing at:
Telephone 843-853-2070
Fax 843-853-0044
E-mail sales@arcadiapublishing.com
For customer service and orders:
Toll-Free 1-888-313-2665

Visit us on the Internet at www.arcadiapublishing.com

*This book is lovingly dedicated to the memory of
Margaret Ann Flattum (1939–2008).*

Contents

Acknowledgments 6

Introduction 7

1. Yountville's Natural History and Early Settlement 9
2. Pioneer Days 19
3. The Veterans Home of California 51
4. Early 20th Century 61
5. Mid-20th Century 71
6. Yountville Today 113

ACKNOWLEDGMENTS

Fours years ago, I was first encouraged to author this book by my colleague and friend Lauren Coodley, dean of history at the Napa Valley College. Professor Coodley had originally suggested that I pursue an internship at the Napa Valley Museum, and today I have the pleasure of serving as the curator of education. The Napa Valley Museum has a treasured collection of historical artifacts, archives, and photographic images. Many thanks go to Rick Deragon, executive director, for opening the doors of the Napa Valley Museum to a community who loves local history. I have made extensive use of the unpublished manuscripts of Yountville's historian, John Wichels. Much of the historical documentation in this collection comes from his outstanding research and scholarship. A special thank-you goes to Kristie Sheppard and the Napa Historical Society. Kristie, Amanda, and a core of volunteers provided a treasure trove of pictures and information for this book. There were also several organizations who greatly contributed to this book: Marcella McCormack and Bart Buechner along with the help of Carol DeBell and Nancy Bueno of the Veterans Home, the Town of Yountville, V Marketplace, and especially Rick Enos of Compadres Bar and Grill.

Yountville is so much more than just an assemblage of historic buildings and structures. Our town's history was created from countless men, women, and children who lived and eventually died here. Some of these lives will fade from our personal and collective memory, and yet others are preserved through treasured photographs and family albums. The following people have shared their pictures and recollections, helping to reveal Yountville's true charm and character. This book would not be possible without the kindness, patience, and generosity of Barbara and Bud Dulinsky, Lee Hart, Phyllis Vallerga, Toni Porterfield, Edgar Beard, Vernon Flock, John Callison, Jim Duff, Neilann Martinez, Jim Atwood, Virginia Crowe, Sue Cole, Mindy Jordan, Maxine Bardessono, Eric Knight, Liz Herr, Liz Stone, Gene Tonascia, Denise Jackson, and Maryanne Stapleton. A huge thank-you goes to my brother-in-law Paul Slavin for writing the introduction—a job well done! Finally, I am deeply grateful to my children, Alora and Aren, and especially to my husband, Stuart. I never could have completed this book without Stuart's research, writing, and editorial assistance. Thanks, honey!

INTRODUCTION

The town of Yountville, nestled in the middle of the beautiful Napa Valley, is located in an area so favored by nature it has been justly termed an "American Eden." Here the rich volcanic soil is warmed by abundant California sunshine; watered by stream, river, and winter rain; and cooled by the kiss of Pacific fog. For thousands of years before the arrival of Europeans, the valley was home to indigenous people who hunted the plentiful elk and deer, fished for steelhead, and avoided the grizzly bears.

The first white settler in the valley was an intrepid, well-traveled frontiersman named George Yount. In 1836, Yount obtained title to the Caymus Rancho, a land grant of 11,814 acres, from the Mexican government. He built a two-story log blockhouse, cleared land, and planted crops—including the valley's first vineyards—and welcomed subsequent settlers with legendary hospitality and sound advice.

In the early 1850s, a town was laid out on land belonging to Yount and several other men who had sizable holdings in the area. It was at first called Sebastopol, but two years after George Yount's death in 1867, it was renamed in his honor. Early Yountville businesses included a store and a blacksmith. One of the oldest buildings, the White House Hotel, served the community from 1857 until it was destroyed by fire in 1903.

Yountville continued to attract newcomers to the area, and some European immigrants noted the similarities between the Napa Valley and the wine-producing areas of their homelands. In 1870, Gottlieb Groezinger planted a vineyard and built a large stone winery in town.

The California Veterans Home was established in 1884 on a 550-acre tract of wooded, rolling hills on the west side of town. In addition to serving the medical and social needs of Civil War veterans, the home offered steady, long-term employment to Yountville residents.

Throughout the early 20th century, Yountville remained a quiet, rural enclave, untouched by developments in nearby San Francisco or the surrounding counties. Residents lived in small, comfortable houses surrounded by gardens and flowerbeds, set along deeply shaded streets. Neighbors knew one another, and a sense of small-town community prevailed. This leisurely pace began to quicken in the early 1960s with a new wave of settlers, young vintners determined to make world-class wines, and other professionals fleeing the cities for the "quiet life." Yountville adapted to new times, welcoming the newcomers' energy, ideas, and lifestyles, while maintaining the town's traditional ambience and character.

So successful has this transition been that today you can stroll through Yountville past world-famous restaurants, fine shops, and galleries (some housed in Gottlieb's original stone winery), and—by merely lifting your eyes to the surrounding mountains and hillside vineyards—imagine yourself having a glass of homemade red with old George Yount himself.

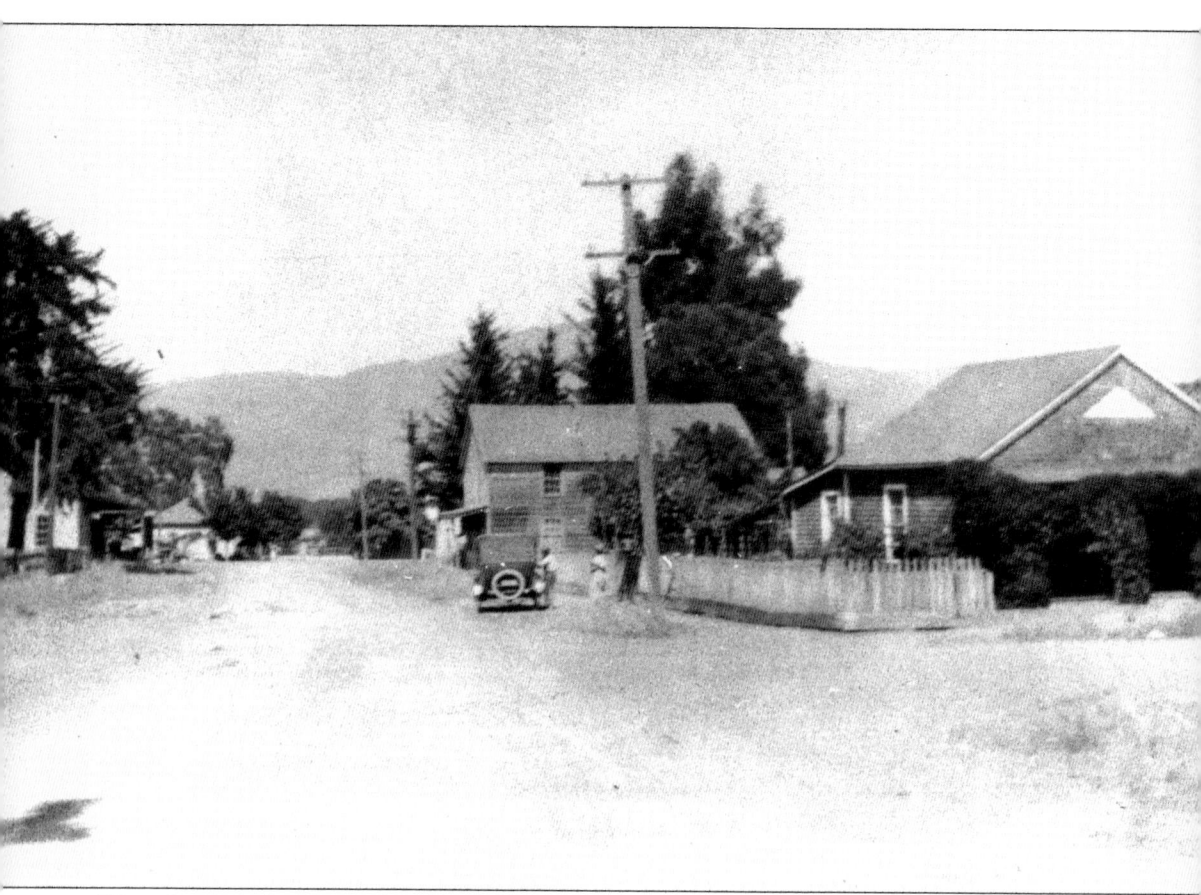

This photograph, taken around the 1920s, shows Madison Street looking east. The road to the right is Jefferson Street. (Courtesy of Lee Hart.)

One

YOUNTVILLE'S NATURAL HISTORY AND EARLY SETTLEMENT

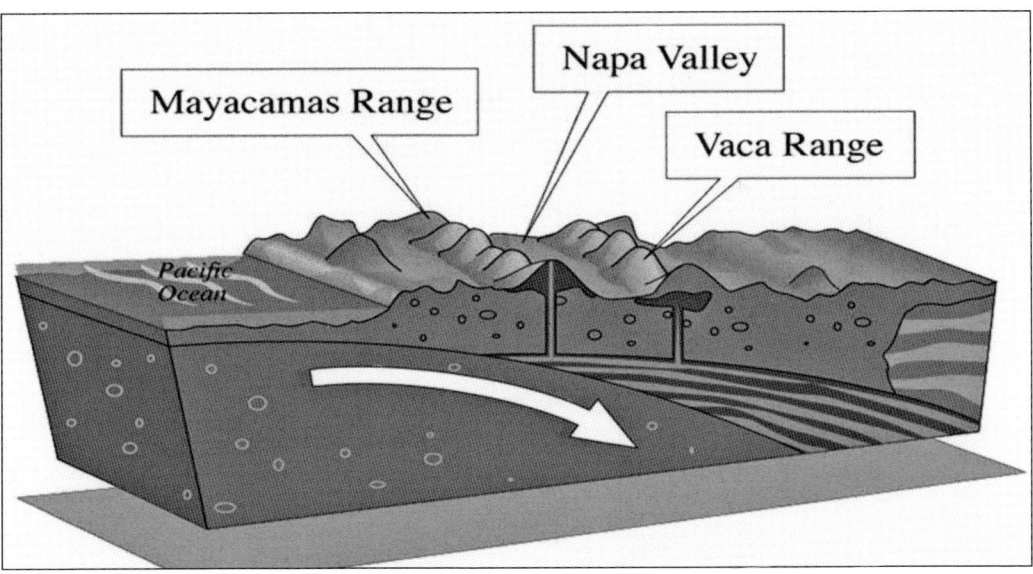

Located on the 38th Parallel, approximately 57 miles north of San Francisco, the town of Yountville occupies the approximate geographic center of the Napa Valley. As part of the California Coast Range, the Yountville Valley floor is bordered by Atlas Peak to the east and Mount Veeder to the west. With seasonal temperatures averaging from 50 degrees in the winter and 80 degrees in the summer, Yountville residents and visitors alike enjoy ideal living conditions. Geologists have revealed that the landforms of Yountville and the surrounding Napa Valley are the result of an ongoing process called plate tectonics, in which two enormous crustal plates, the Pacific and North American plates, have collided over time. For 100 million years, large portions of seabed have been uplifted into mountain ranges, creating a series of peaked folds with valleys sandwiched between. Added to this landscape are vast regions of igneous rock deposited by volcanic activity that occurred between two and five million years ago. (Courtesy of Dr. John Livingston.)

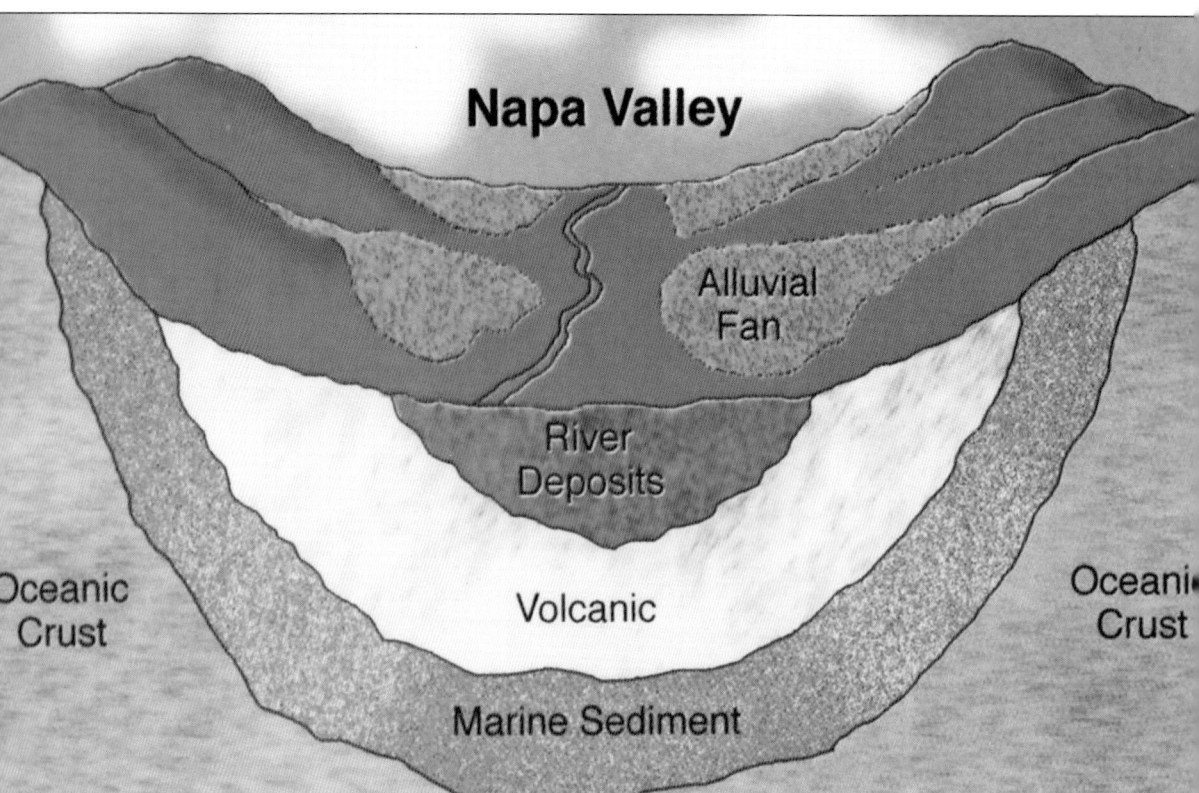

According to local geologist John Livingston, the tectonic collision of both oceanic and continental plates created a U-shaped fold along the floor and sides of the Napa Valley. This syncline shape has four layers that consist of oceanic crust, marine sedimentary rock, volcanic rock, and, at the surface, Napa River alluvial soil deposits. Over millions of years, this unique mixture of inorganic and organic soils created one of the most fertile valleys in the world that would later sustain large plant, animal, and human populations. (Courtesy of Dr. John Livingston.)

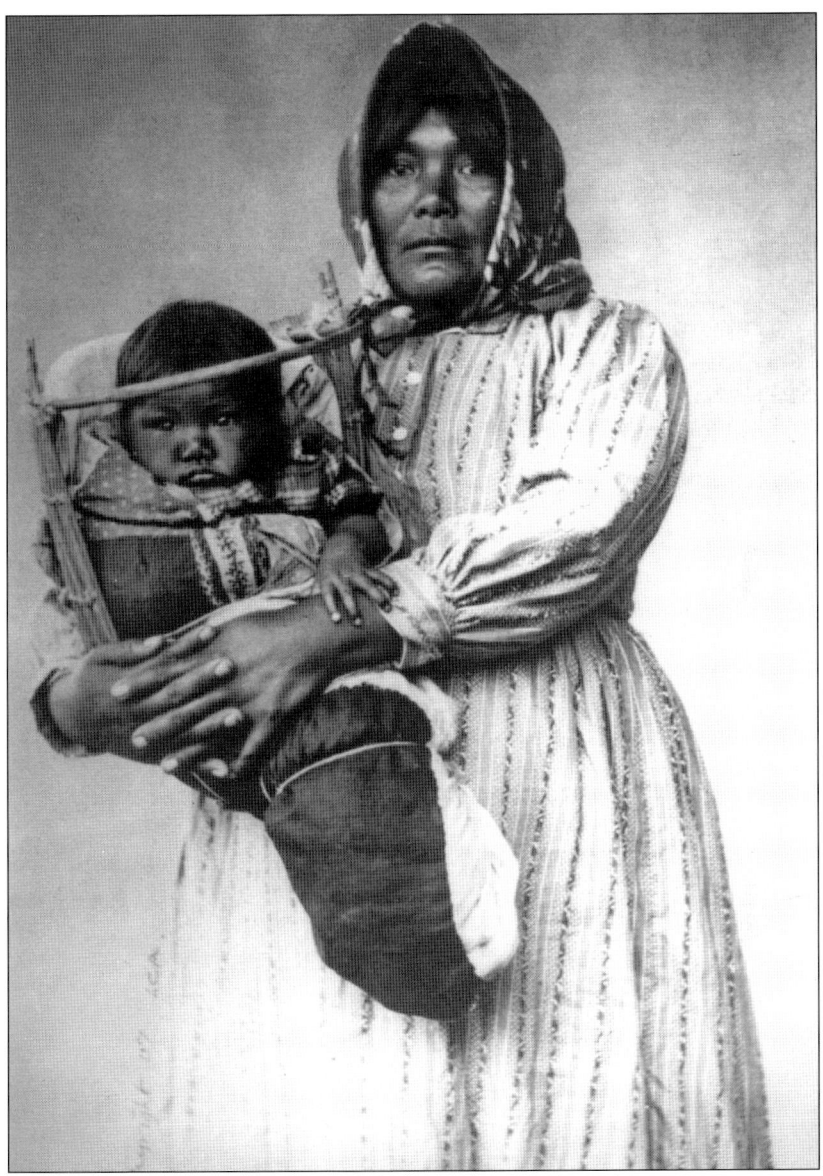

Yountville's temperate weather, rich soils, and serene environs have been attracting visitors to the area for thousands of years. Known as the Caymus (Kaimus) or, as they called themselves, "the People," the inhabitants of this area lived for thousands of years by the banks of the Napa River fishing for salmon, trout, otters, and fowl. The Caymus people hunted deer, elk, and rabbit, as well as raccoon and squirrels. Like many other California indigenous people, the Caymus collected, processed, and ate several varieties of acorns, especially those of the Black Oak tree. The earliest inhabitants of Yountville formed the Caymus village and lived for thousands of years before the arrival of European settlers. In the early 1800s, Mexican settlers encountered this indigenous population and called them *Guapo*, the Spanish word for handsome, courageous, and brave. The word Guapo, unfamiliar to many of the non-Spanish-speaking early settlers, became commonly pronounced as "Wappo" to describe Yountville's original inhabitants. Taken in Calistoga, this rare *c.* 1907 photograph shows a Wappo woman holding her baby. Note the intricate artisanship of the cradle basket. (Courtesy of the Sharpsteen Museum.)

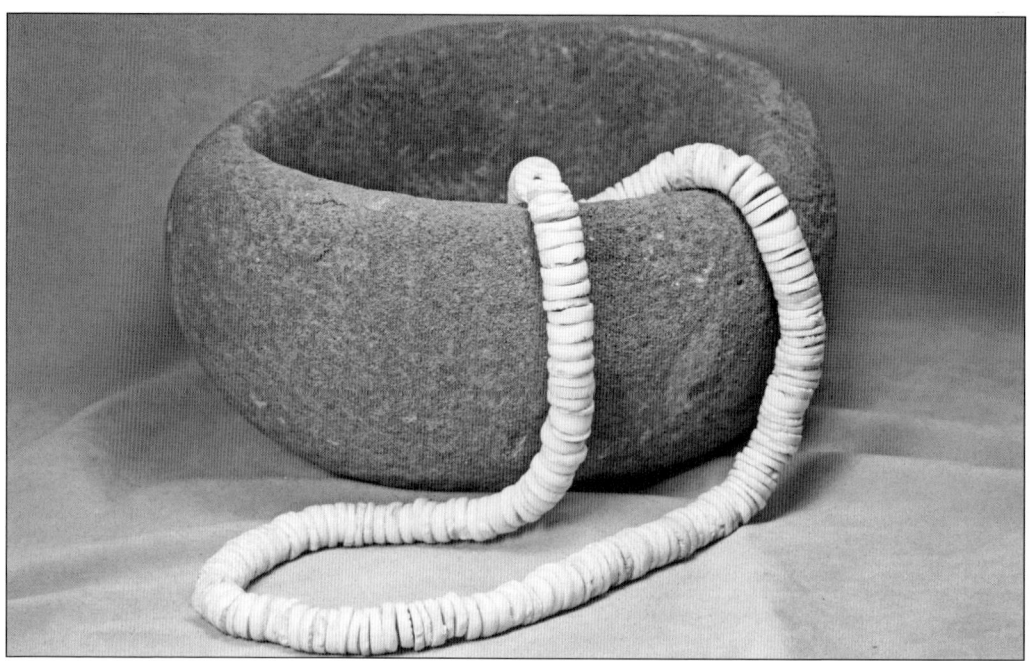

This photograph shows a fine example of a 20-inch clamshell disk necklace. In addition to ceremonial decorations that included the use of feathers, wood, bone, and body painting with colorful earth and charcoal, the Wappo wore bracelets and necklaces made from a variety of mineral and shell materials. While abalone shells were popular throughout much of Northern California, this type of shell jewelry was not as common in the Napa Valley. (Courtesy of the Napa Valley Museum; photograph by Stuart Alexander.)

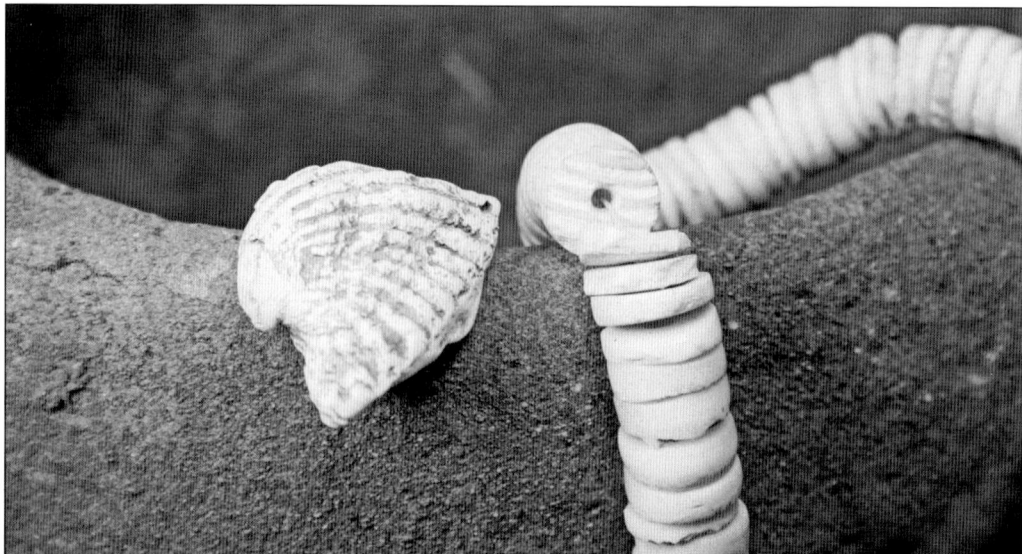

Disk beads made from clamshells were used by the Wappo and are known from examples that date to several thousand years old. The Wappo probably obtained finished clamshell disk beads and raw clamshell material through seasonal treks to the coast and through trade with the Clear Lake Pomo and Coast Miwok Indians. (Courtesy of the Napa Valley Museum; photograph by Stuart Alexander.)

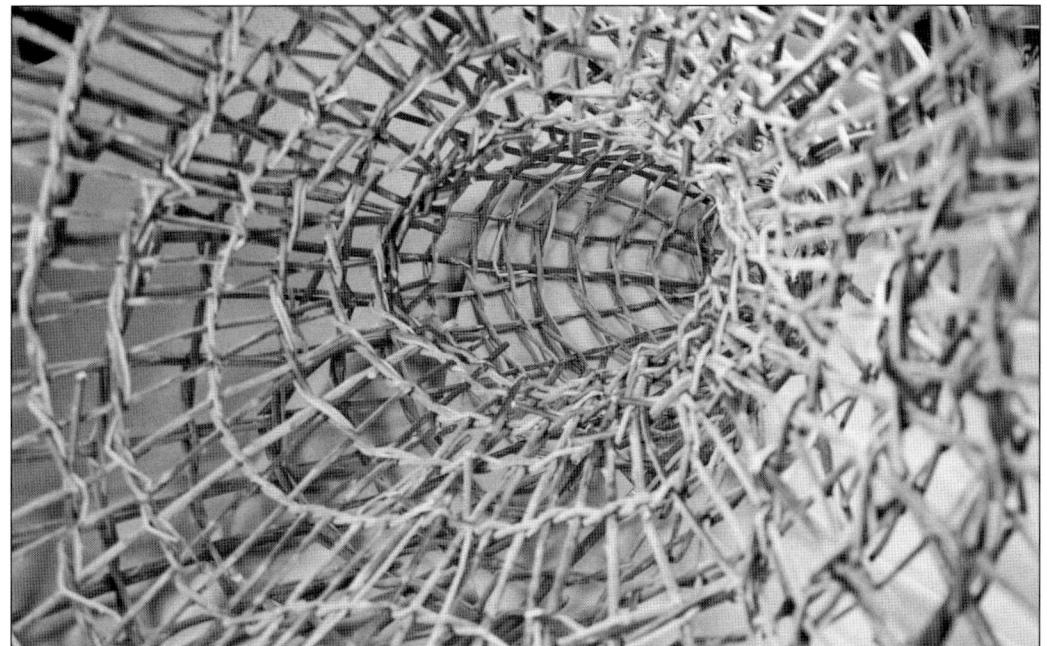

The Wappo employed spears, nets, and traps to collect fish from local streams and waters and fluted basket traps to catch small birds. One fishing method was to place a woven wicker basket trap into a narrow or dammed area of a waterway to drive nearby fish into the trap. Efficient restraining baffles woven within the basket trap prevented trapped fish from swimming back out of the trap, and sometimes a plant known as soap root (*Chlorogalum pomeridianum*) was introduced into the water to stun the fish. (Collection of the Napa Valley Museum; photograph by Stuart Alexander.)

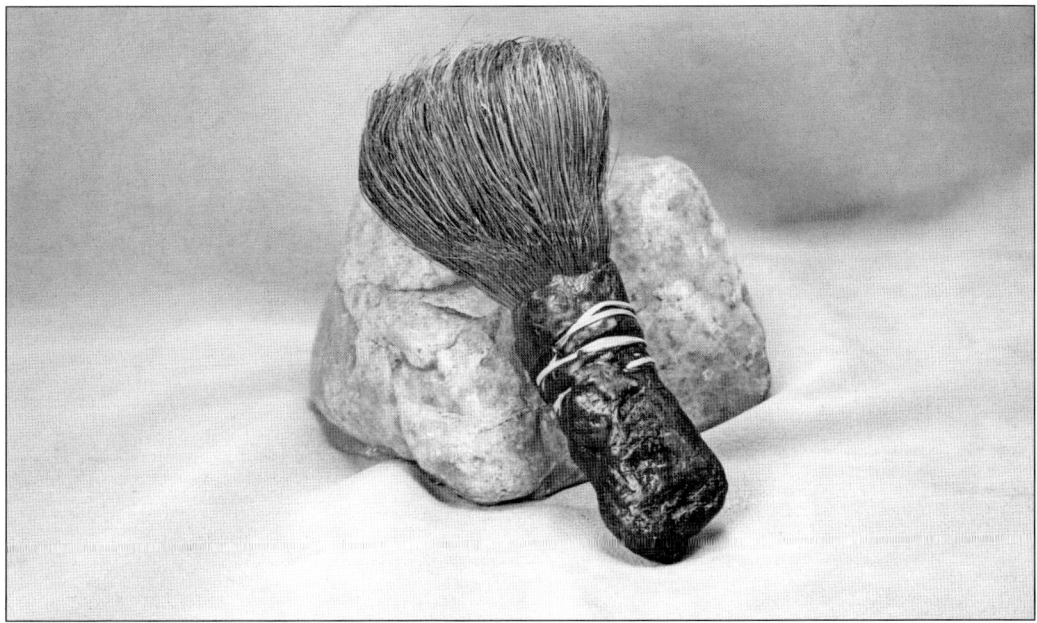

The soap root pictured above is one of the artifacts found in the Wappo Native American Trunk Program. (Collection of the Napa Valley Museum; photograph by Stuart Alexander.)

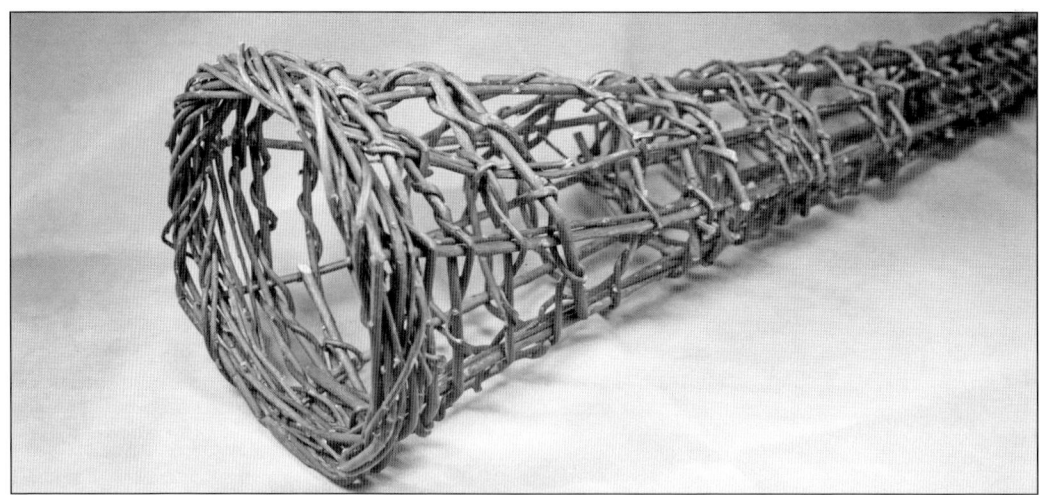

While the activity of basket weaving was typically undertaken by Wappo women, men conducted the weaving of fishing traps, nets, and other coarse weaving projects. Pictured is a fluted basket trap for catching small birds. (Collection of the Napa Valley Museum; photograph by Stuart Alexander.)

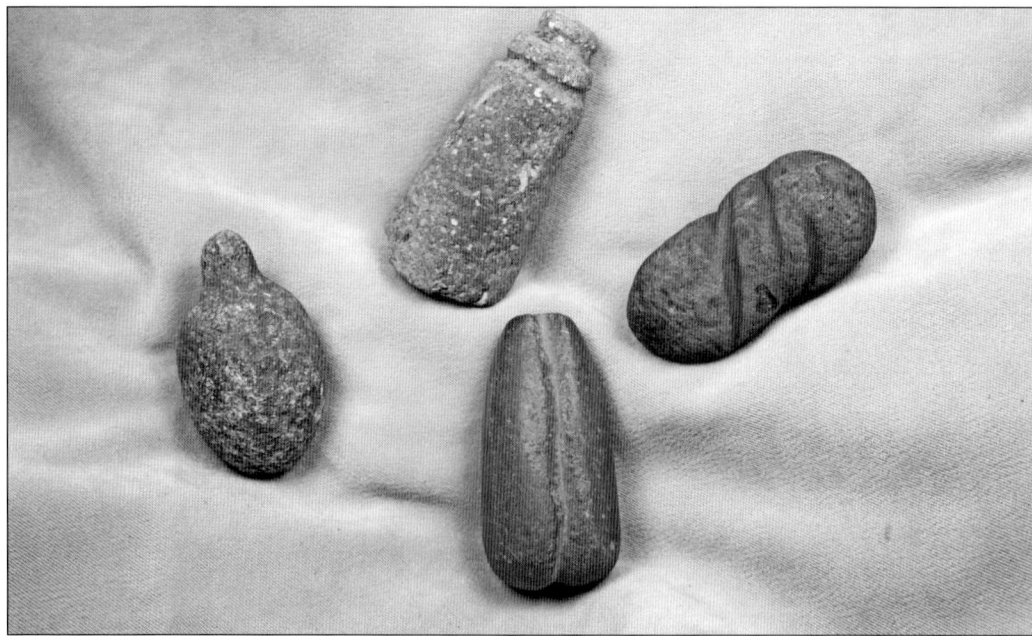

Carefully ground and crafted stones found in a variety of shapes and carved patterns, which do not appear to have had a utilitarian use for the Wappo, are known under the general term of "charmstones." Some insight into these unusual and singular stones is provided in an ethnographic record published by L. G. Yates in 1889. Yates described his discussions with an elderly Wappo man who stated that the plummet-shaped stones were hung from poles over the bank of local fishing holes or suspended in mountainous areas where hunting was favorable. Similarly, the stones were sometimes placed on rock ledges or mountain peaks. The belief was that the stones, possessing mystical properties, traveled through the water during the night to drive fish to favorite fishing places, or through the air to drive land game toward good hunting grounds. (De La Cruz Collection courtesy of the Napa Valley Museum; photograph by Stuart Alexander.)

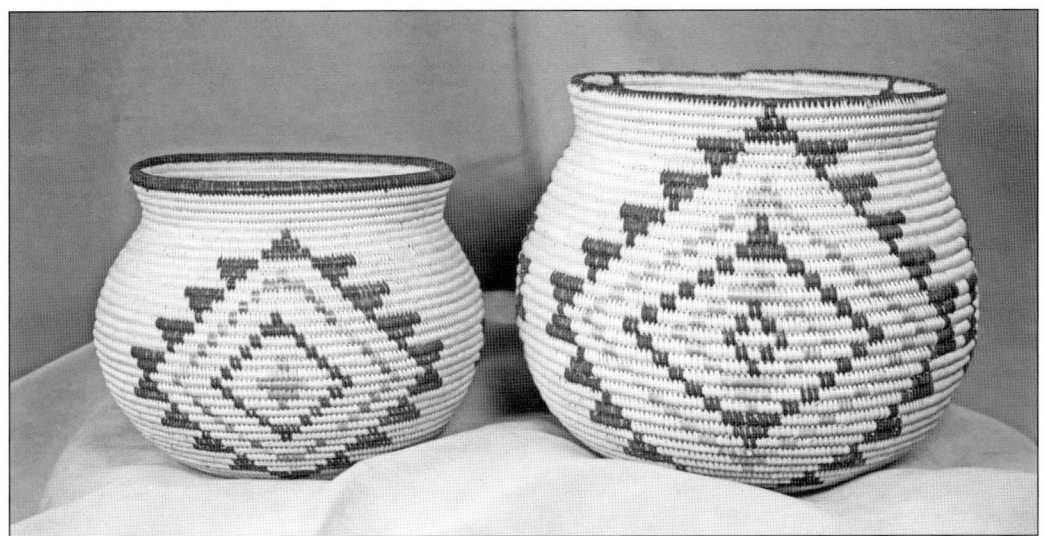

Wappo women were primarily responsible for weaving the basketry used in daily domestic life, and they produced finely made baskets used as plates, cups, pots, and storage baskets. Cooking baskets were so finely woven that they could hold water; the water-holding integrity of these baskets was sometimes further increased by lining the inside of the baskets with pitch. Both men and women used large conical baskets, carried on the shoulders and supported with the aid of a headband, for transport of heavy loads. Babies were protected in basket cradles while carried on their mother's shoulders, and the cradles could be leaned against an object when the mother needed to set the baby down while conducting her daily activities. Wappo baskets were made from locally collected materials that included willow stems and bark, sedge roots, marsh grass, and digger pine roots. The exquisite baskets pictured above are carefully stored in the archives of the Napa Valley Museum. The pictured baskets are believed to have come from the eastern Mojave region of Southern California and are attributed to the Chemehuevi. (Courtesy of the Napa Valley Museum; photograph by Stuart Alexander.)

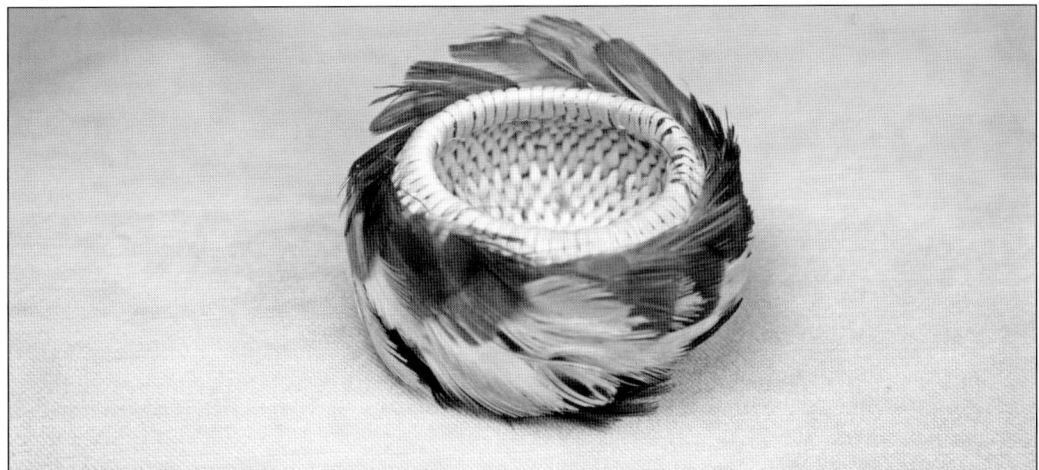

Small, tightly woven miniature baskets that ranged in size from less than a dime to a few inches in diameter were sometimes referred to as thimble or finger baskets. These tiny baskets were usually given as gifts to demonstrate the skill of the maker. This perfectly woven example of a feather basket is attributed to maker Elsie Allen. (Courtesy of the Napa Valley Museum; photograph by Stuart Alexander.)

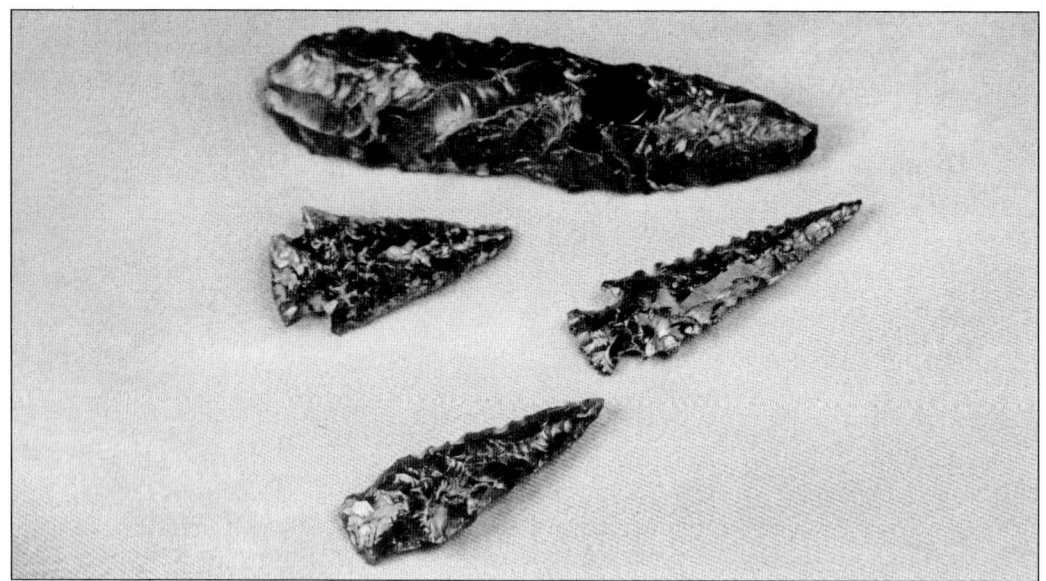

Chipped stone tools and weapons were extensively crafted and used by the Wappo, with most of the chipped stone artifacts found in the Napa Valley made from black obsidian. The source of this obsidian is primarily from the area of Glass Mountain, near the modern city of St. Helena. Quality obsidian such as the material from Glass Mountain was highly sought after and traded in early times, and obsidian from this source has been found in many ancient sites throughout California. Chipped stone tools, including spear and arrow points, knives, scrapers, and large ceremonial blades, were manufactured by Wappo men through two processes: percussion flaking, where stone flakes were struck from a rock core, and pressure flaking, where small pieces of stone were pushed away from the obsidian object by using a pushing tool such as an antler tip. In some cases, if obsidian was not readily available or if another stone was preferred for a particular application, some chipped stone tools were made of chert, basalt, and sandstone. (Both images contain objects from the De La Cruz and Callizo Collections courtesy of the Napa Valley Museum; photograph by Stuart Alexander.)

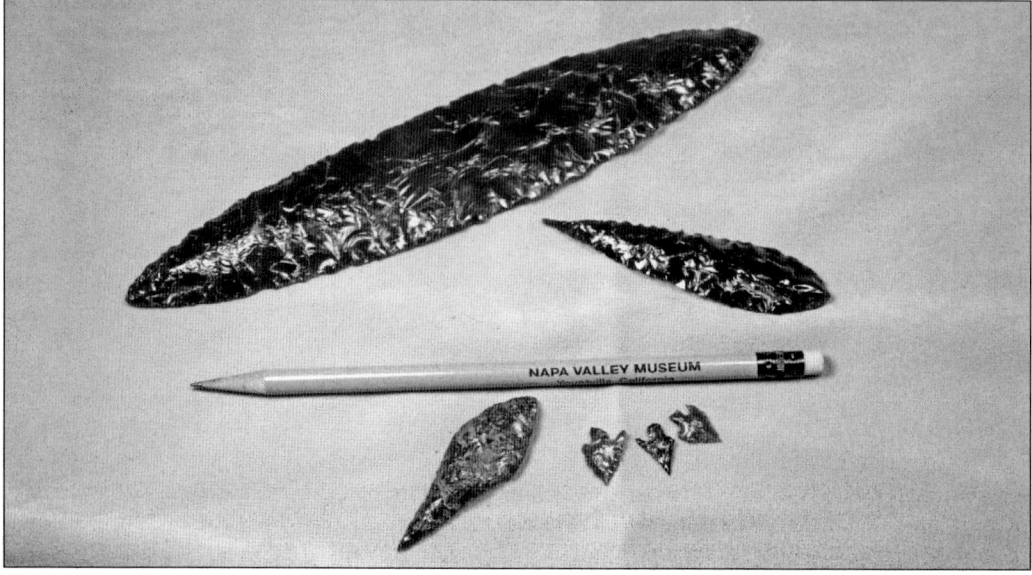

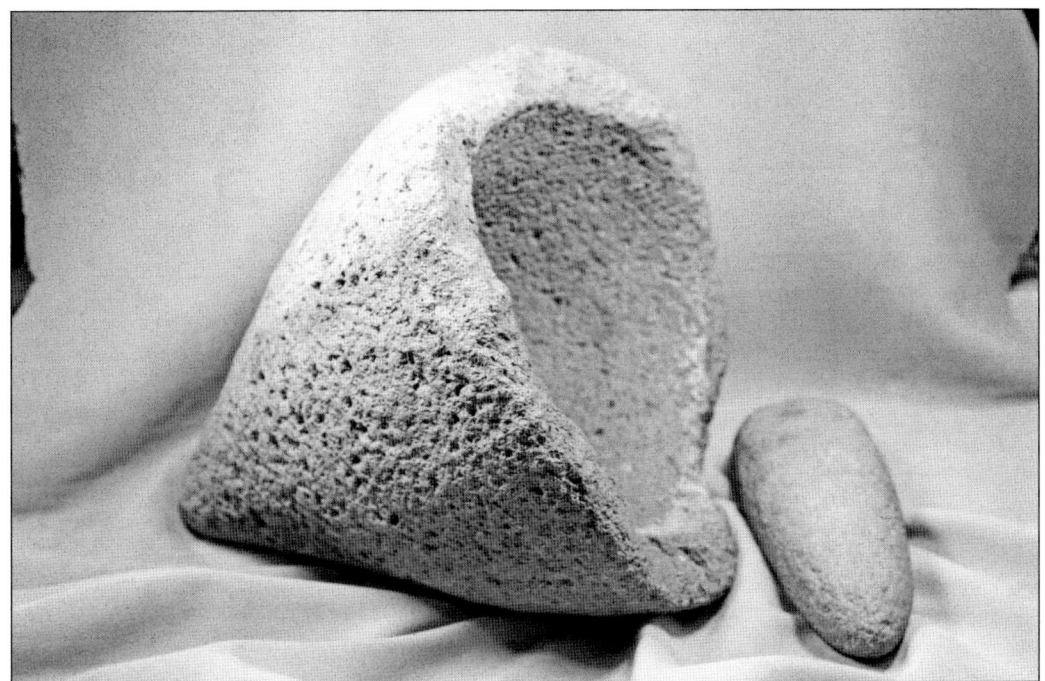

Ground stone artifacts consist of tools and other objects used by the Wappo in daily living that were shaped through abrasion, or grinding, of a base stone material. Bowl-shaped mortars and their associated grinder pestles, represented by both permanent bedrock mortars and portable individual mortars, are some of the most publically recognized of the Wappo ground stone artifacts. (Both images courtesy of the Napa Valley Museum; photograph by Stuart Alexander.)

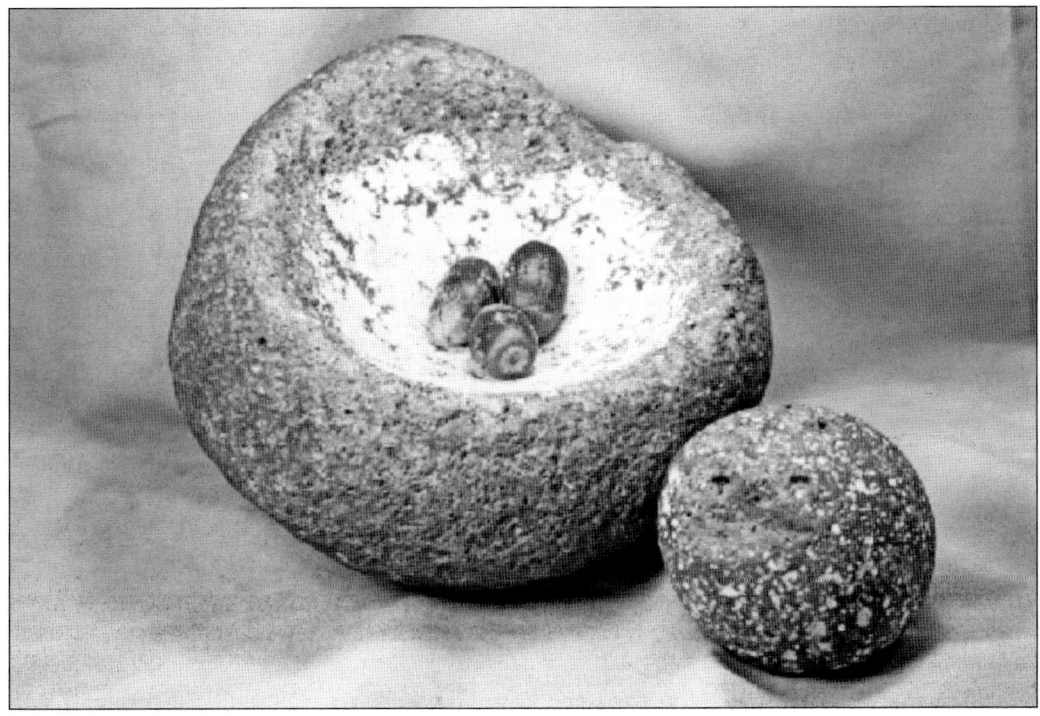

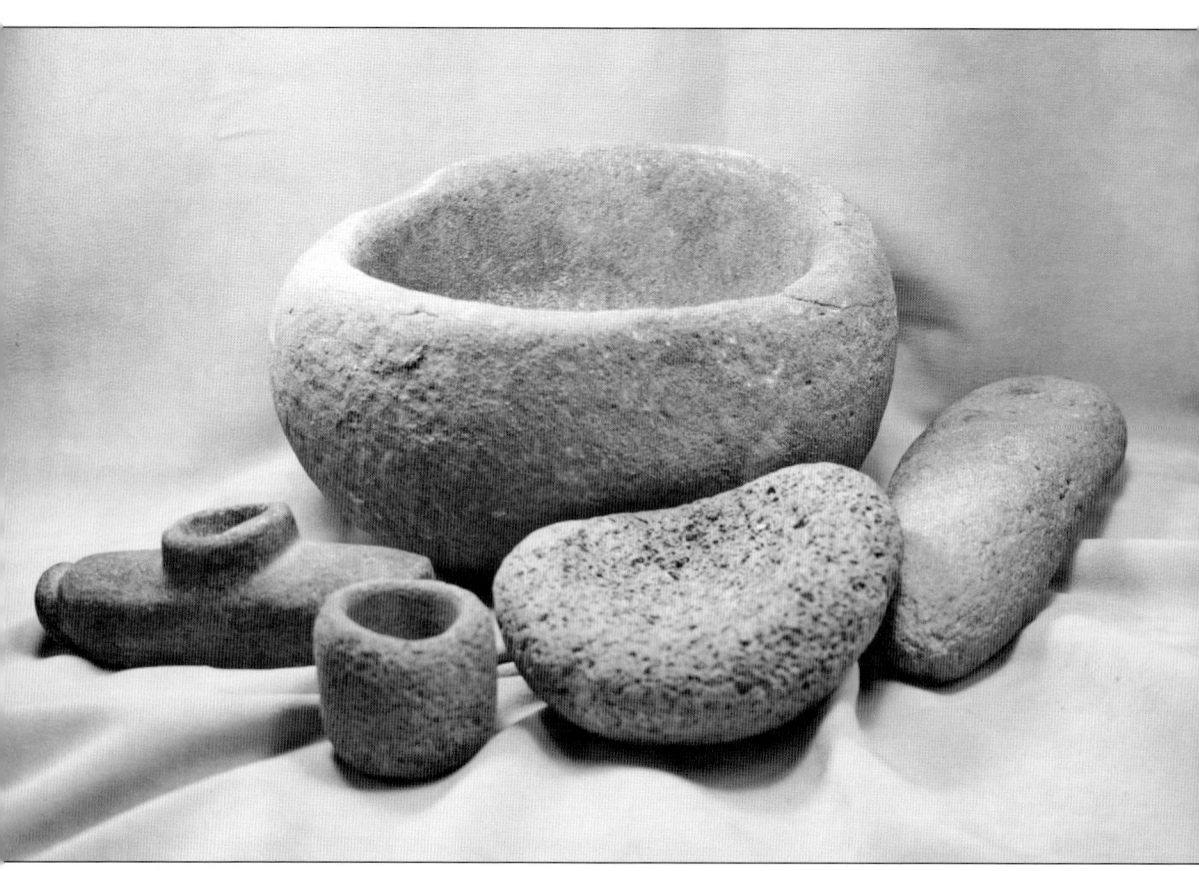

Hard black basalt stone appears to have been preferred by the Wappo for both mortars and pestles, but sandstone and other rock was sometimes used. Mortars were extensively used to grind acorn meal and were also used to grind pigments, extract plant juices, and pulverize bone and dried meat. Other ground stone objects included boiling and cooking bowls, pipes, saws, finger bowls, and slabs for bead grinding. (Courtesy of the Napa Valley Museum; photograph by Stuart Alexander.)

Two

Pioneer Days

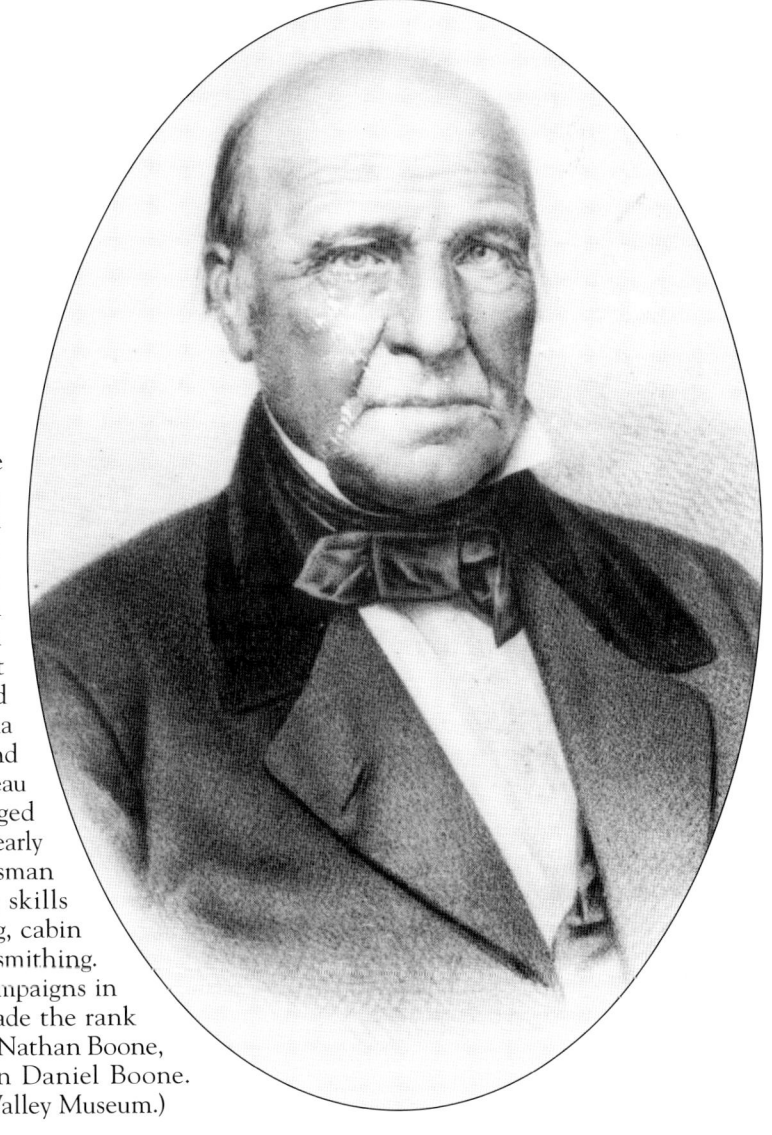

George Yount, namesake of the town of Yountville, was the first non-Mexican settler to receive a Mexican land grant in the Napa Valley. Born to Jacob and Amarilla Yount in 1794, the Yount family (originally spelled Jundt) left North Carolina when George was 10 and migrated to Cape Girardeau in Missouri. In the rugged wilderness, Yount gained early experience as a frontiersman and trapper, acquiring skills such as hunting, logging, cabin construction, and blacksmithing. He served on several campaigns in the War of 1812 and made the rank of lieutenant under Col. Nathan Boone, the son of frontiersman Daniel Boone. (Courtesy of the Napa Valley Museum.)

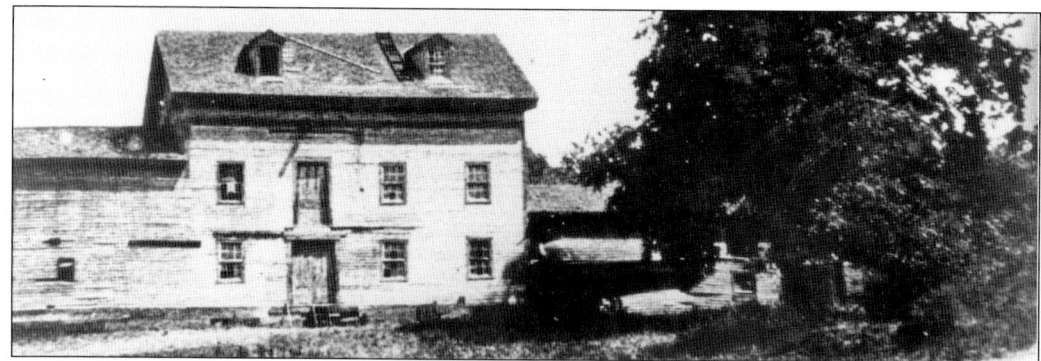

Intent on improving his land, Yount began construction of a two-story log blockhouse and adobe dwelling in 1837. With the assistance of the local Caymus Indians, Yount planted crops and vineyards, raised cattle and sheep, and later constructed a gristmill. Yount's Star of the Pacific Premium Mill produced up to 30 barrels of flour per day. This photograph was taken around 1910, shortly before the demolition of the mill. (Courtesy of the Napa Historical Society.)

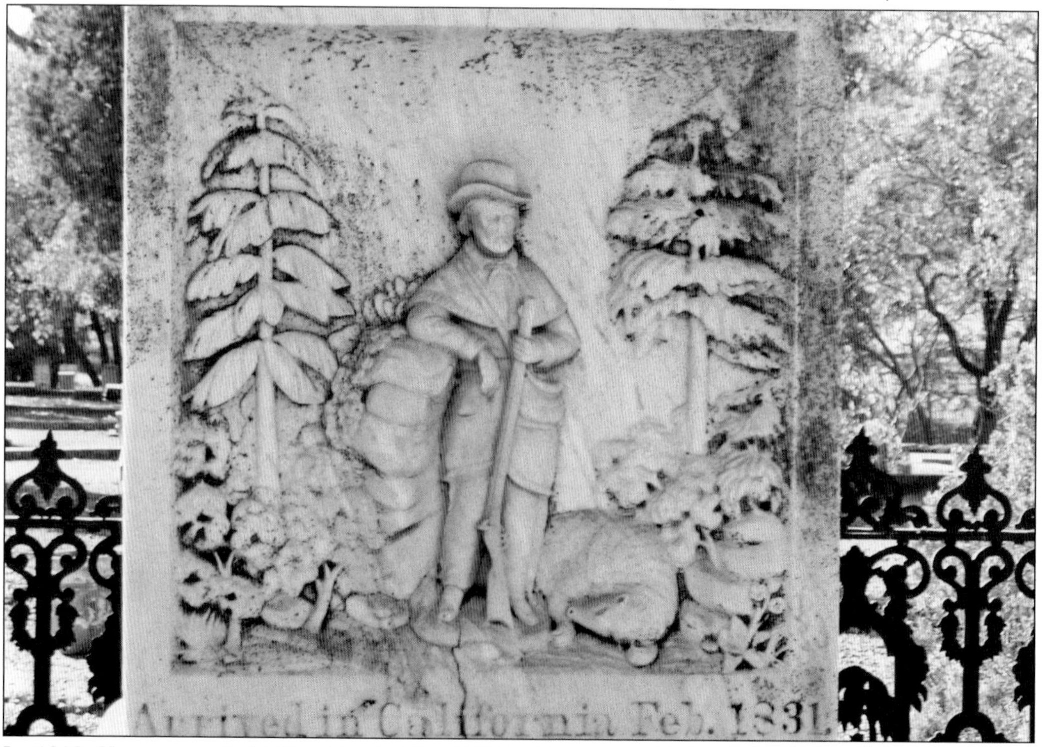

In 1818, Yount married Eliza Cambridge Wilds. George and Eliza had three children: Robert Wilds Yount, Frances Yount, and Elizabeth Ann Yount. George Yount made his way west, joining the company of history's most famous mountain men, such as Ewing Young, Thomas "Pegleg" Smith, and William Wolfskill. By 1833, Yount had reached the Sonoma Mission, where his good character and ability commended him to local Mexican officials. In 1836, assisted by Fr. Jose Quijas, Gen. Mariano Vallejo, and Gov. Juan Alvarado, Yount obtained the title to Rancho Caymus, an 11,814-acre land tract in the heart of the Napa Valley. After a full and adventurous life, Yount died on October 5, 1865. He was laid to rest in the Yountville Pioneer Cemetery, California Historical Landmark No. 693. This photograph shows a detailed close-up of the exquisite marble carving on one side of the George Yount gravesite monument. (Courtesy of the Napa Valley Museum.)

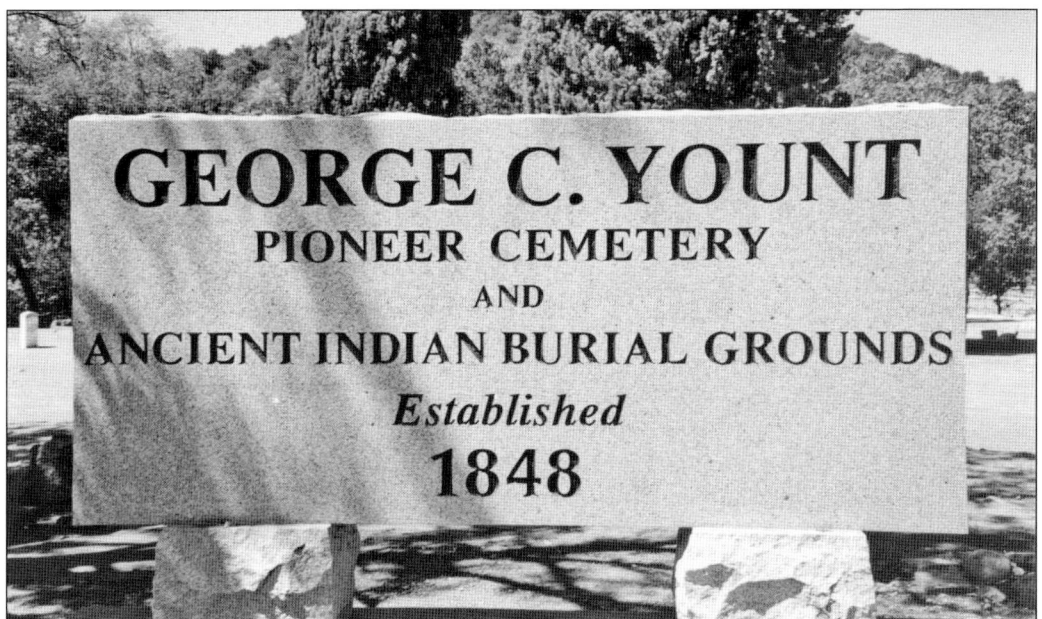

The first people to inter human remains in the George Yount Pioneer Cemetery and Ancient Indian Burial Grounds were not Yountville's pioneers but the indigenous people who resided near Yountville. This group of people had been burying cremated remains along the northern edge of the cemetery for many centuries before George Yount received the title to his 11,814-acre Caymus Ranch in 1836. When George Yount died in 1865, his will instructed that all of his property, including the cemetery, would not be sold until five years after his death. Yount's son-in-law Eugene Sullivan bought the cemetery for $1, thus keeping it in the Yount family. (Courtesy of Lee Hart.)

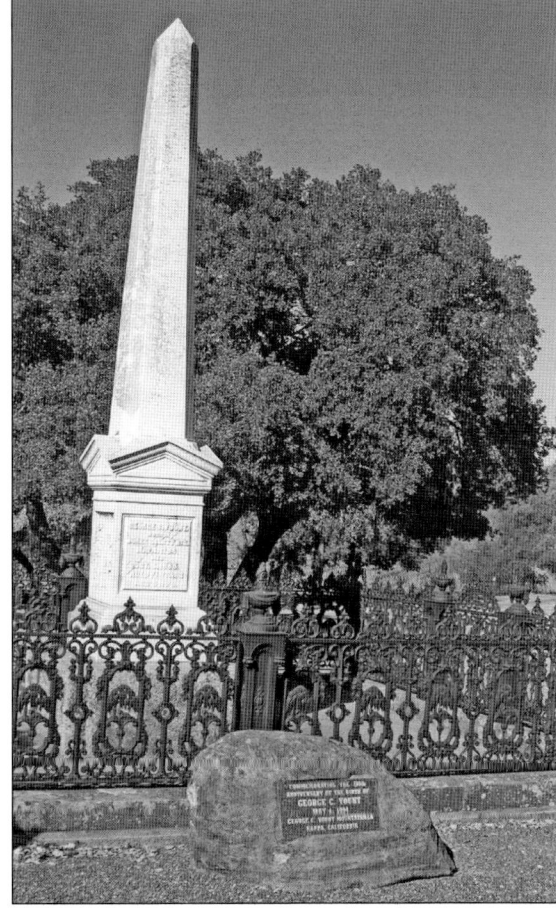

In 1894, Yount's descendant Margarethe Davis sold the cemetery to the Yountville Cemetery Association. The association's mission to protect the beauty and integrity of the cemetery has been faithfully honored for over 115 years. The grave of George Yount Yountville Cemetery is California State Historical Landmark No. 693. (Courtesy of Stuart Alexander.)

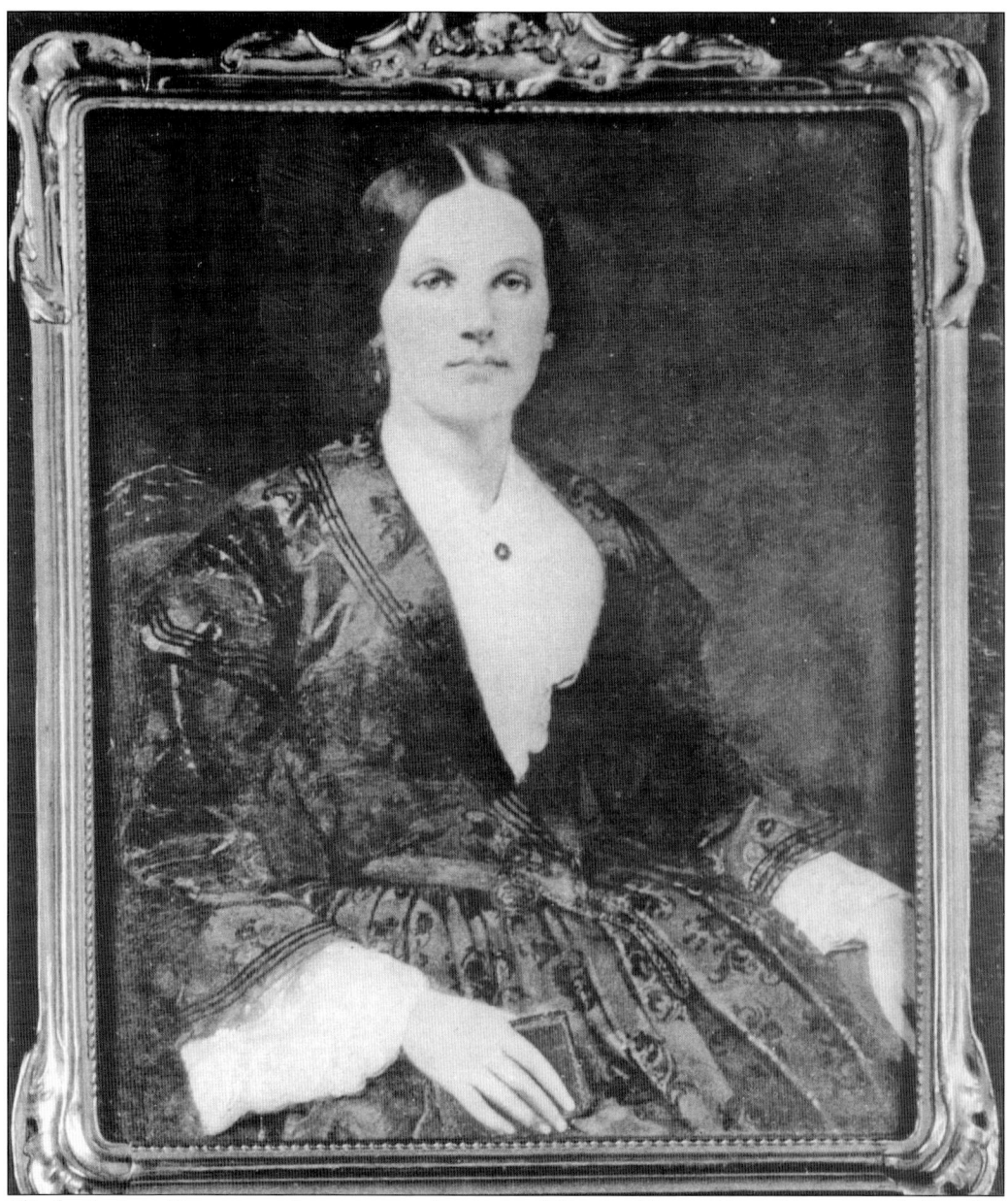

Elizabeth Ann Yount was the youngest daughter of George Yount. Once he was settled on his Caymus Ranch, Yount asked his friend and fellow Missourian Joseph Chiles to bring his family to California. In 1843, Elizabeth Ann and her sister Frances Yount Vines crossed the plains in the Chiles Walker Party to rejoin their father in the Napa Valley. Soon after arriving in Yountville, Elizabeth made the acquaintance of London-born shipbuilder John Calvert Davis. Davis was the owner of a shipbuilding and merchant marine company located in San Francisco. Elizabeth married Davis in 1844, and one year later on April 1, 1845, gave birth to her first daughter, Mary Eliza Davis. In 1848, John Davis died and Elizabeth Ann married Eugene L. Sullivan. Sullivan was a San Francisco attorney who later helped George Yount in litigation suits against land squatters. This image shows Elizabeth, whose likeness was painted in 1850. (Courtesy of the Sharpsteen Museum and Meredie "Toni" Porterfield.)

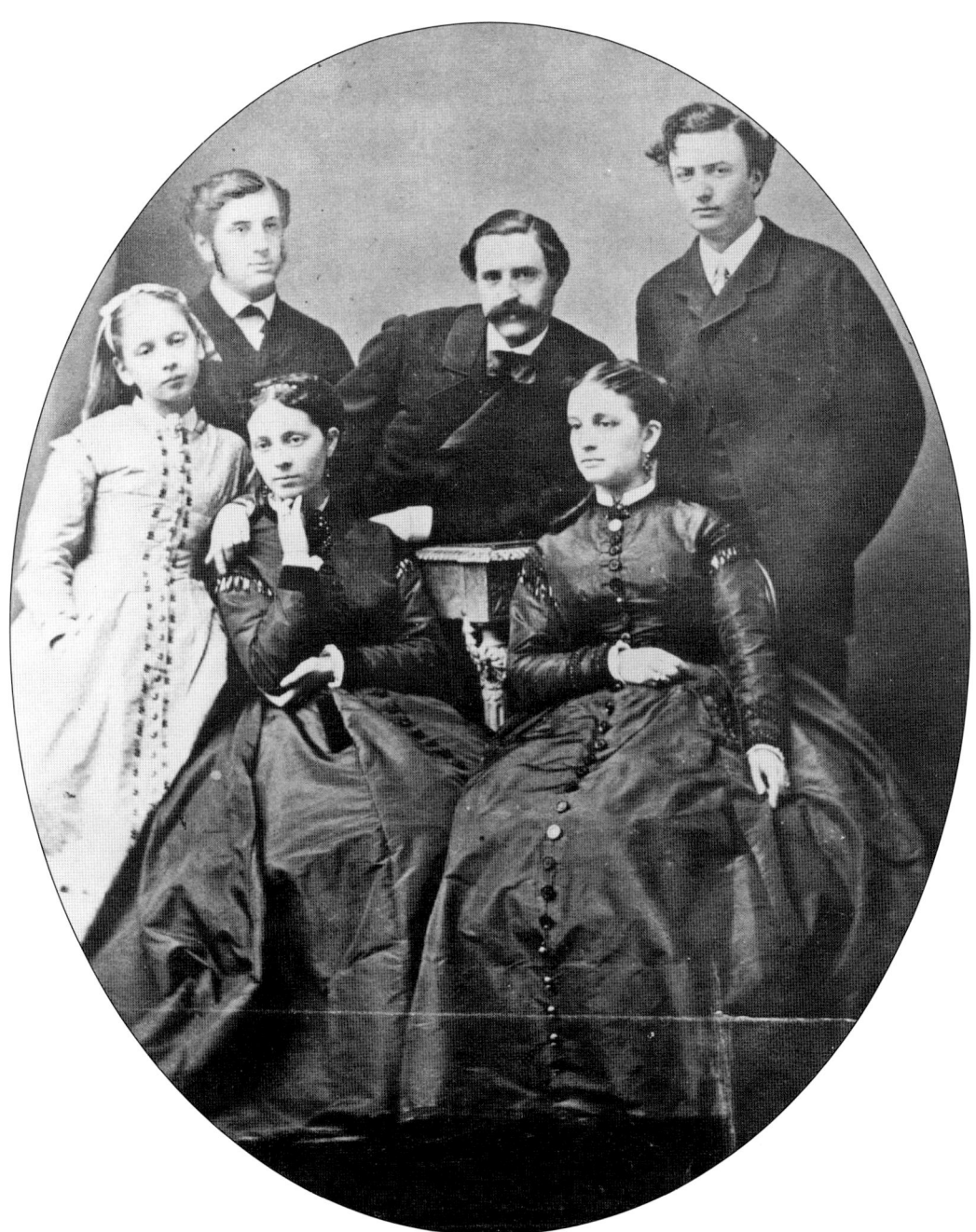

Yount's first granddaughter, Mary Eliza Davis, was distinguished as the first Anglo child born in the pueblo of Yerba Buena (later known as San Francisco). As a young child, Mary Eliza was featured in several state inaugural celebrations held in San Francisco as "California's Infant State." Her mother, Elizabeth Ann, had two more children: Elizabeth and John Davis. Pictured in the early 1870s from left to right are (seated) Yount granddaughters Mary Eliza (Davis) Bucknall and Elizabeth (Davis) Watson; (standing) granddaughter Georgiana (Sullivan) Jones, grandson John Davis, and sons-in-law W. C. Watson and Dr. George Bucknall. (Courtesy of the Napa Historical Society and Meredie "Toni" Porterfield.)

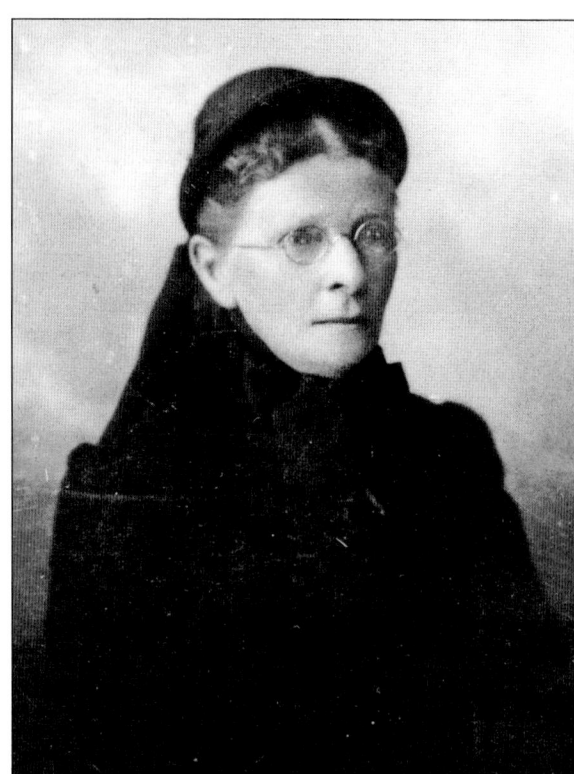

Eliza Gashwiler Yount, believed to be photographed here in the 1880s, was the second wife of George Yount. In a ceremony officiated by minister John Ver Mehr, Eliza Gashwiler married Yount at the Yountville Baptist Church in 1855. Eliza Gashwiler Yount was laid to rest in the Yountville Pioneer Cemetery. Yount's first wife, Eliza Cambridge Wilds, divorced Yount during his long absence from Missouri and subsequently remarried Missourian Joseph Wright. (Courtesy of the Sharpsteen Museum.)

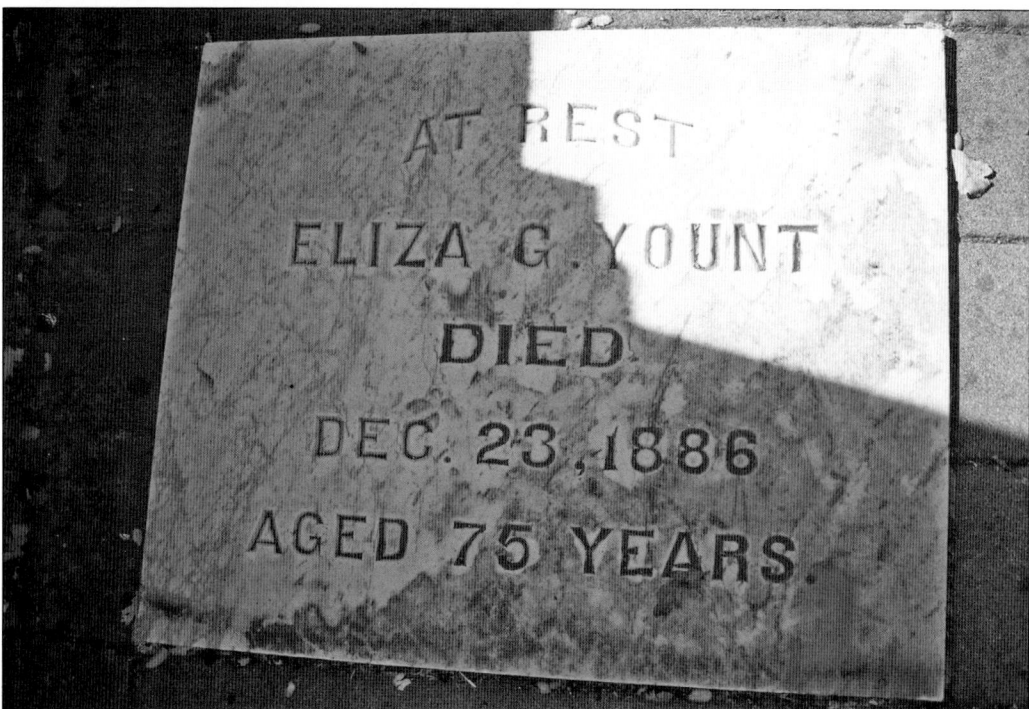

Eliza Gashwiler Yount was interred next to her husband at the Yountville Pioneer Cemetery. (Courtesy of Stuart Alexander.)

In 1867, Elizabeth Davis Watson posed with her six-month-old daughter, Maude Watson, in Frankfurt, Germany. Elizabeth Davis Watson and her daughter Maude represent the third and fourth generations of George Yount. Returning to the United States years later, Maude Watson married Thomas Dozier of Redding, California, and on October 15, 1894, produced a son, Erwin Yount Dozier, belonging to the fifth generation. (Courtesy of Meredie "Toni" Porterfield.)

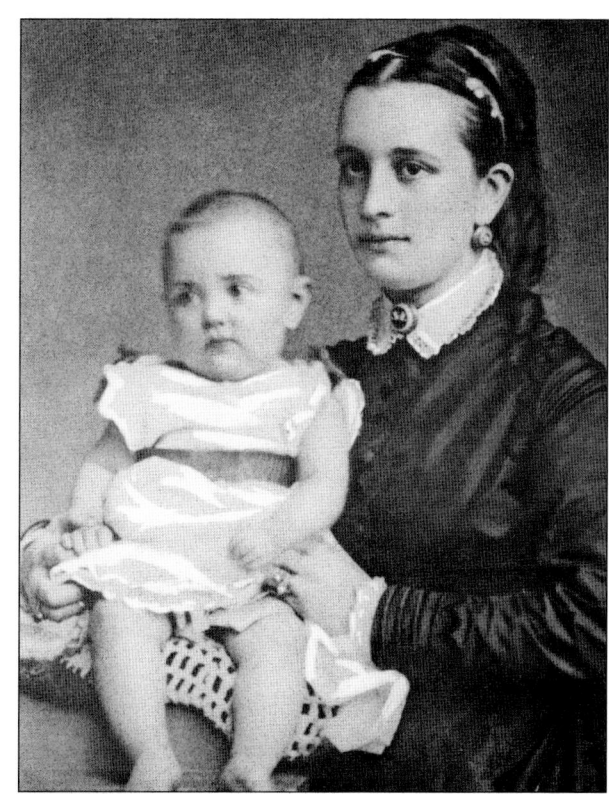

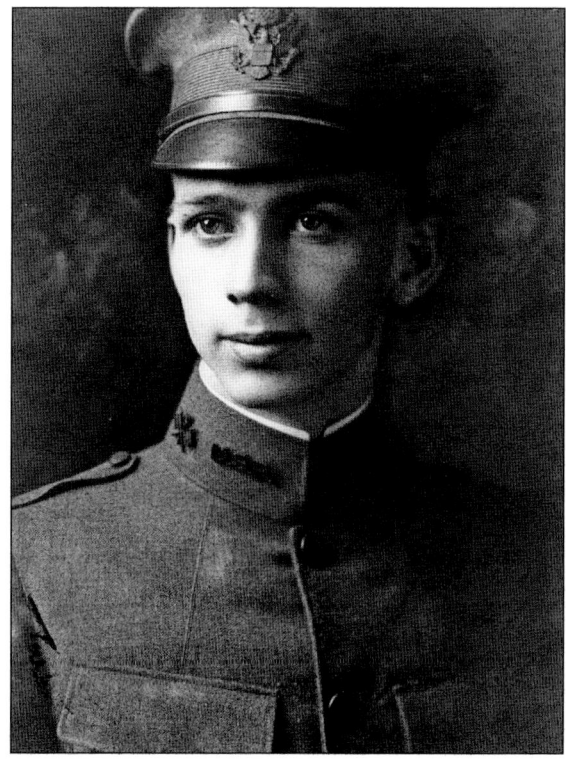

Following the tradition of his great-great-grandfather George Yount, Erwin Yount Dozier served his country in both the National Guard in 1914, and again in World War I, where he served as a second lieutenant in France. This c. 1918 photograph was taken shortly before Yount's departure to France. (Courtesy of Meredie "Toni" Porterfield.)

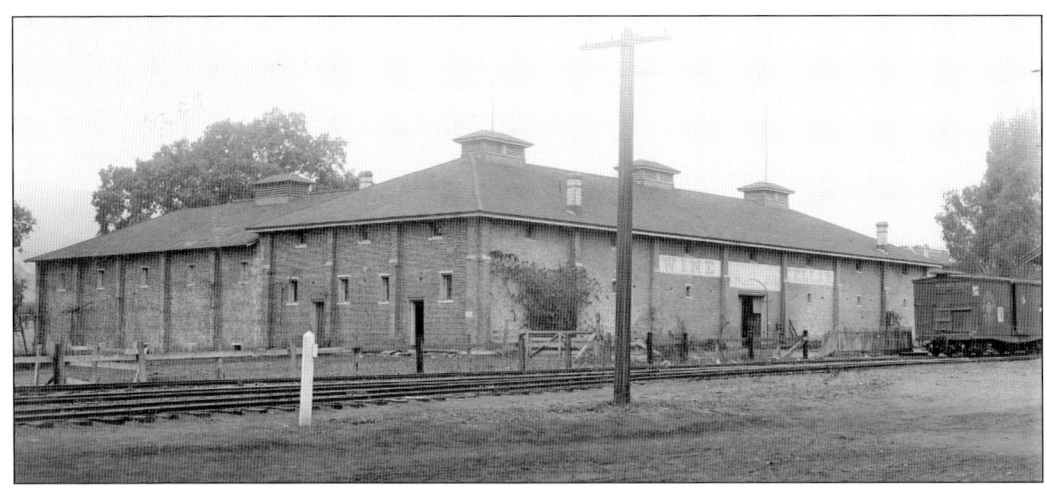

In 1870, German-born San Francisco wine merchant Gottlieb Groezinger built the first large-capacity wine cellar complex in the Napa Valley. The Groezinger Estate included a brick distillery and winery (constructed with bricks made in Yountville), a stable and barn, a cream-of-tartar manufacturing center, as well as a steam power plant to run the complex. He hired St. Helena contractor John Steves to lay two miles of pipe from John Hopper's canyon water supply to the steam equipment room at the Groezinger complex. Gottlieb continued to operate his winery until 1891, when the Groezinger Winery went bankrupt. The above image, taken in the beginning of the 20th century, shows the Groezinger Winery still in operation. The winery continued to operate under several other owners until 1955. Finally, in 1968, Don Schmidt and several partners bought the 23-acre estate and converted the winery buildings into small gift and specialty shops. For many years, the Groezinger Winery complex was known as Vintage 1870, and in 2008 residents and visitors know the property as V Marketplace. The Groezinger Wine Cellar Buildings are on the National Register of Historic Places, No. 1982002218. The photograph below was taken around 1977. (Above photograph courtesy of the Napa Historical Society; below photograph by Charles Wharff, courtesy of the Town of Yountville.)

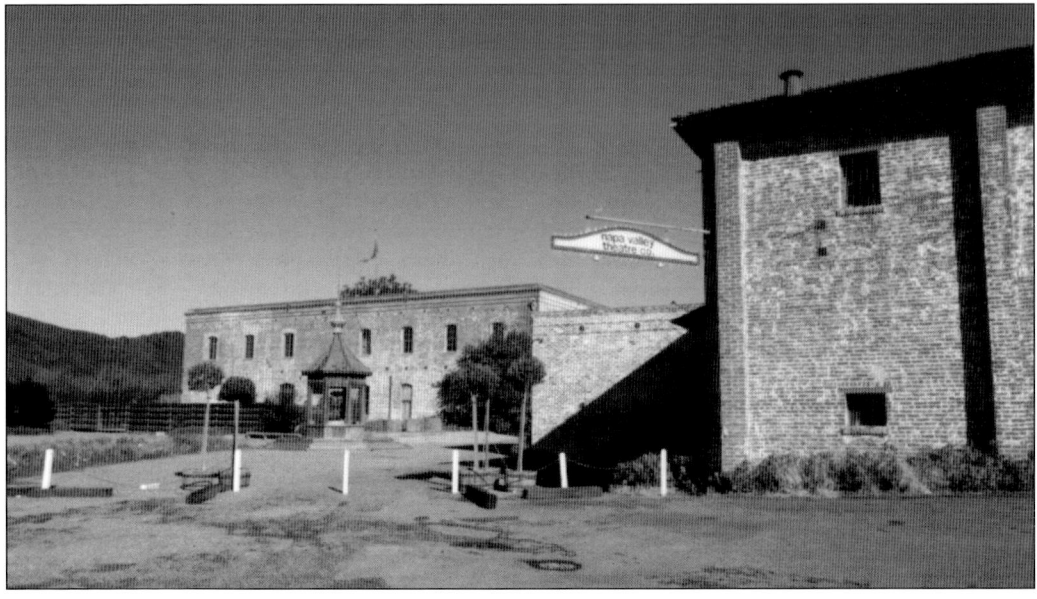

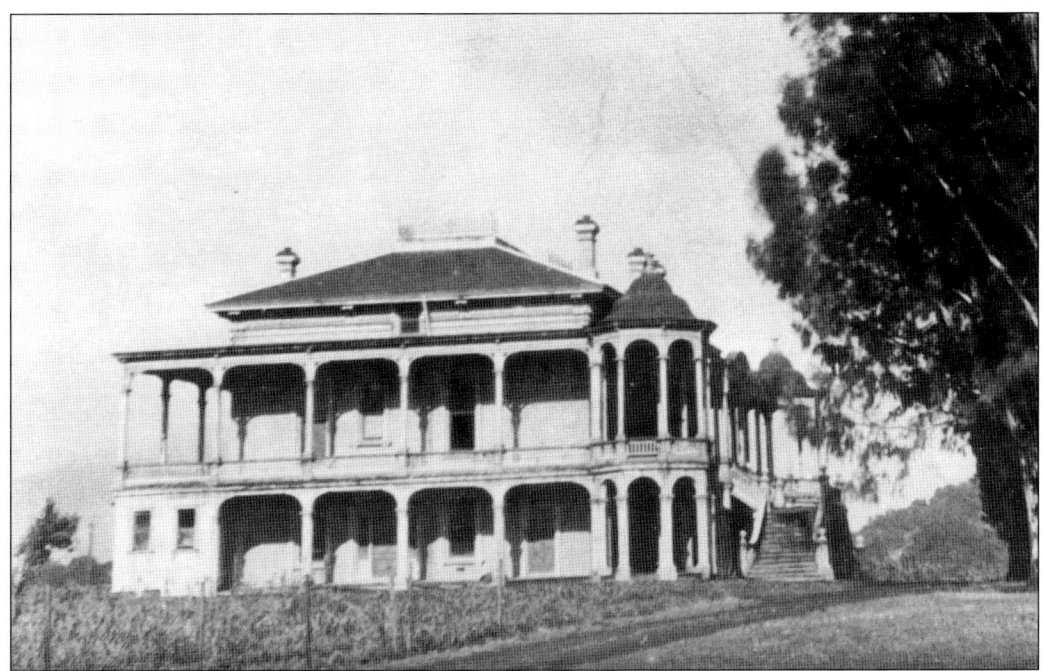

In 1880, Groezinger built a mansion on the north portion of his winery estate for his family in San Francisco. Pictured here around 1910, the original structure was a two-story brick building measuring 40-by-70 feet. The manor had over 20 rooms, and the upstairs had a large veranda. The front of the mansion contained an elegantly manicured flower garden and a large fountain surrounded by a lily pond. During the 1950s, the second story was removed and the mansion was rebuilt as a single-story building. Over the years, this building was used as a residence, a storage area, and for over 15 years as the popular Yountville restaurant Compadres Mexican Bar and Grill. (Above photograph courtesy of the Napa Historical Society; below photograph by Chuck Wharff, courtesy of the Town of Yountville.)

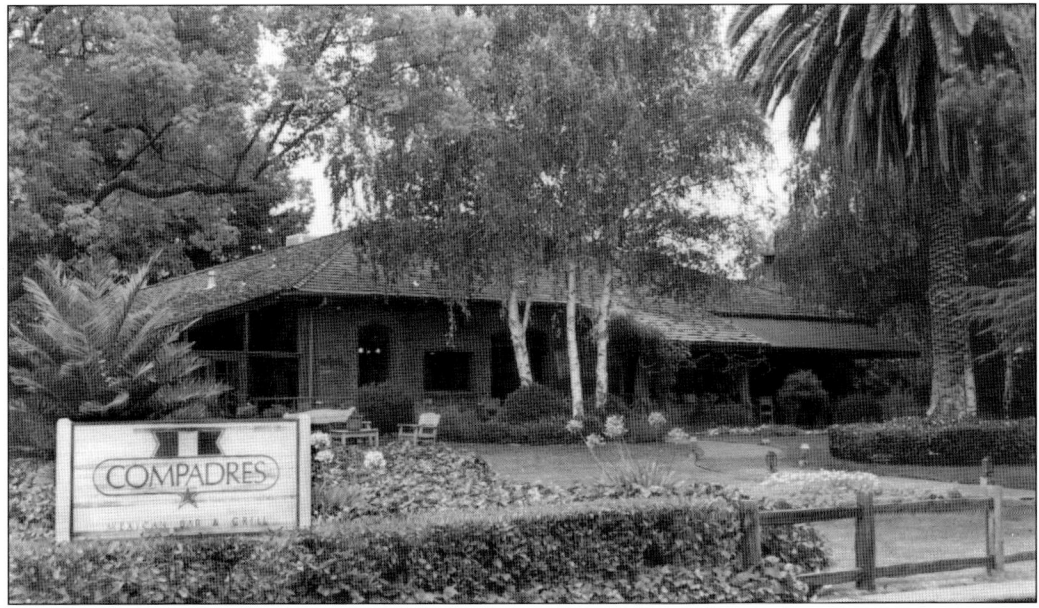

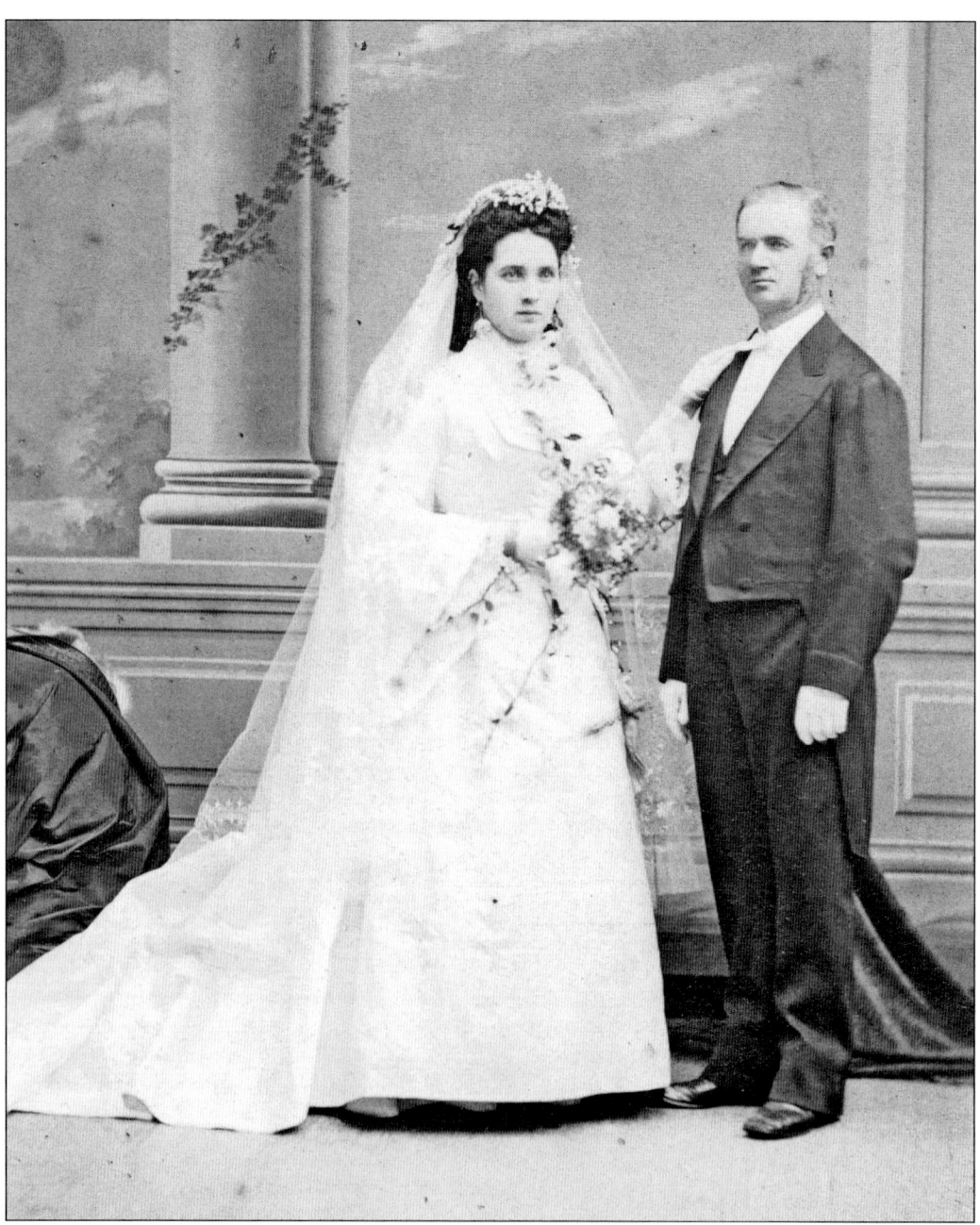

Gottlieb Groezinger married Rosalie Trondle in the mid-1800s. This c. 1890 wedding portrait was probably taken in San Francisco prior to the family's relocation to Yountville. Groezinger, in addition to supplying local job opportunities in his winery, was also responsible for the expansion of the community of Yountville. In 1874, the town increased its size with the "Groezinger addition," which added 10 additional blocks and eight streets to the town. Several of these lots were intended by Groezinger to be set aside for public use. One such triangular lot, the current site of Van de Leur Park and the former site of the historic Yountville Fire House, was bordered by Rosalia Street, which was renamed Jefferson Street by the Napa County Board of Supervisors in 1922. (Courtesy of Phyllis Vallerga.)

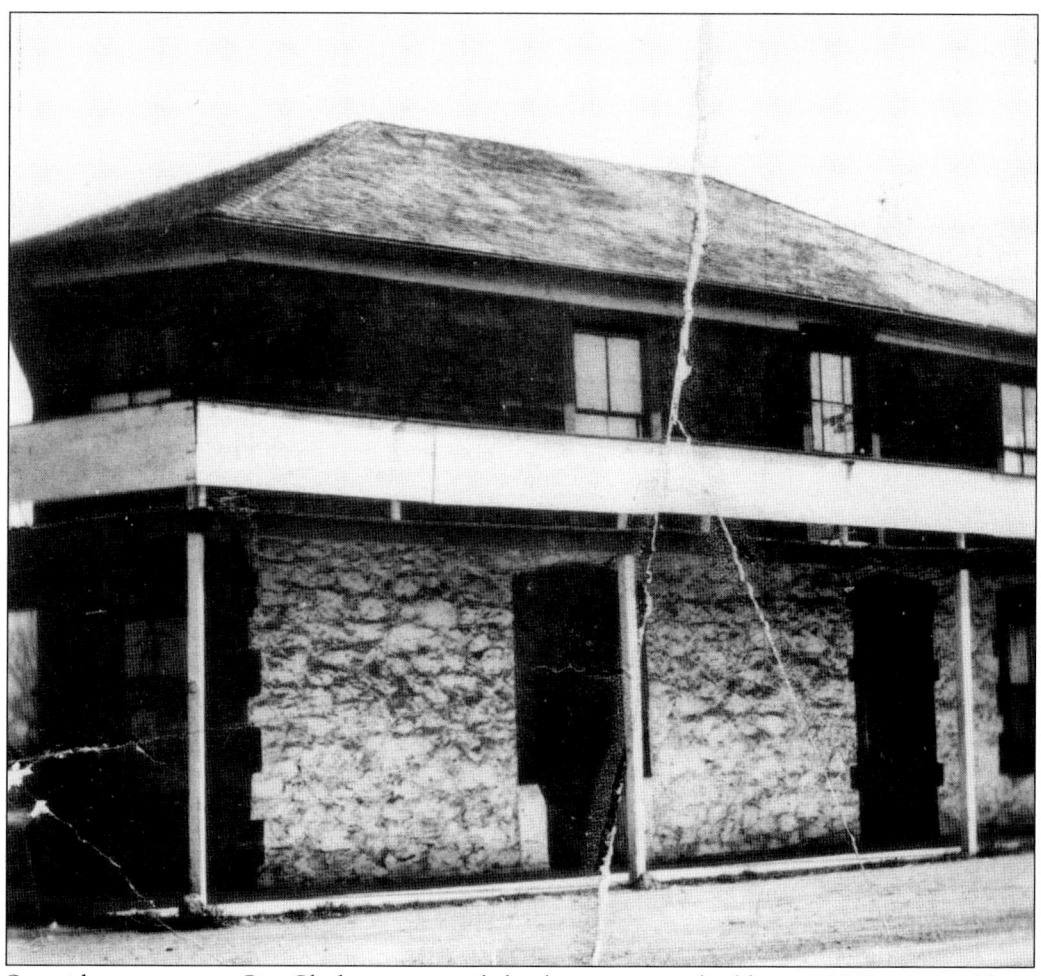

Scottish stonemason Gus Clark constructed this historic stone building in 1900, pictured here around 1910. The architecture is remarkable because of its stone craftsmanship and 22-inch-thick double-wall construction. The historic significance of this building reflects the architectural influence of the Swiss, French, and Italian immigrants who used stone from local areas to construct houses, wineries, bridges, and civic buildings. Owner Pierre (Peter) Guillaume operated the Eagle Saloon until 1907, when the property was sold to the Lande family. The saloon was then converted into a French-style steam laundry and later a boardinghouse. In 1974, the building was sold to Yountville mayor Don Schmidt. The Schmidt family remodeled the building and opened a restaurant called the French Laundry. Finally, in 1992, Schmidt sold the property to chef Thomas Keller. The French Laundry is listed on the National Register of Historic Places, No. 78000728. (Courtesy of the Napa Historical Society.)

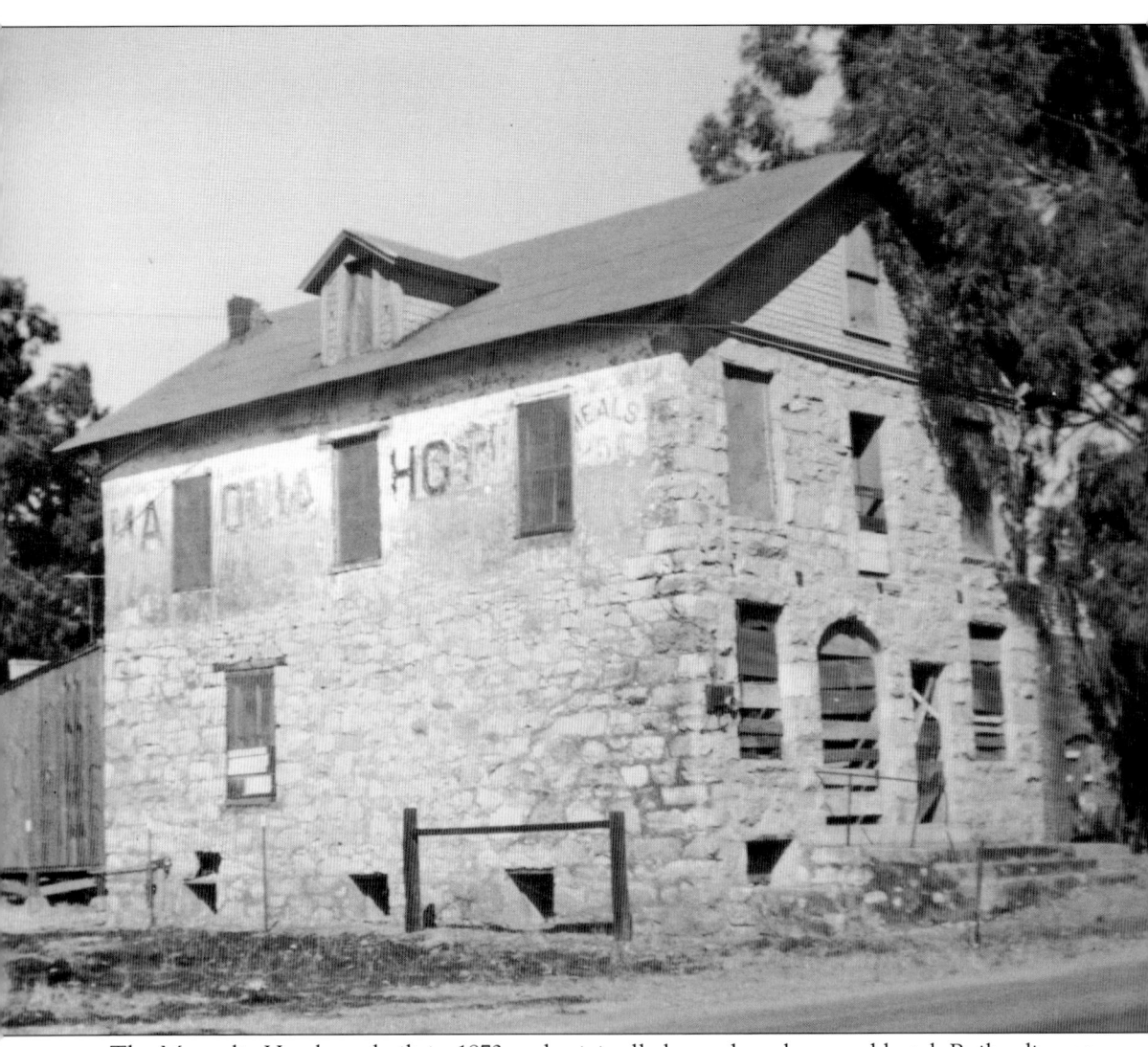

The Magnolia Hotel was built in 1873 and originally housed a saloon and hotel. Built adjacent to the railroad and the Groezinger Winery complex, the Magnolia Hotel is one of three historic stone structures in Yountville made with stone from local quarries. The stone exterior also includes bricks that were reused from the Disciples of Christ Christian Church, which was demolished in 1897, as well as a balcony that was obtained from San Francisco's old French Hospital. Today the Magnolia Hotel operates as Maison Fleurie, a bed-and-breakfast. This photograph was taken just after 1920. (Courtesy of the Napa Historical Society.)

Charles Hopper (pictured below) was one of the original immigrant pioneers of California to help settle the Yountville area. Born in North Carolina in 1800, he was an expert trapper and frontiersman. Crossing the plains in 1841, he came to Yountville via Sutter's Fort with the famous Bidwell-Bartelson Party. After his initial exploration of the Napa and Sonoma Valleys, Hopper returned to Missouri via New Mexico. After Hopper offered assistance to George Yount in an errand to retrieve Yount's children from Missouri, Yount sold 650 acres to Hopper in 1850 for the sum of $1. The historic Hopper House, pictured above around 1940, is located north of Yountville on the west side of Highway 29, situated near a canyon and seasonal creek that was named in his honor. (Above photograph courtesy of Liz Herr; below photograph from the John Wichels manuscripts, courtesy of Edgar Beard.)

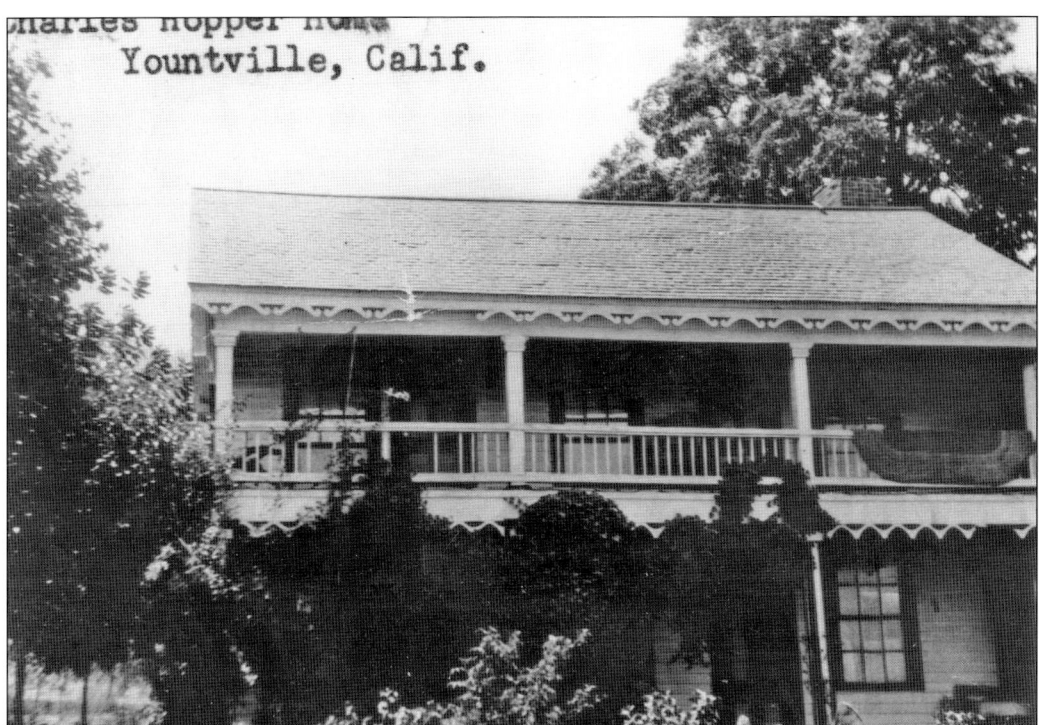

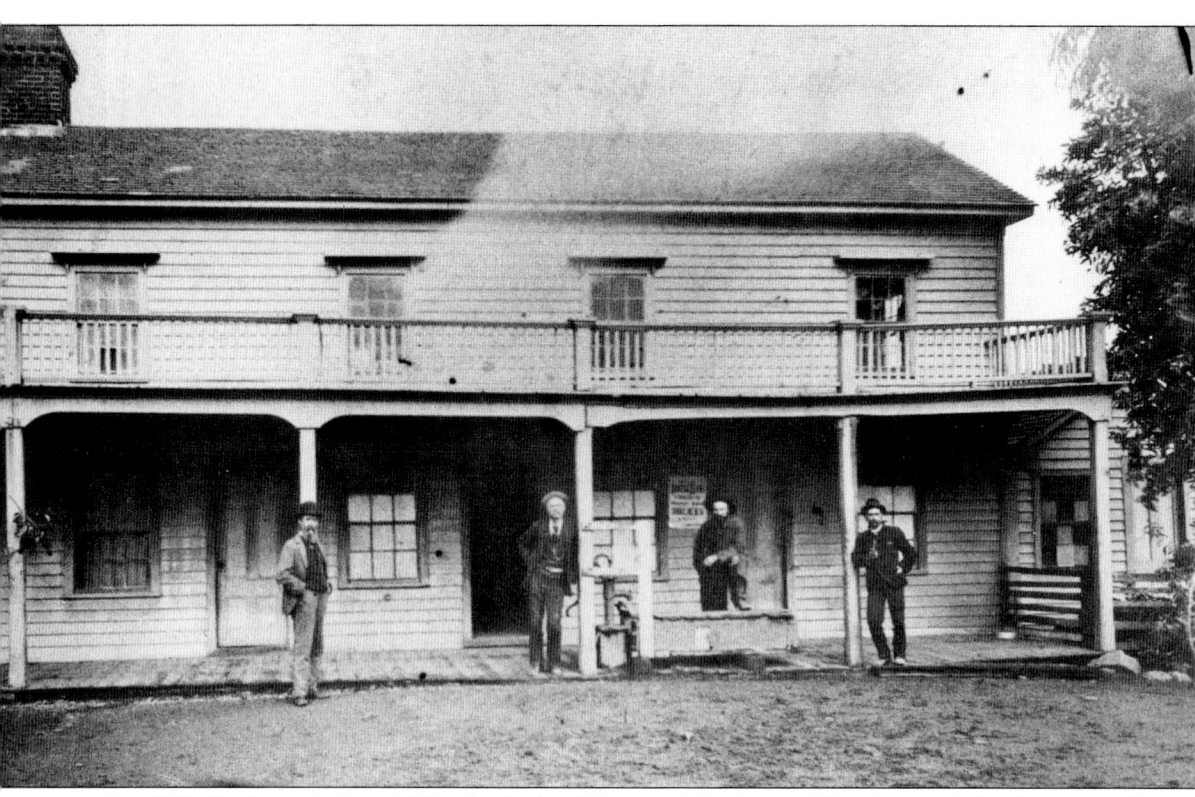

In 1856, blacksmith David Wise built the Sebastopol Exchange Hotel, one of the first several buildings to be constructed in the village of Sebastopol (later renamed Yountville). This two-storied wooden building was located on the east side of Yount Street near the corner of Madison Street. This photograph is believed to have been taken in the late 1890s, several years before the structure burned. (Courtesy of Phyllis Vallerga.)

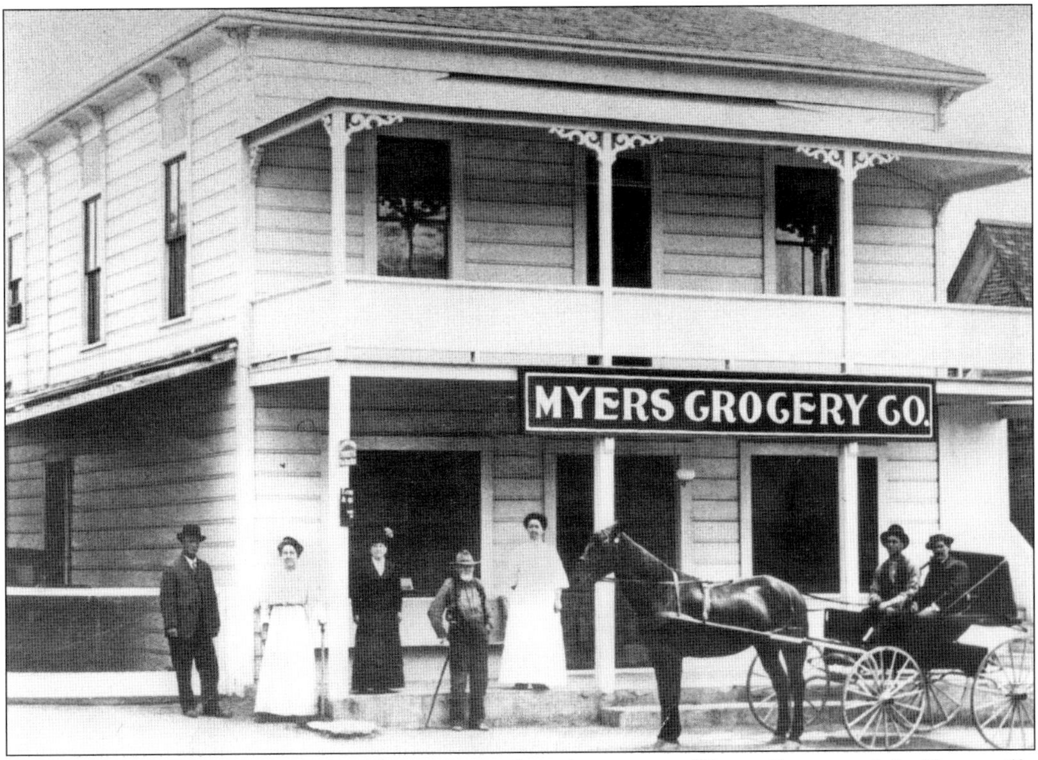

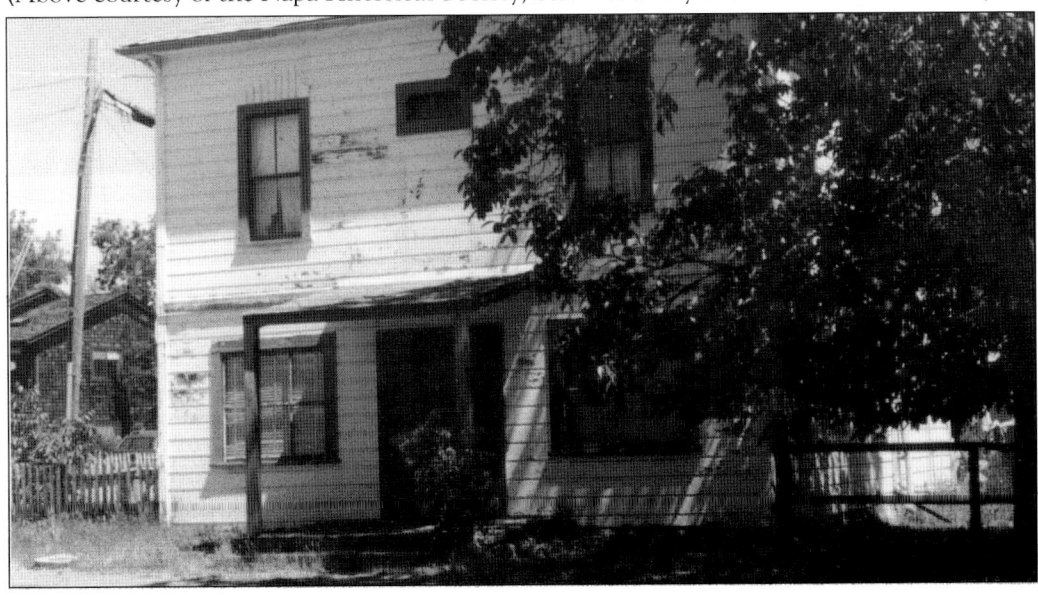

The Myers Grocery Company building is located on the corner of Yount Street and the Yountville Crossroads. This store was believed to have belonged to Hattie and Reese Myers in the early 1910s. Functioning as a grocery store until 1921, the building was purchased by the Aragon family, longtime Yountville residents. In later years, the property was purchased by Betty Maxwell, who converted the structure into a rooming house. Remodeled in the 2000s, the historic architectural design has remained intact. Pictured below around 1977, the building now serves as a multifamily dwelling. (Above courtesy of the Napa Historical Society; below courtesy of the Town of Yountville.)

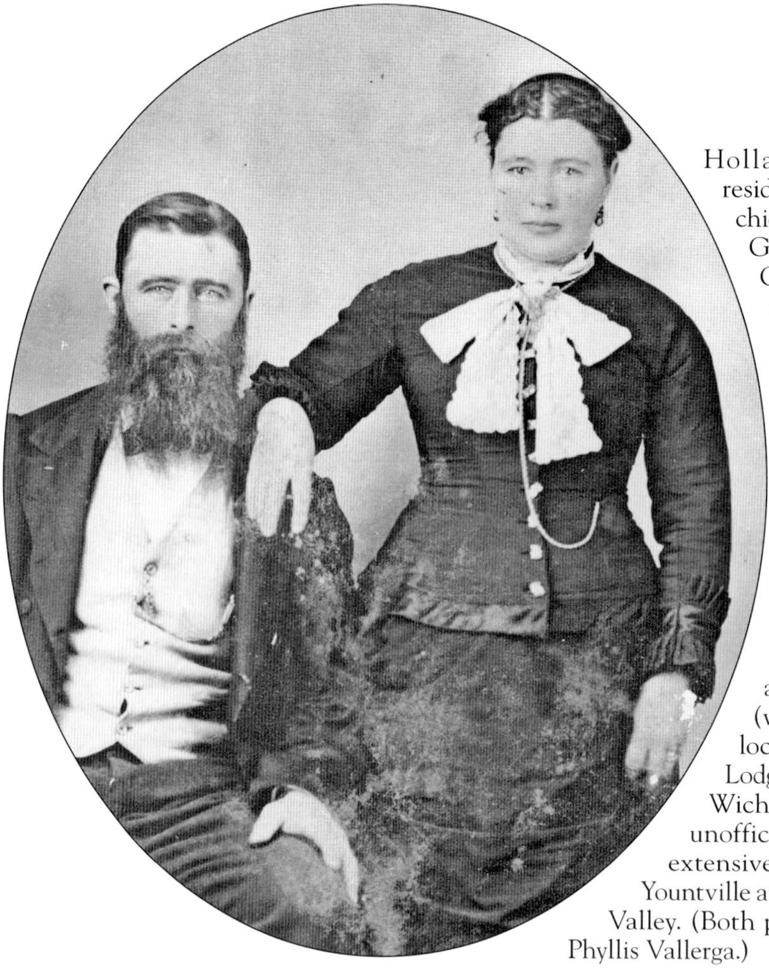

Holland-born Yountville resident Simon Sax was the chief accountant for Gottlieb Groezinger, owner of the Groezinger Winery. Sax also served as justice of the peace for one term in 1892. Probably taken in the 1880s, the portrait above shows a young Simon and Anna Sax in a formal portrait studio. The second photograph, taken in the early 1900s, shows Simon and Anna Sax in front of their residence on Madison and Washington Streets (which is the current location of the Napa Valley Lodge). Anna's grandson John Wichels became Yountville's unofficial historian and wrote extensively about the history of Yountville and the surrounding Napa Valley. (Both photographs courtesy of Phyllis Vallerga.)

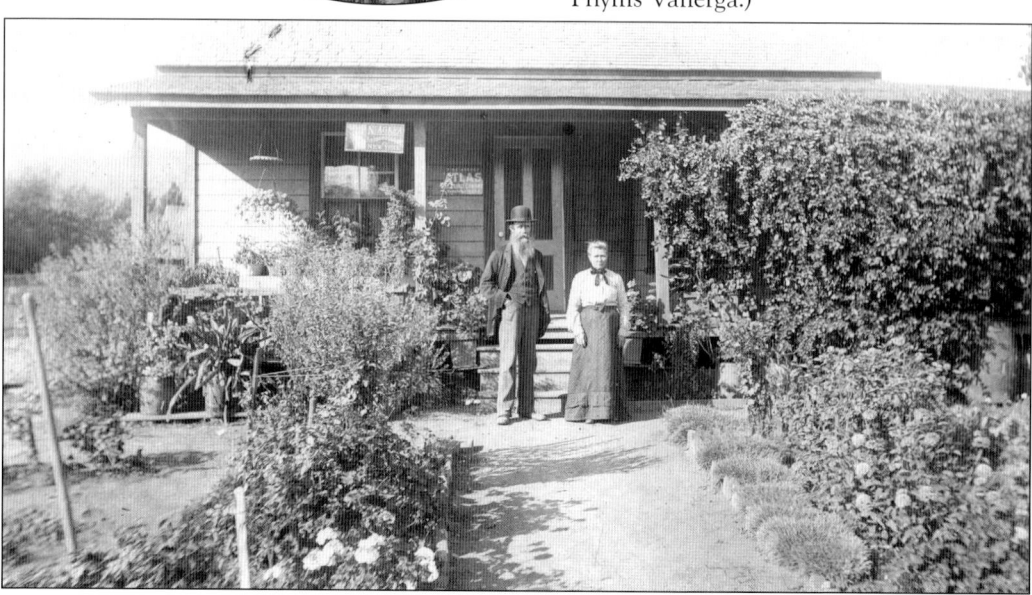

In 1881, German-born businessman Fredrick Volz and his wife, Mary Magdalena, purchased 188 acres approximately one mile south of the Veterans Home property. Taken in the late 1800s, this formal portrait features Frederick and Mary Magdalena Volz. The Volz ranch was sandwiched between the Veteran's Home to the north and the Grigsby property to the south. Fredrick Volz was able to finance his purchase with the interest earned from his San Francisco–based brewery, the National Brewery. (Courtesy of Phyllis Vallerga.)

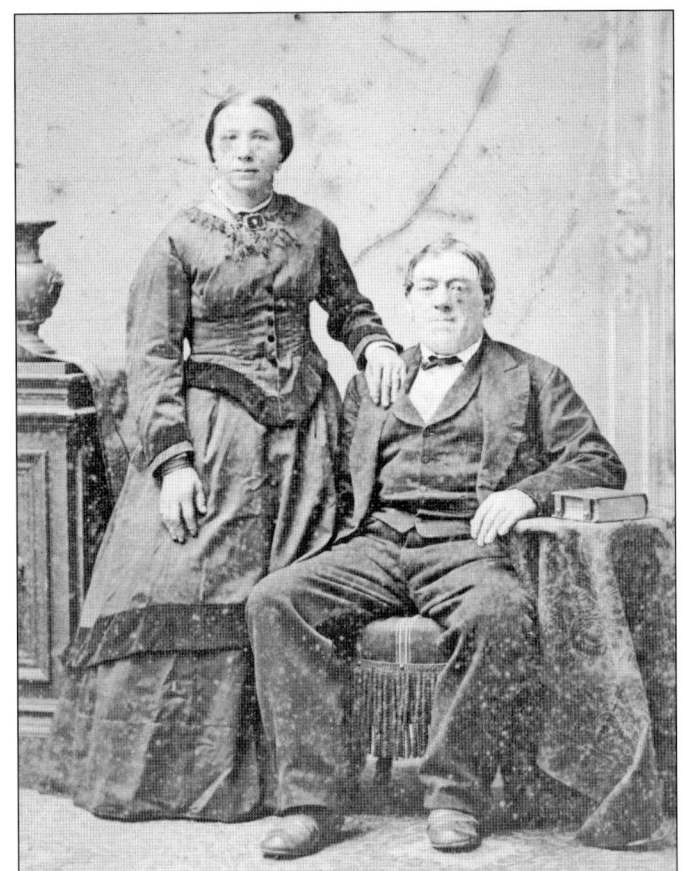

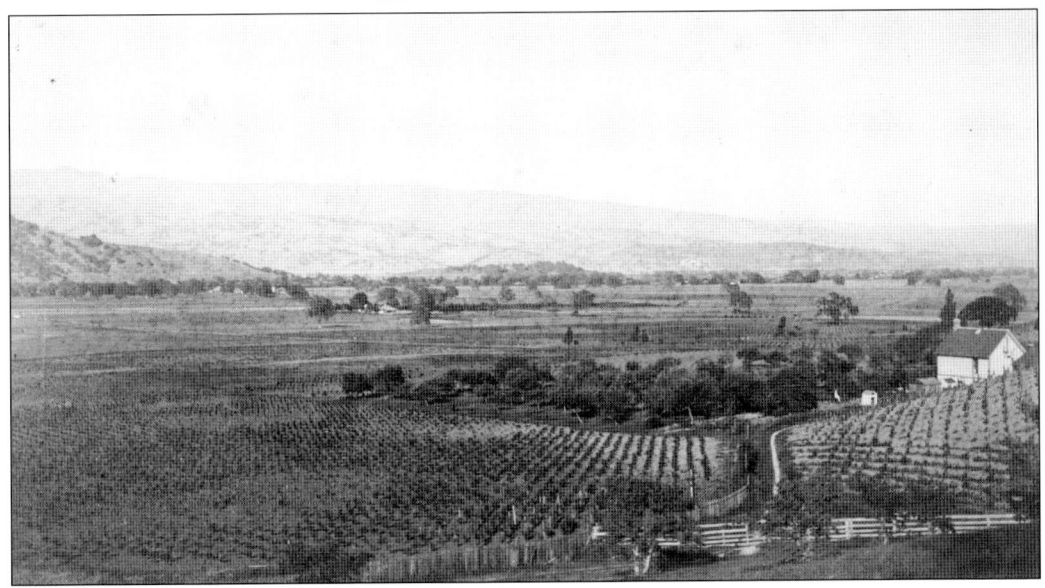

The Volz family was able to keep the ranch for over 80 years; it was sold in 1972. Taken in the late 1880s, this photograph shows the view from the Volz ranch looking southeast. (Courtesy of Phyllis Vallerga.)

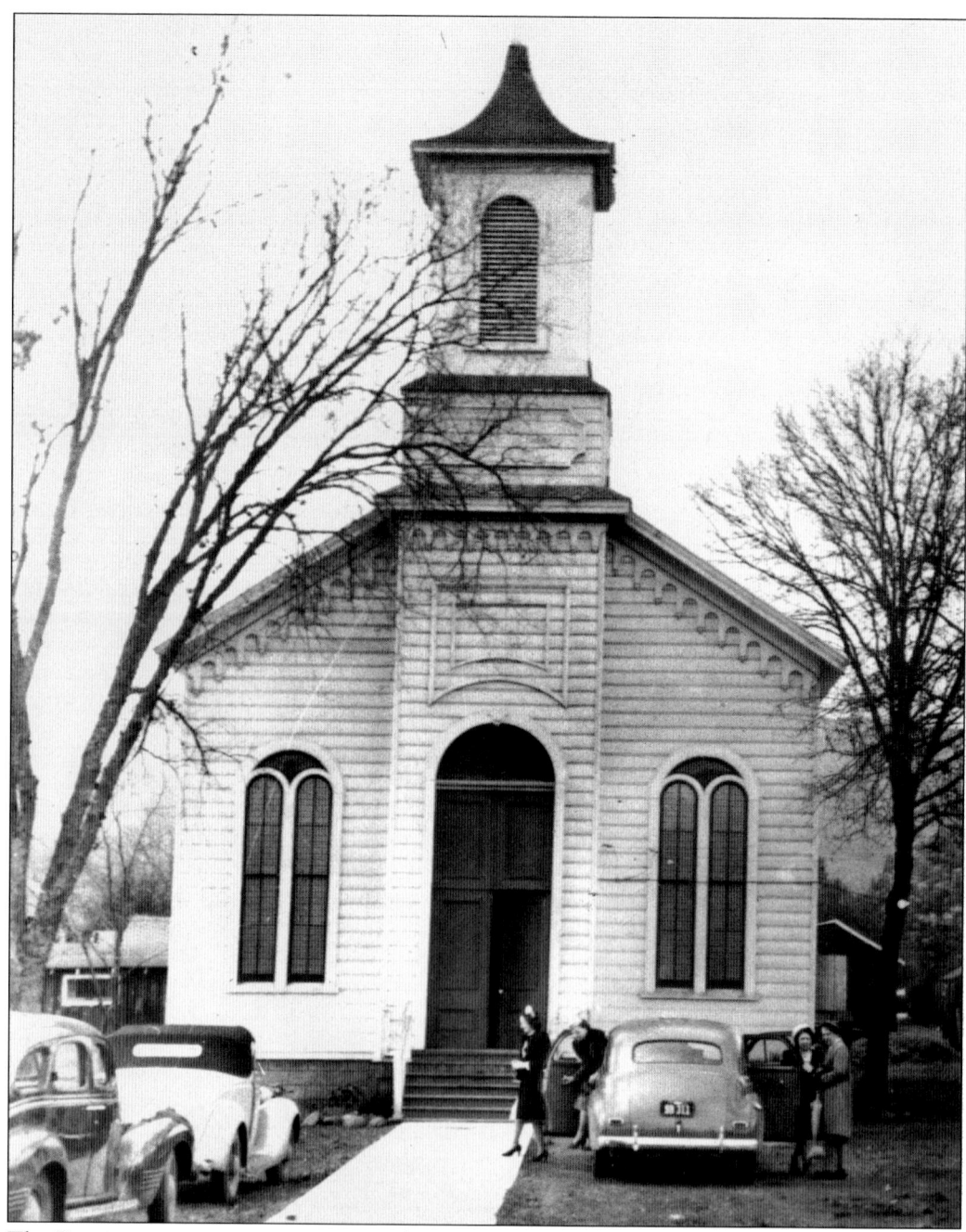

The Baptist congregation was organized in 1874 as the Union Sunday School, and the church building was constructed in 1876. The lot was donated by Yountville residents on land that had originally been purchased from Salvador Vallejo by pioneer John Grigsby in 1848. In 1930, the nondenominational church was renamed the Yountville Christian Church, and it continues by that name today. Pioneer Charles Hopper was credited with the donation of the church bell. Both Charles Hopper and his wife, Rebecca's, funeral services were held at the Yountville Christian Church in the late 1880s. This photograph was taken around 1950. (Photograph by John Wichels, courtesy of Edgar Beard.)

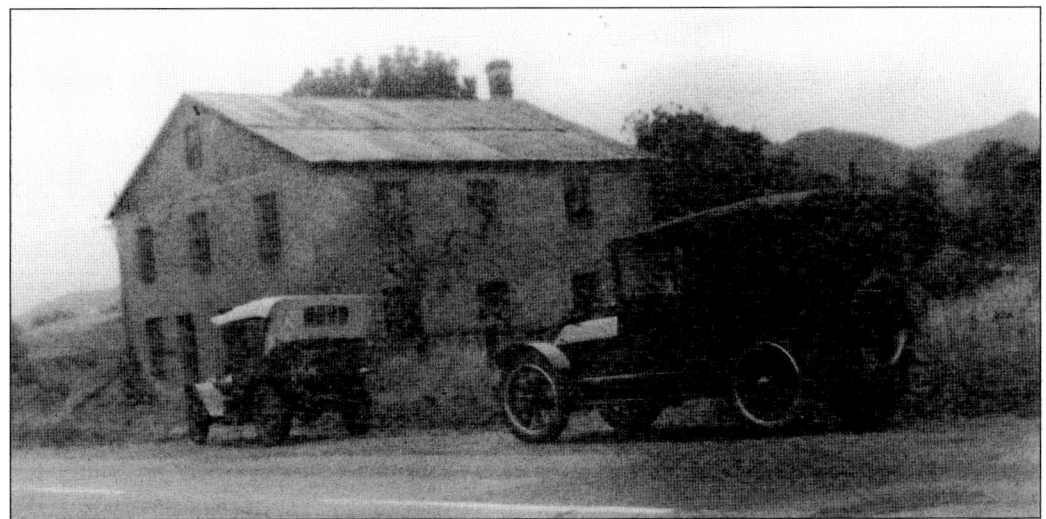

This beautifully constructed stone building was constructed in 1894 by Italian stonemason Carlo (Charles) Rovegno, with the help of Angelo Brovelli. Similar to the French Laundry and the Magnolia Hotel, the walls of the Rovegno house are 22 inches thick and were quarried from local hillsides. Over the next 50 years, the beautifully constructed home served as the residence of Mr. Rovegno. This early 1900s photograph shows the Rovegno house on County Highway 29—the present-day location of Washington Street. The lot to the north of this historic house was the site of Yountville's very small Chinatown. Sing Go and Sing Gee had a common interest in a laundry business that also functioned as a community gathering site for Chinese residents living in Yountville. (Courtesy of Barbara and Bud Dulinsky.)

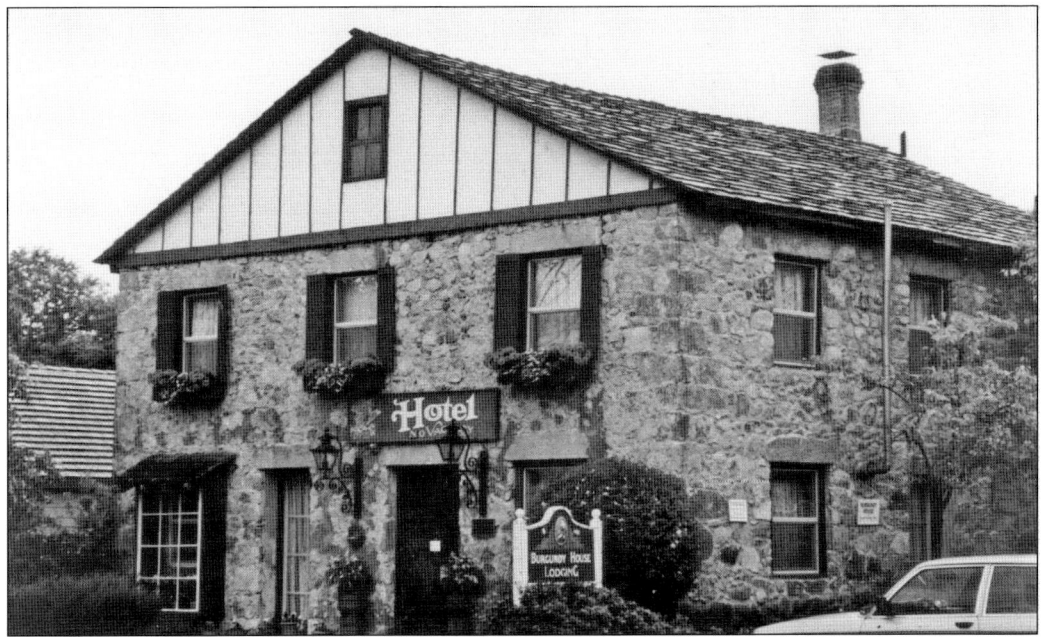

In 1954, Carlo Rovegno died. His historic home remained vacant for many years. Under new ownership and after extensive renovation, the house is pictured here in 1970. For over 25 years, it was the famous Burgundy House Bed and Breakfast Inn. This property is listed on the Napa County Historic Resources Inventory. (Courtesy of the Napa Historical Society.)

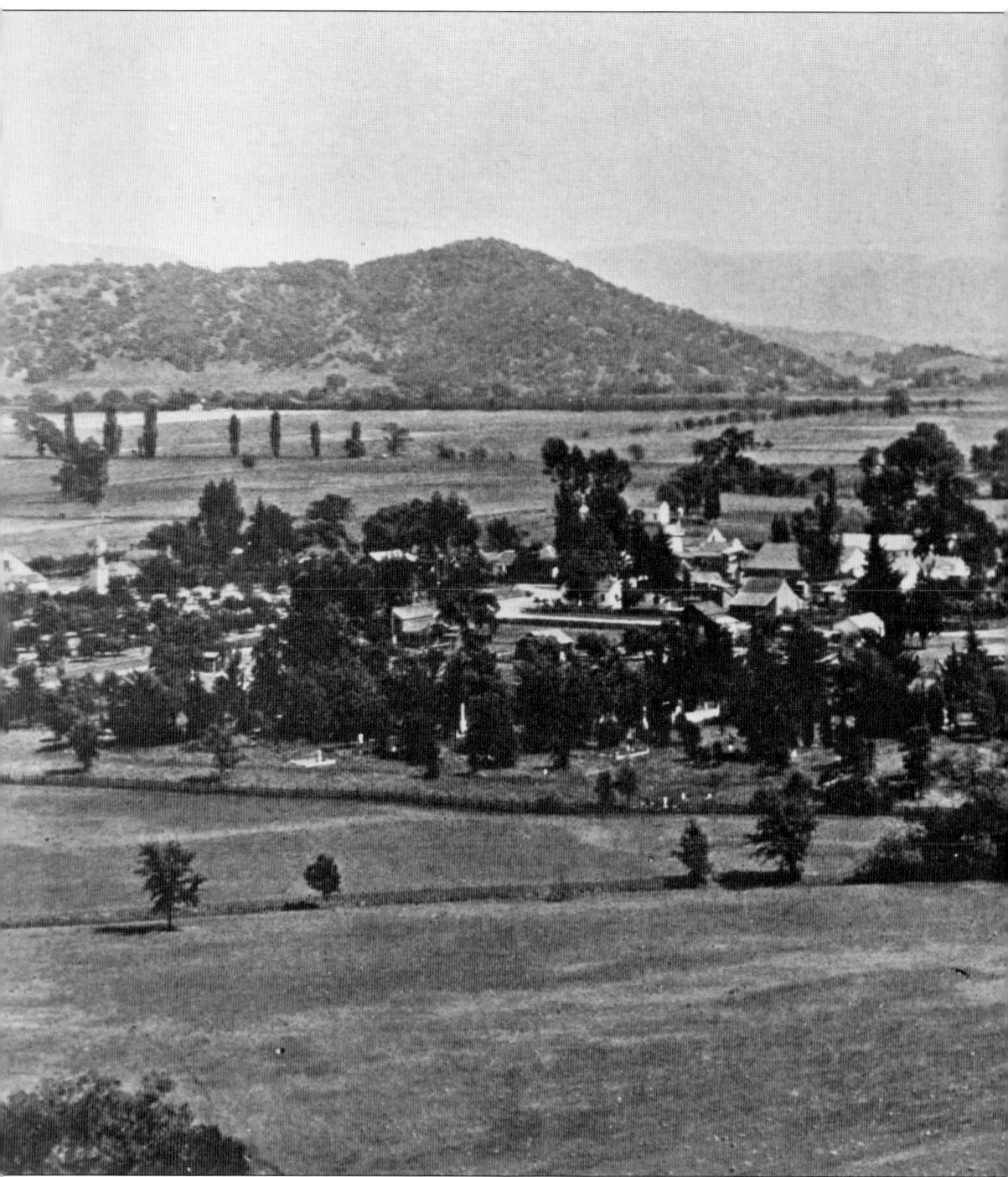

This rare 1901 photograph of Yountville shows a wide southern-facing panoramic view from the top of Yountville Butte. In the upper right, the two-story Groezinger Mansion can clearly be seen on what was then called County Highway 29. This road would later become known as Washington Street. Below the Groezinger Mansion, the roof of the Charles Rovegno house and the northern face of the stone walls can be seen. The steeple and roof of the Yountville Community Church

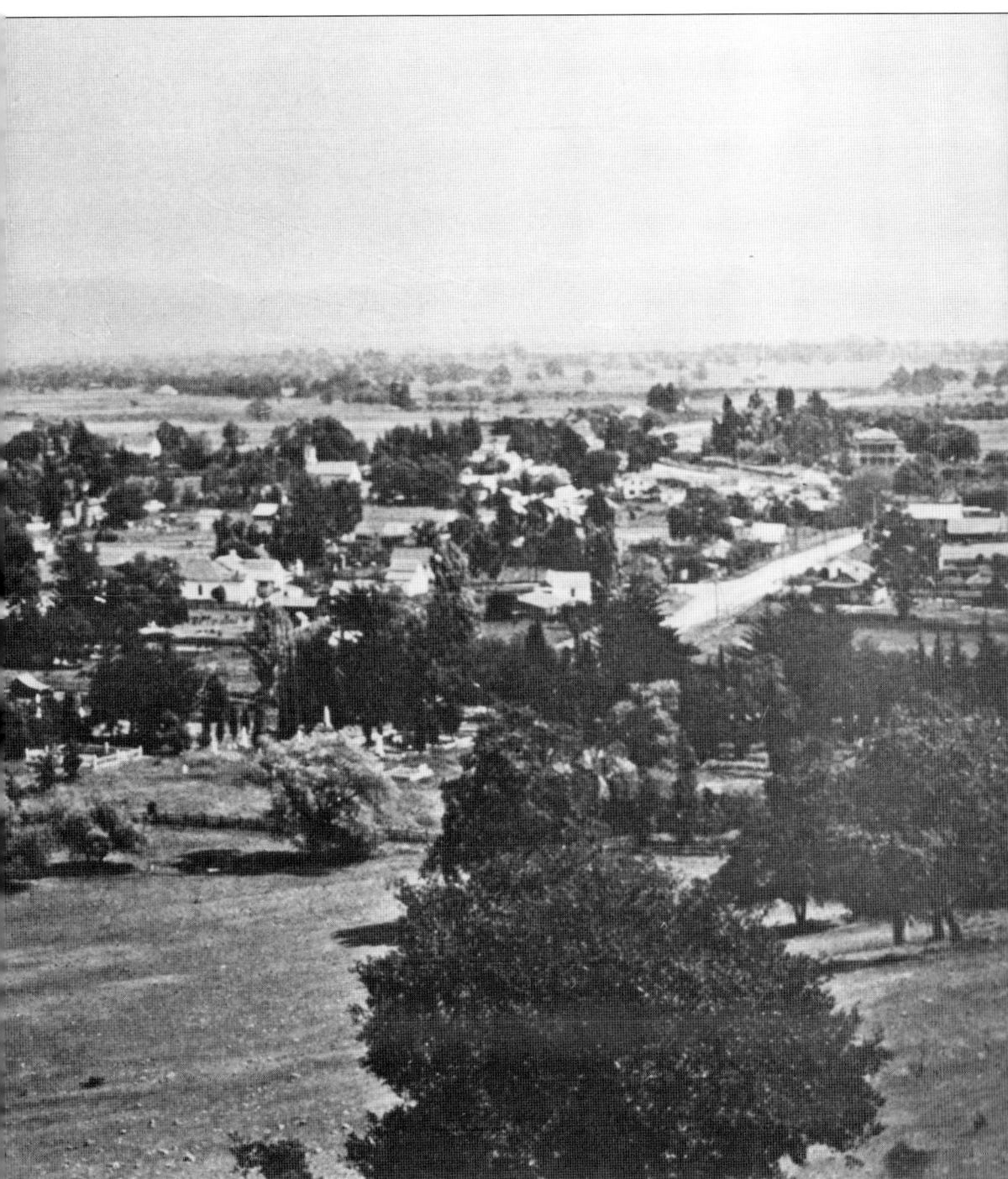

is also visible to the left and center of the photograph. Clearly visible is the entire length of the Yountville Pioneer Cemetery. The graves in this cemetery bear witness to the lives of many residents who made Yountville their home and final resting place. Some of these names include the following: Yount, Hopper, Guillaume, VandeLeur, Rovegno, Wichels, Whitton, Volz, Myers, Reed, Forrester, and Casaday. (Courtesy of Phyllis Vallerga.)

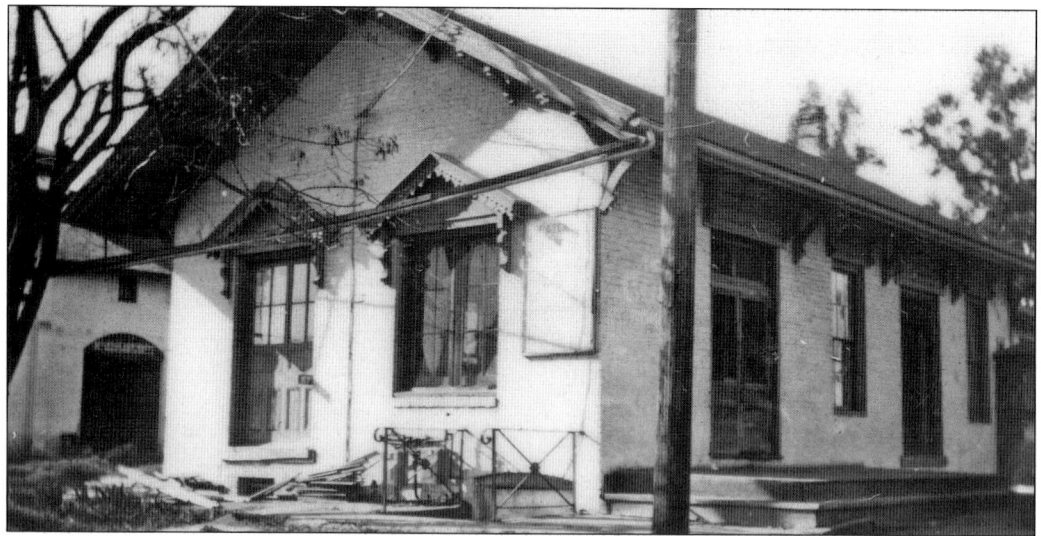

Constructed in 1868, this brick building is among several historic brick structures built in Yountville that are still in existence. It was originally constructed as a depot by the Napa Valley Railroad Company for the transport of building materials, passengers, and agricultural products up and down the valley. When the Southern Pacific Railroad took over the rails and constructed the new depot, the old building served countless other businesses in Yountville as the Old Depot for years. Over time, the Old Depot housed several grocery stores, the Yountville Telephone Exchange (mid-1930s), a barbershop, the Cash 'n' Carry Grocery (1946), the Vintage Café, the Red Rock Café, and finally, by 2008, the Pacific Blues Café. (Courtesy of Barbara and Bud Dulinsky.)

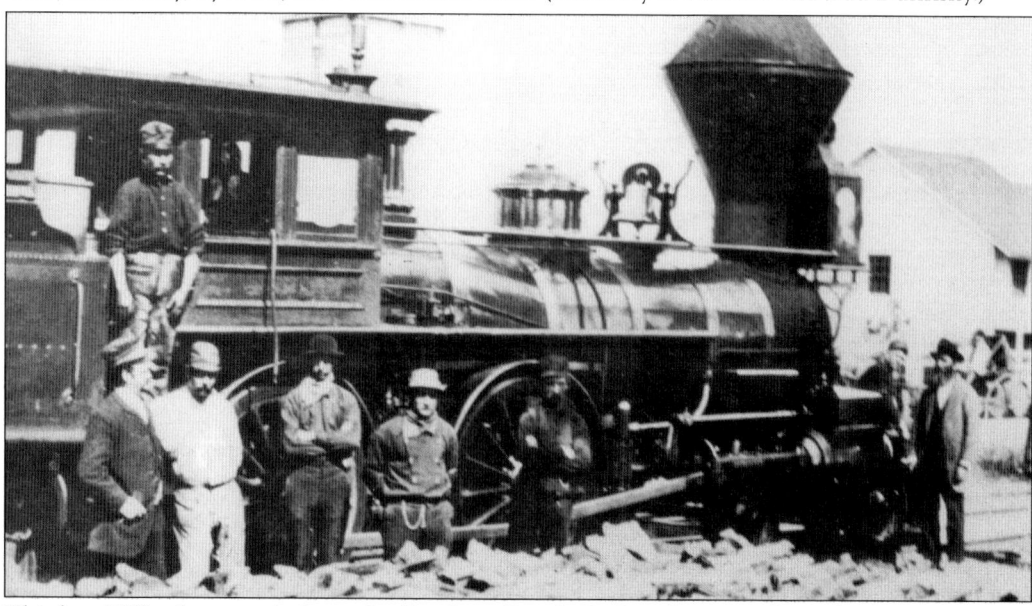

This late-1880s photograph shows the Southern Pacific Railroad train at the Oakville train station heading south to Yountville. Note the wood at the bottom of the image. Early planners believed that the eucalyptus tree would provide inexpensive fuel and track for the railroad; therefore, trees were planted along the length of the railroad line. Although the tree potential never came to fruition, many of the eucalyptus trees remained and date back to the mid-1880s. (Courtesy of the Napa Historical Society.)

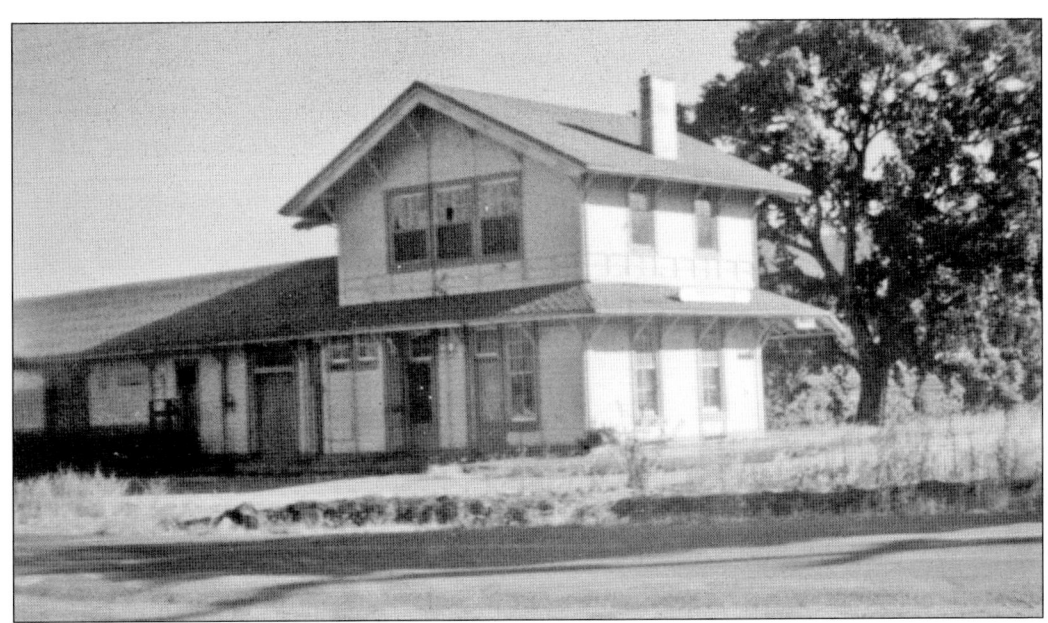

Since the railway in this area was originally used as both freight and passenger transportation, a larger depot was needed to accommodate the expanded agricultural growth of Yountville and the entire Napa Valley. In 1888, the Whistle Stop was constructed by the Southern Pacific Depot in Yountville, California. With power generated from the Veterans Home, the Southern Pacific Depot was the only building in Yountville with electric lighting. By 1907, however, both passenger and freight demand began to decline due to the introduction of the Napa Valley and Calistoga Electric Railroad and the rise of the automobile and trucking industries. In 1929, the Southern Pacific Railroad discontinued service for passengers. Note that the tracks that were located in back of the depot have been diverted to the west side of the highway. Over the next 70 years, the Whistle Stop station was used as a post office, a blacksmith shop, a local bar and grill, and in 2008, a retail business operated by the Overland Sheep Company. This photograph was taken in the mid-1960s, prior to the incorporation of the town of Yountville. (Courtesy of Barbara and Bud Dulinsky.)

In 1958, Hollywood came to the Southern Pacific Railroad stop in Yountville. The Yountville Depot station was featured in the 1959 movie *This Earth Is Mine* starring Rock Hudson and Jean Simmons. "Boots" Dulinsky is standing in the center of this c. 1957 image, facing the train. (Courtesy of Barbara and Bud Dulinsky.)

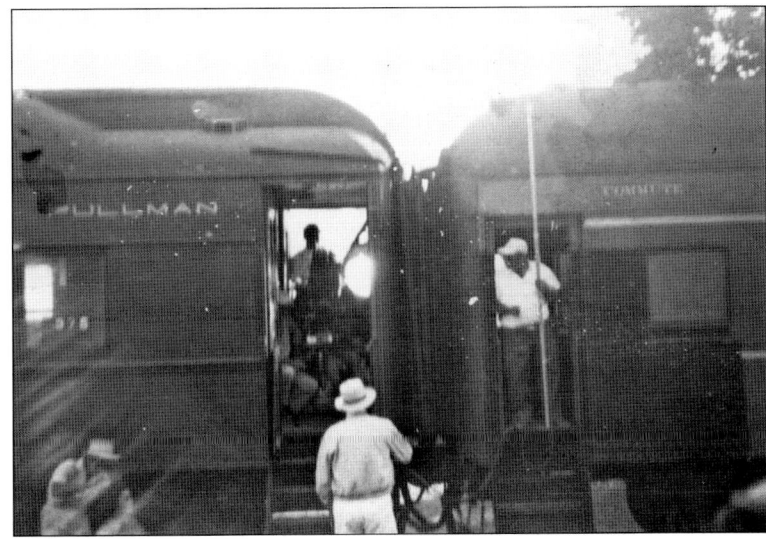

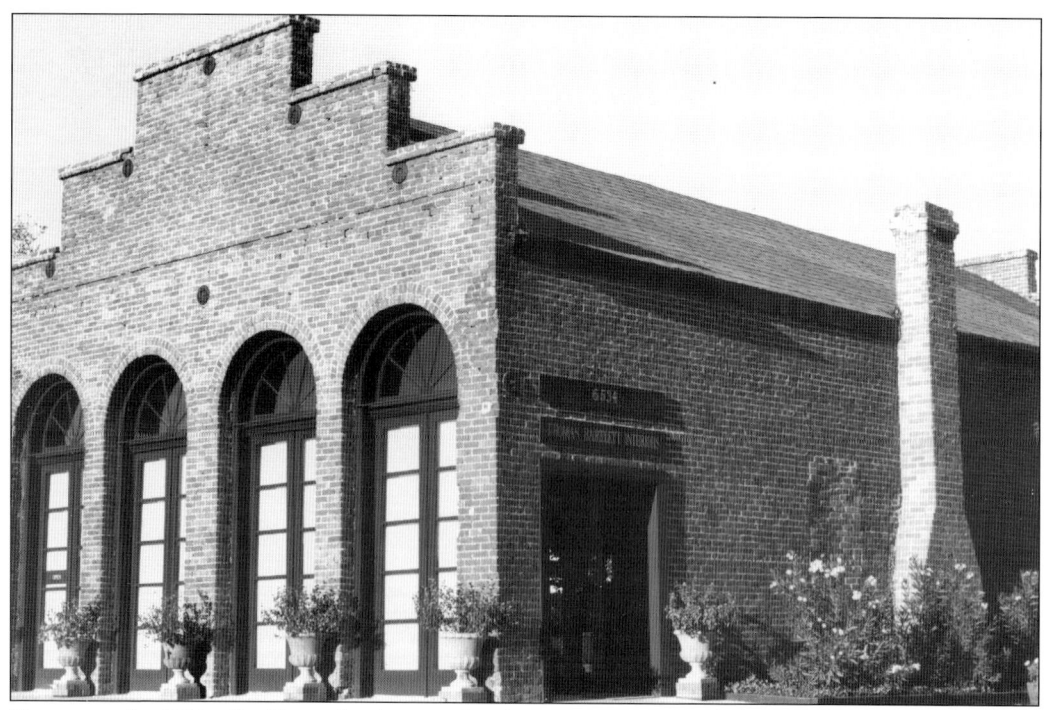

Known as the Gibbs Building, this historic brick structure, pictured above around 1977, may have been built in 1870, near the same time as the construction of the Groezinger Winery. Historians and architects have been unable to accurately trace the origins of construction, yet county records show that William Gibbs, a prominent Yountville landowner and businessman, purchased the lot from Gottlieb Groezinger in 1876. The building has been used for a variety of businesses in Yountville including a Wells Fargo stagecoach office, a saloon, Boots Coffee Shop (pictured below in the mid-1940s), an interior design showroom, and, more recently, Bouchon Restaurant. In the c. 1940 photograph below, the wooden building to the left is the Gibbs dance hall. The building to the left of the dance hall was the Veterans Pool-Hall. (Above courtesy of the Town of Yountville; below courtesy of Barbara and Bud Dulinsky.)

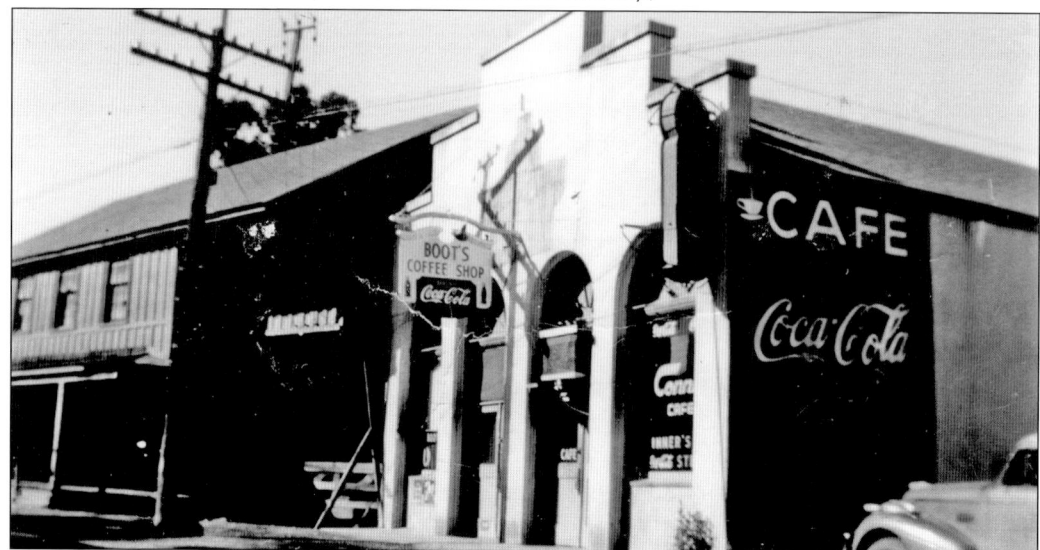

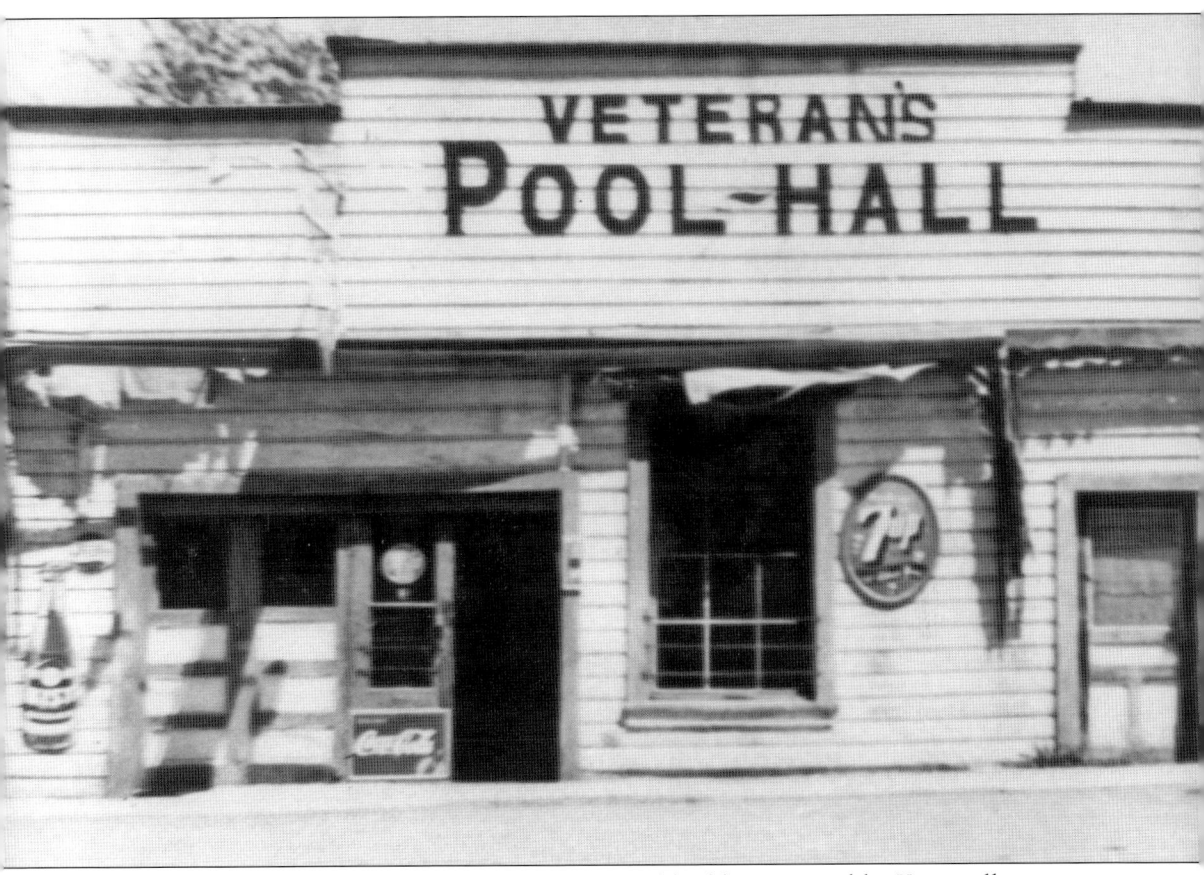

The Veterans Pool-Hall was housed in one of several buildings owned by Yountville pioneer Wallace Beard. Initially opened as a grocery store, the several structures located on this property burned down twice before the construction of the Veterans Pool-Hall. Aptly named to serve the members of the Veterans Home, the Veterans Pool-Hall remained in business until 1959 when a third and final fire destroyed the building. This photograph was taken in the 1950s shortly before the last fire. (Courtesy of the Napa Historical Society.)

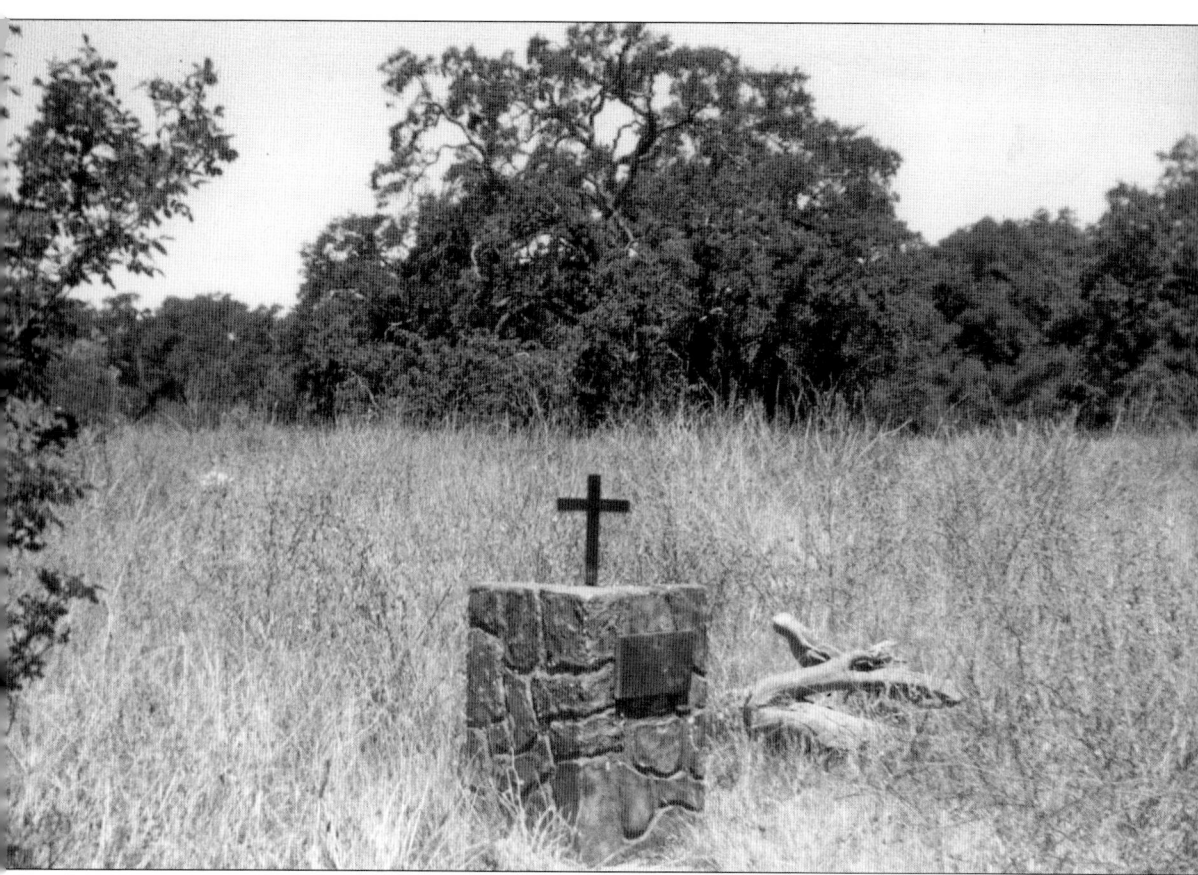

This photograph shows the plaque commemorating the site of Yountville's "Old Camp Ground" located near the current site of the Yountville Ecological Preserve. The large clearing, owned first by George Yount and later by John Finnell, was used as a place for camp meetings for Methodist, Disciples of Christ, and Seventh-Day Adventist congregations. In October 1874, the Seventh-Day Adventists held a statewide camp meeting to raise funds for a publishing house in Oakland. The campground fund-raising efforts were so successful that the Adventist newspaper was soon created. In 1980, 100 years later, the Signs Memorial Yountville Seventh-Day Adventist Church was dedicated at 1920 Finnell Road. (Courtesy of the Napa Historical Society.)

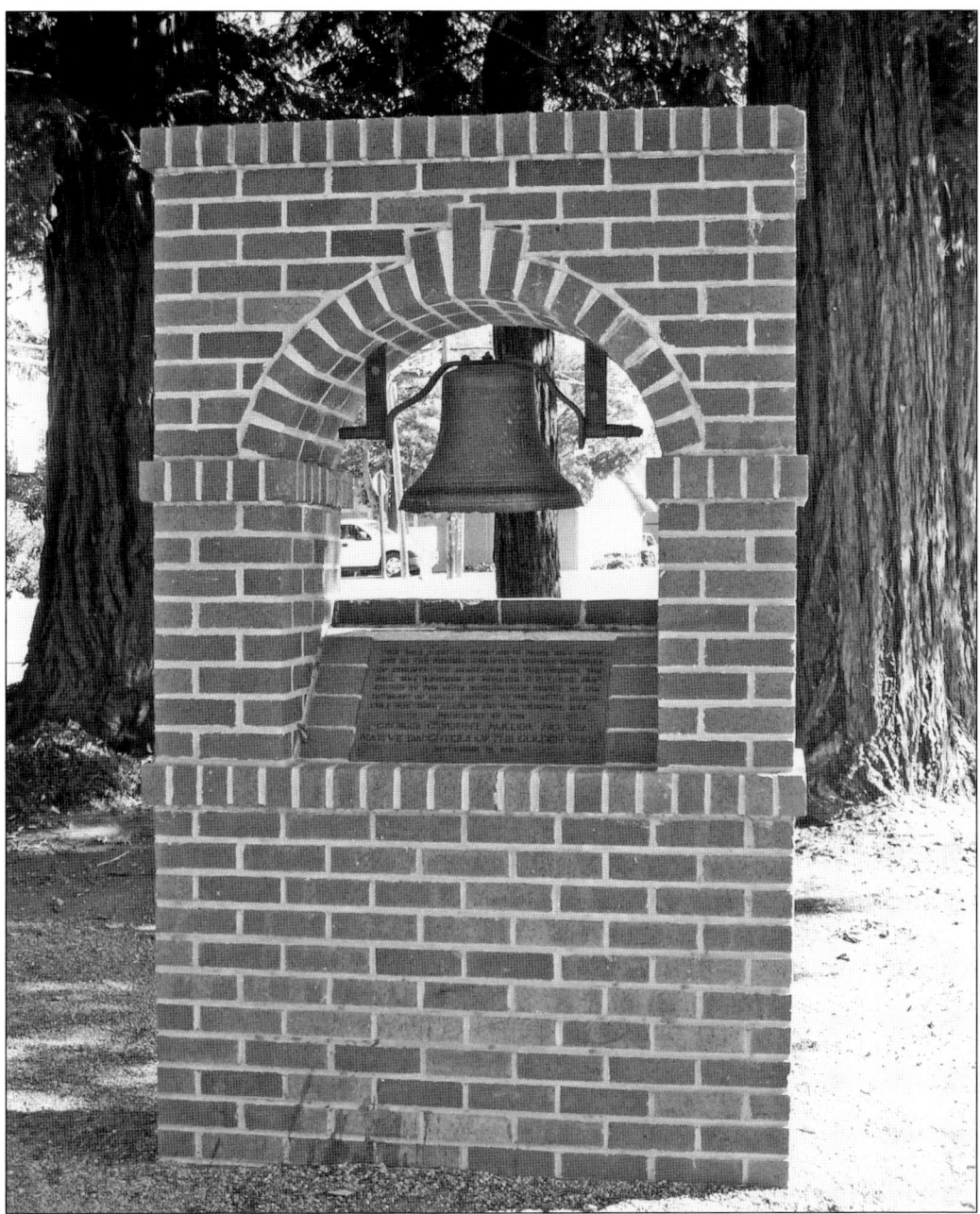

On November 14, 1859, George Yount donated land to the trustees of the Disciples of Christ Christian Church. Located on historic lot No. 25, a brick church, along with a bronze bell, was erected near the corner of present-day Madison and Washington Streets. In 1896, the church was dismantled and the locally fired bricks were sold to Yountville resident Johann (John) Wichels and the proprietors of the Magnolia Hotel. The bronze bell's location was unknown until 1983, when it resurfaced on a private ranch where it had been preserved. This recent photograph shows a monument in Yountville Park near the historic site of the Disciples of Christ Christian Church. The monument was erected by the George Yount Parlor No. 322, Native Daughters of the Golden West. (Courtesy of Stuart Alexander.)

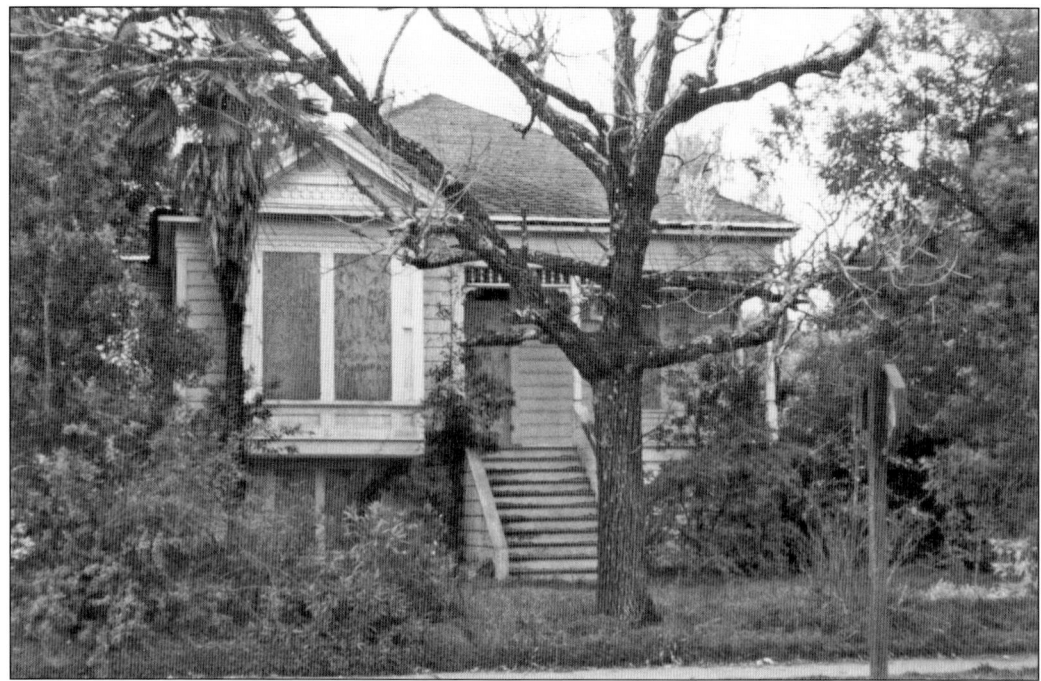

Noted for its Queen Anne bungalow style of architecture, the Whitton House, located on Washington and Humboldt Streets, was constructed in 1896. Greene and Sarah Whitton arrived in Yountville in the mid-1800s and raised their three children: Elmina, Theodore, and Charles. Both generations of Whitton men engaged in ranching and, later on, farmed a small vineyard. The home pictured here belonged to son Theodore as an adult. The front-door entrance originally faced Humboldt Street, but in the 1980s the Whitton House was extensively remodeled. During the remodel, architects raised the single-story structure, added a first story, and rotated the building to face the east. This 1983 photograph shows the Whitton House before renovation. (Courtesy of Liz Stone.)

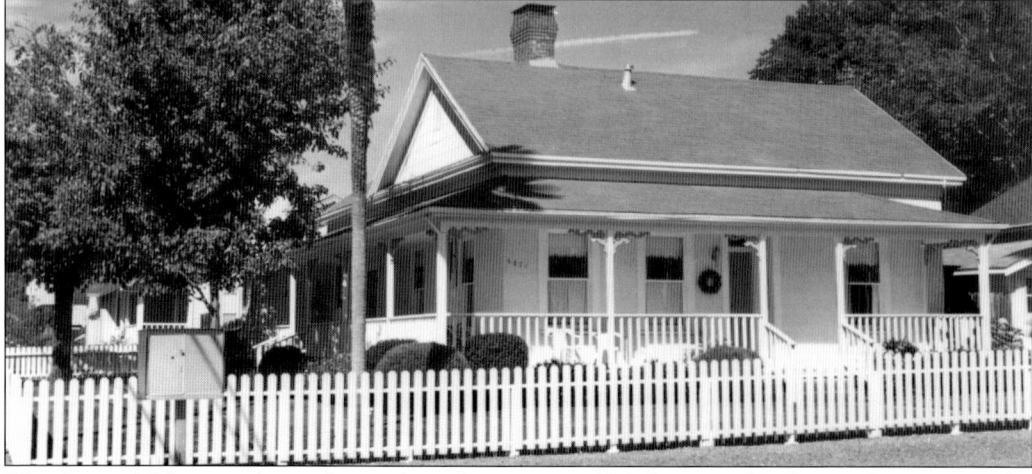

This beautiful historic home located on the corner of Madison and Jefferson Streets was the residence of famed historian John Wichels, whose pioneer grandfather Simon Sax maintained the bookkeeping duties at the Groezinger Winery in 1870. (Photograph taken in 1987, courtesy of the Town of Yountville.)

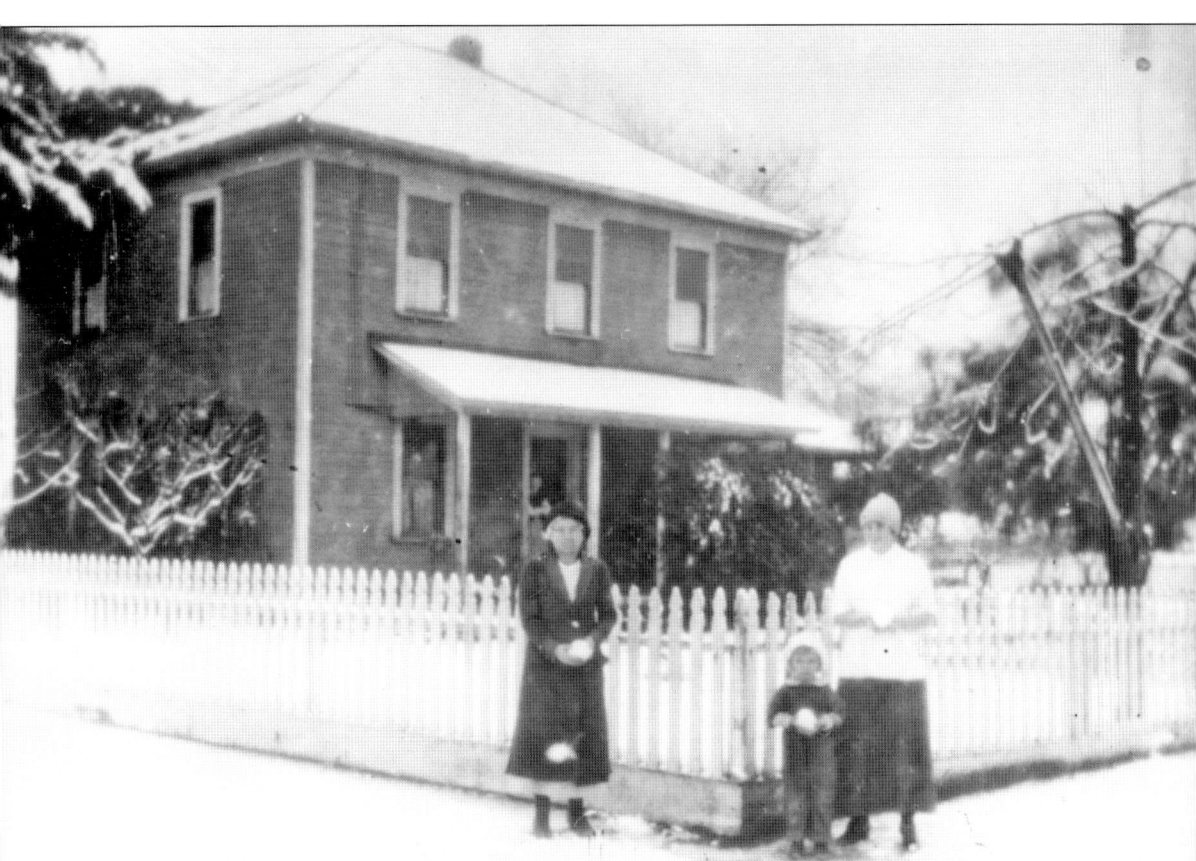

The Casaday House (sometimes spelled Cassaday), located at 6903 Jefferson Street, was built by David Casaday in 1894. The two-story, hip roof architecture of this house represents Victorian Yountville at the turn of the century, featuring landscaping details such as walking paths and perimeter picket fencing, as well as manicured lawns and gardens. The lot is located on land originally designated by George Yount for use as a public square. This early 20th-century photograph shows the Casaday House sprinkled in rare Yountville snow. The two women, left to right, are believed to be Grace Casaday and Mabel Frost Casaday. The small child standing to the left of Mabel is unidentified. (Courtesy of Mary Anne Stapleton.)

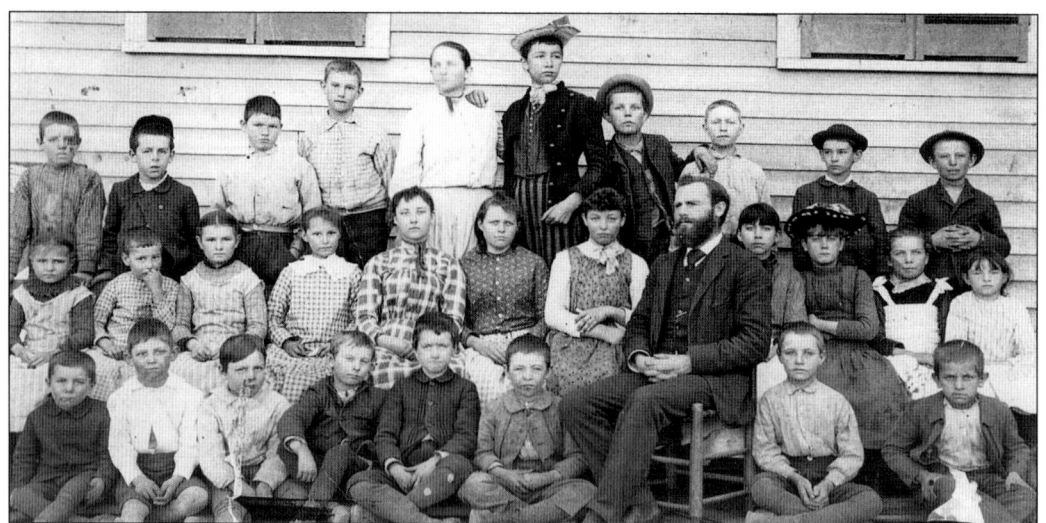

The original Yountville Grammar School was located near the site of the present-day Yountville Elementary School soccer field. Constructed in the 1860s, the original Yountville Grammar School was a one-room schoolhouse. In 1880, a second building was erected. Still a third building was erected in the current location of the Yountville Town Hall in 1942. This picture shows the school as it appeared in 1903. (Courtesy of Lee Hart.)

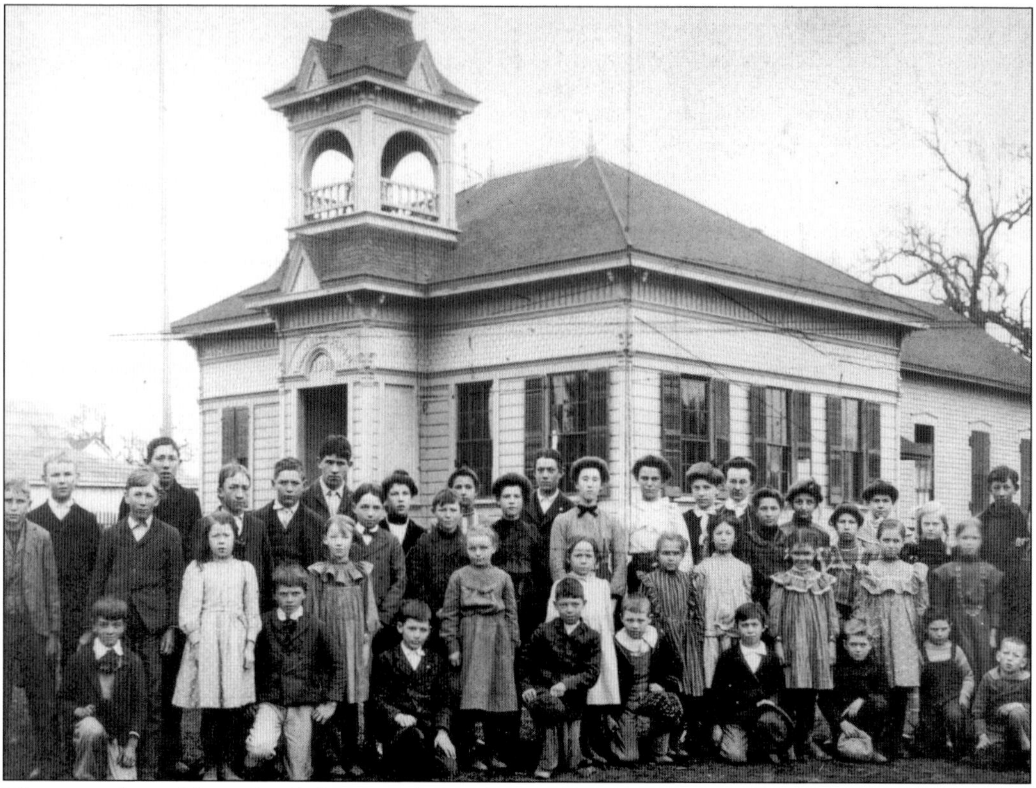

The exact date of this school photograph is unknown. With only one school in the town, there are several Yountville students in 2009 who have attended the same school as their great-grandparents. The school pictured above is actually the second Yountville School. (Courtesy of Rick Enos.)

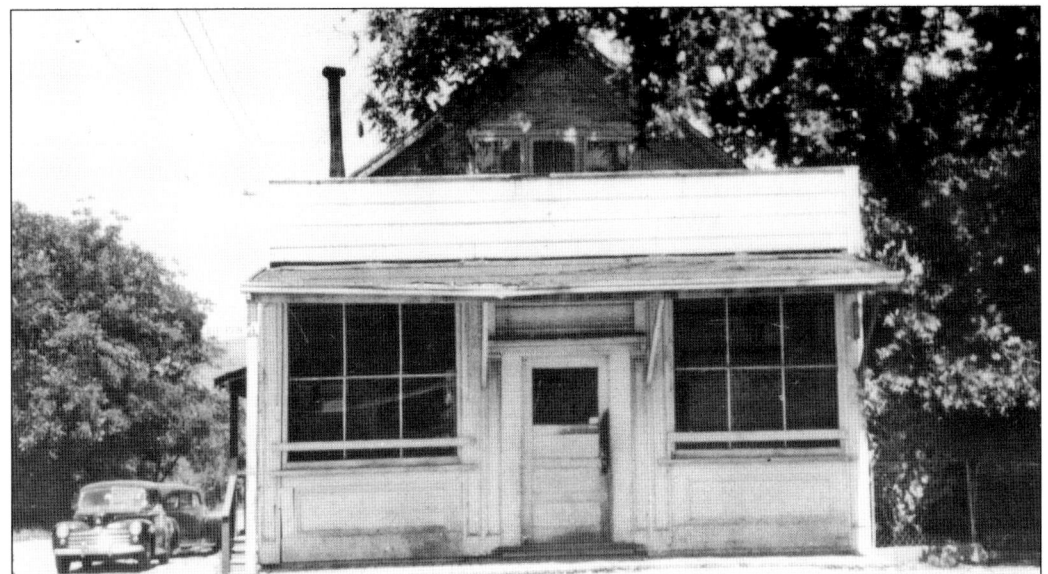

The U.S. Postal Service first assigned the name of Sebastopol to the town on May 19, 1856, and assigned Donald M. Johnson as postmaster. This may have caused some initial confusion, because there was already another post office with the name (Sebastopol) located in Sonoma, California. The name remained for 11 more years until 1867, when the U.S. Postal Service changed the name to Yountville. The post office in Yountville changed locations at least four times before it ended up on the corner of Washington and Humboldt Street in 1915. Prior to 1915, Yountville had two daily mail deliveries, six days per week.

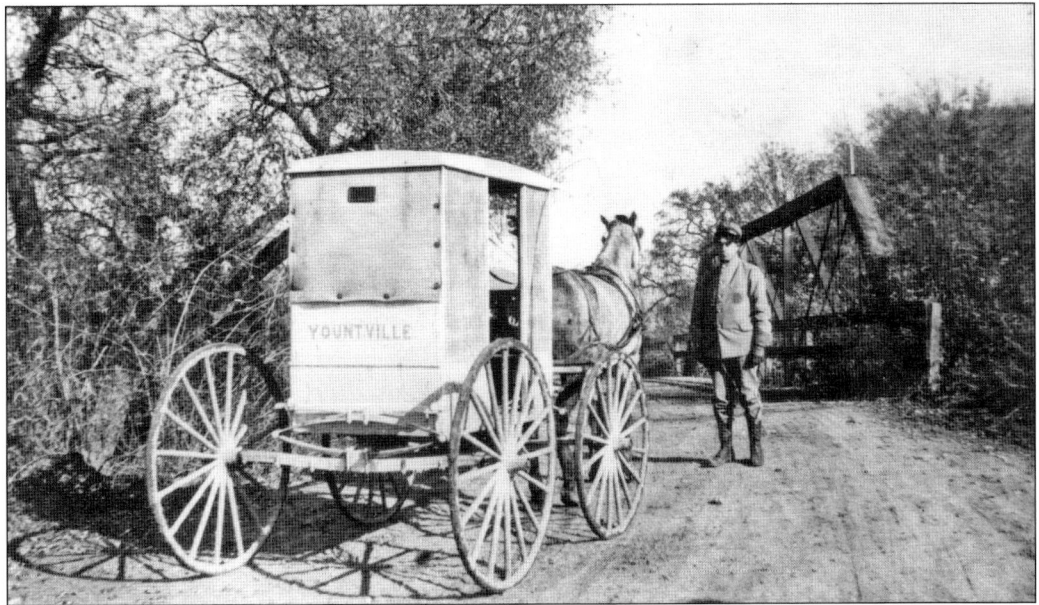

In 1906, the Yountville Post Office began rural free delivery service (RFD No. 1) with Chancellor Walt Whitton as the first carrier. In 1907, Chancellor E. W. Johnson was appointed to deliver the mail and faithfully preformed this duty for the next 39 years. This picture shows Johnson on duty in the early 1900s. In 1922, Gladys E. Beard assumed the duty of postmaster of Yountville and operated the Yountville Post Office for the next 33 years. (Courtesy of the Napa Historical Society.)

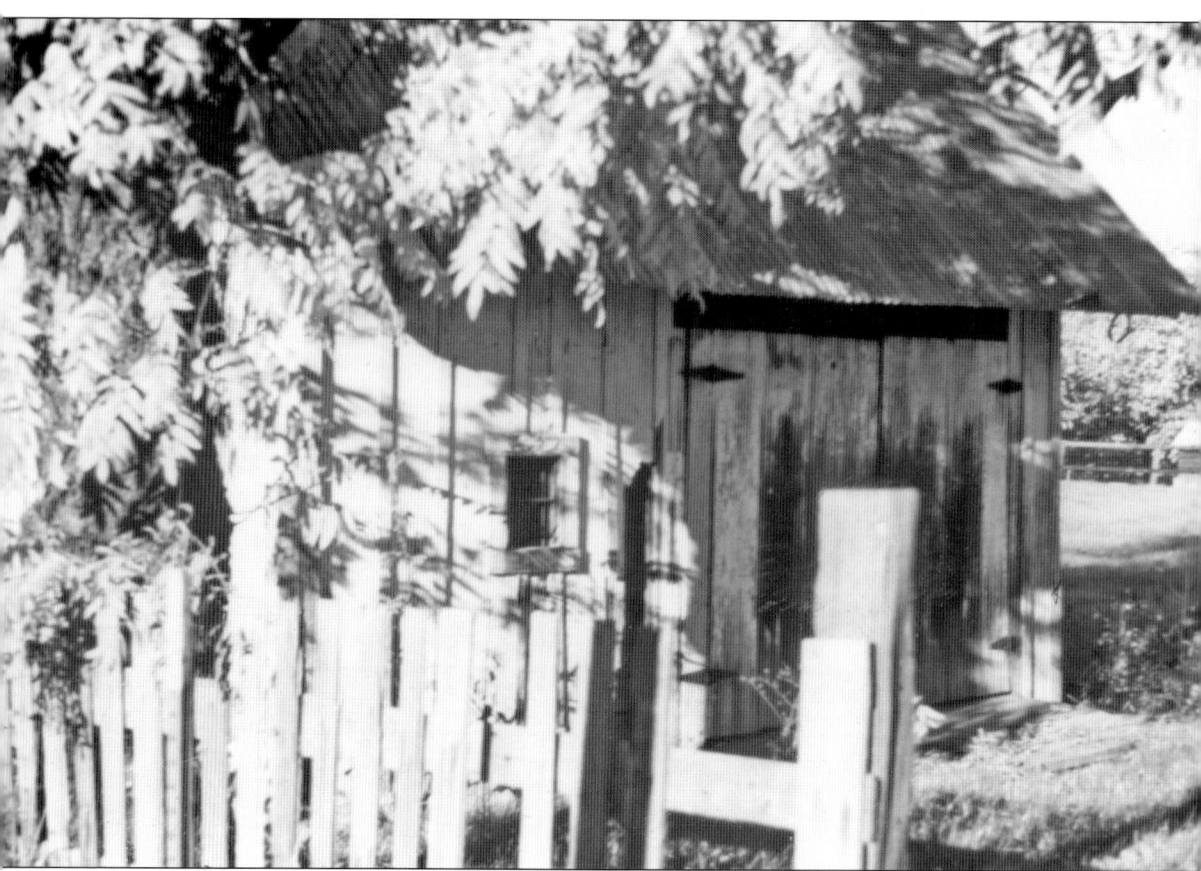

The original Yountville Jail, often used to house inebriated Yountville bar patrons, was located on the north side of Monroe Street, west of Jefferson Street. Although the structure's original location is unknown, historians can confirm it was built in the mid-1800s and moved to the Monroe Street location in the early 1900s. This two-room, 9-by-9-foot cell, shown here around 1970 complete with a wooden bench and barred windows, was torn down shortly after this photograph was taken. (Courtesy of Mindy Jordan.)

Three

THE VETERANS HOME OF CALIFORNIA

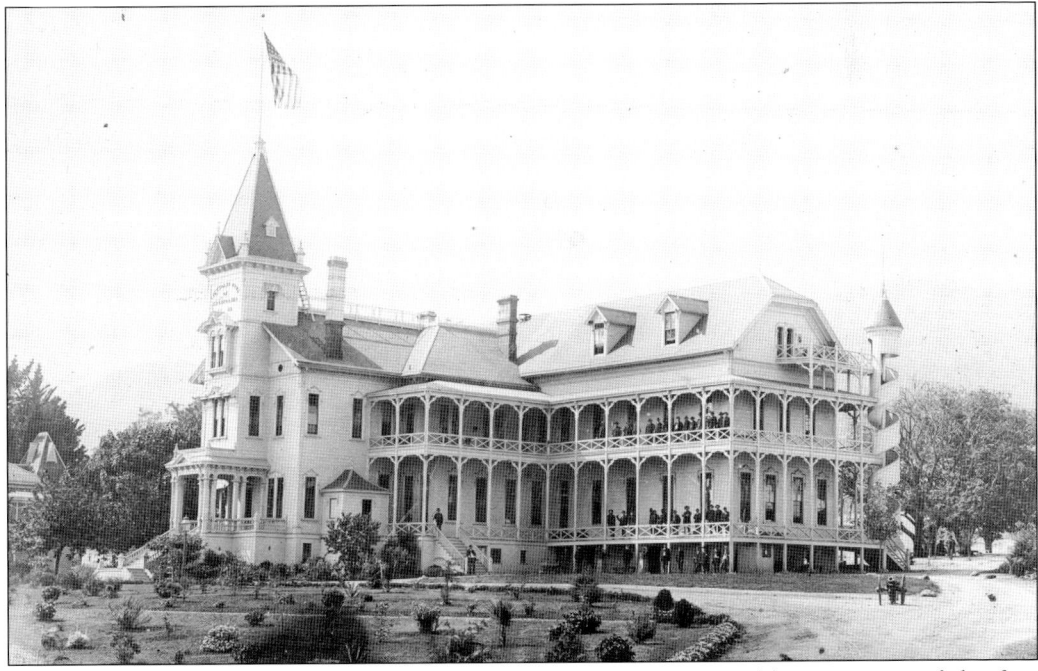

Opening its doors in 1884, The Grand Mark Administration Building was one of the first buildings constructed by the Veterans Home Association. Originally proposed by the Associated Veterans of the Mexican-American War with the help of the Lincoln Post of the Grand Army of the Republic, both organization members recognized the need for a care and support facility for disabled veterans. Upon incorporation in 1882, the newly created Veterans Home Association purchased 910 acres near Yountville on a parcel of land known as the A. G. Clark Place. This vintage postcard shows the administration building as it appeared in the late 1890s. The Grand Mark had rooms for officers, staff, library, chapel, kitchen, dining room, hospital, and dormitories for the veterans. Note the rounded fire escape on the right-hand side of the picture. The Veterans Home of California is listed as California Historical Landmark No. 828. (Courtesy of Barbara and Bud Dulinsky and the archives of the Veterans Home of Yountville.)

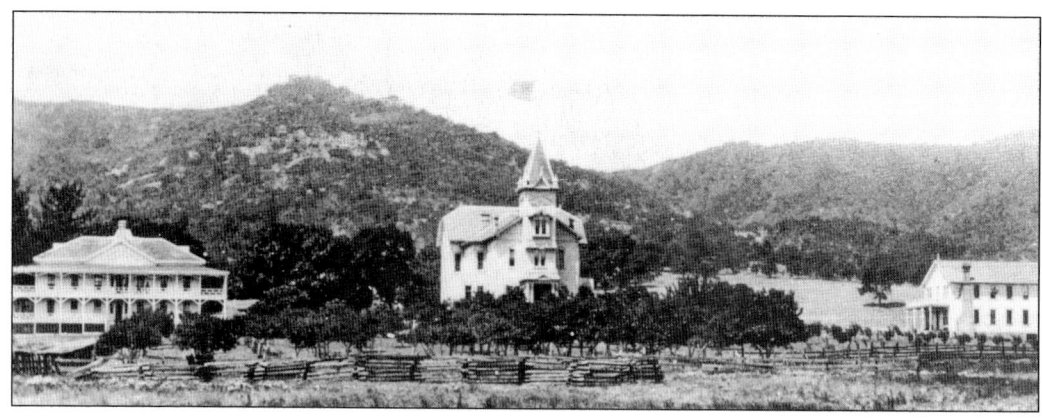

This is the Veterans Home as it appeared in the late 1880s. The facility was completely rebuilt in the 1930s when its leadership passed to World War I hero and Congressional Medal of Honor recipient Col. Nelson Miles Holderman. Under his direction, the old Victorian-style buildings which had housed Civil War veterans were replaced by more modern Mission Revival architectural design. In the c. 1922 photograph below, the tree-lined drive is called Los Angeles Avenue. This street name reflects the Mediterranean style of landscape found throughout the entire Veterans Home grounds. (Above courtesy of Bud and Barbara Dulinsky; below courtesy of the archives of the Veterans Home of California-Yountville.)

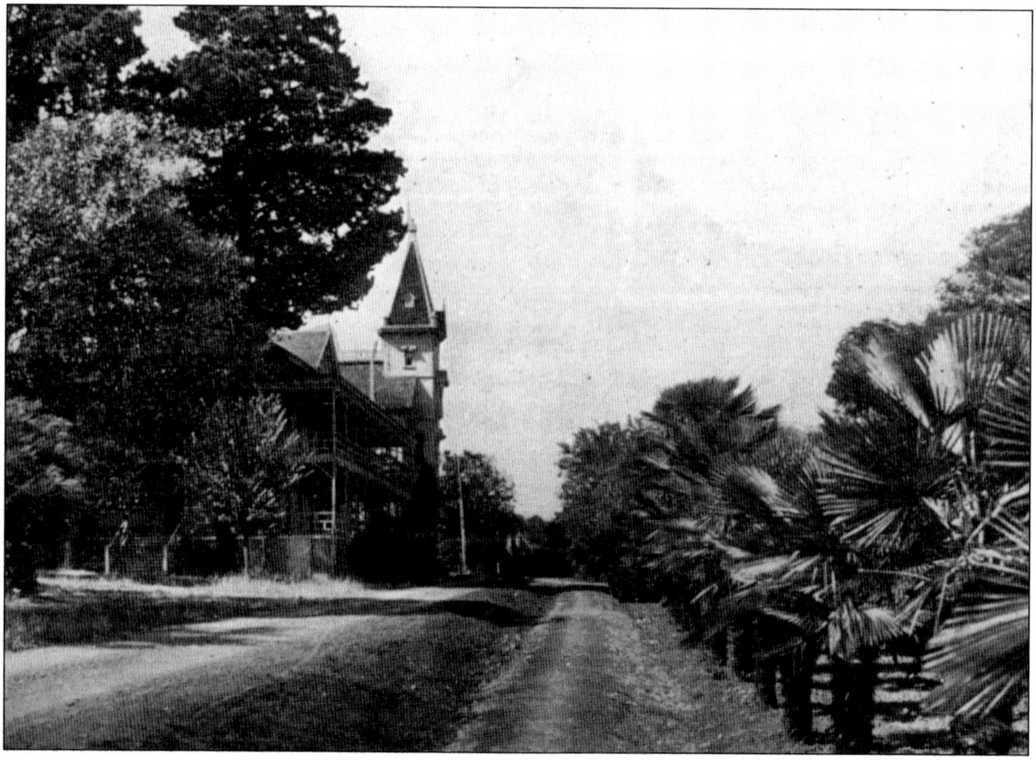

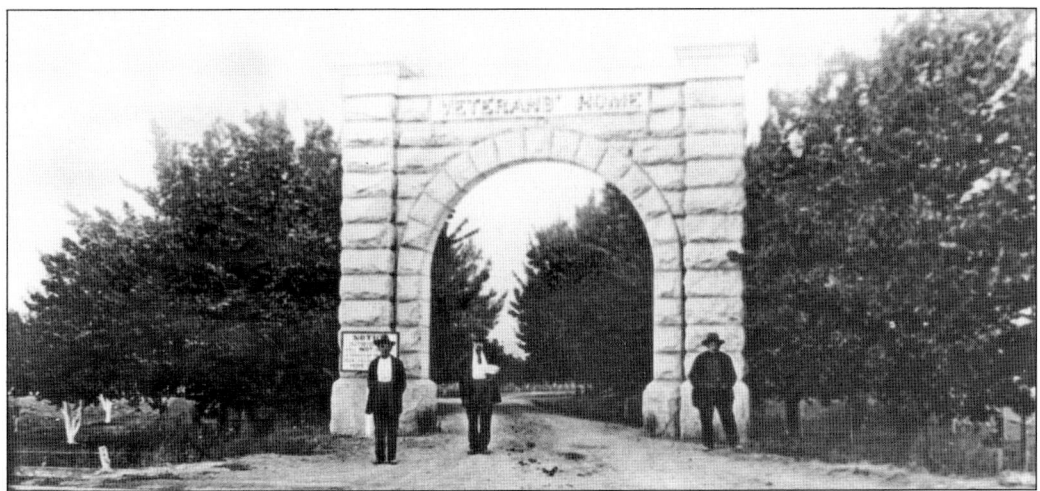

Initially, the Veterans Home received partial funding from both the state and federal governments. In 1896, the federal government declared it would no longer provide funds to privately operated soldiers' homes. Because of this new policy, the Veterans Home Association sold the home and associated property to the State of California for a single $20 gold coin. Under the ownership of the State of California, the name was officially changed to the Veterans Home of California. Taken in the late 1880s, this photograph shows several unidentified gentlemen in front of the home's entrance. This entrance location was to the south of the present-day entrance on California Drive, shown below. (Courtesy of the Napa Historical Society.)

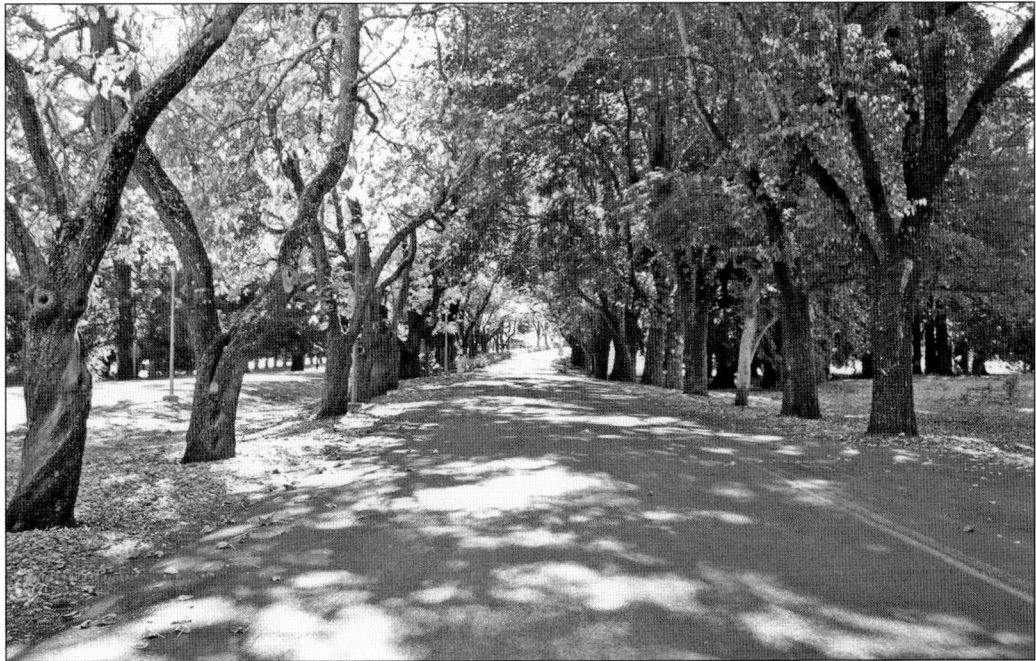

When visitors come to the Veterans Home, they pass under a tunnel of beautiful elm trees along California Drive. These historic elms came from the 1939 World's Fair and Exposition on Treasure Island in San Francisco. At the closing of the world's fair, the San Francisco Presidio donated several dozen trees in pots that were to be planted along California Drive. (Courtesy of Beau Alexander.)

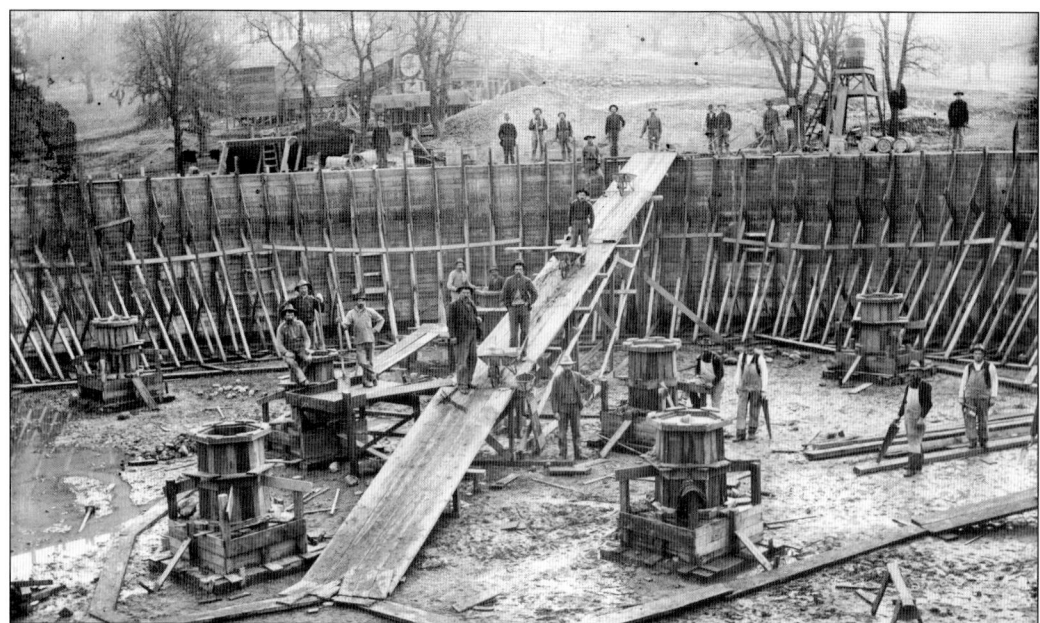

The water reservoir tank in this c. 1906 photograph was designed by civil engineer Clement Fusier and was built in the early 1900s. Originally the water source for the tank came from the Hinman Lake and Dam project located approximately one mile west of the reservoir, also on the Veterans Home grounds. The tank was covered in 2008 and is still in use holding over one million gallons of water. The water source that currently fills the reservoir comes from the Rector Dam and Reservoir project located on the Silverado Trail and is also operated by the Veterans Home. (Courtesy of Phyllis Vallerga.)

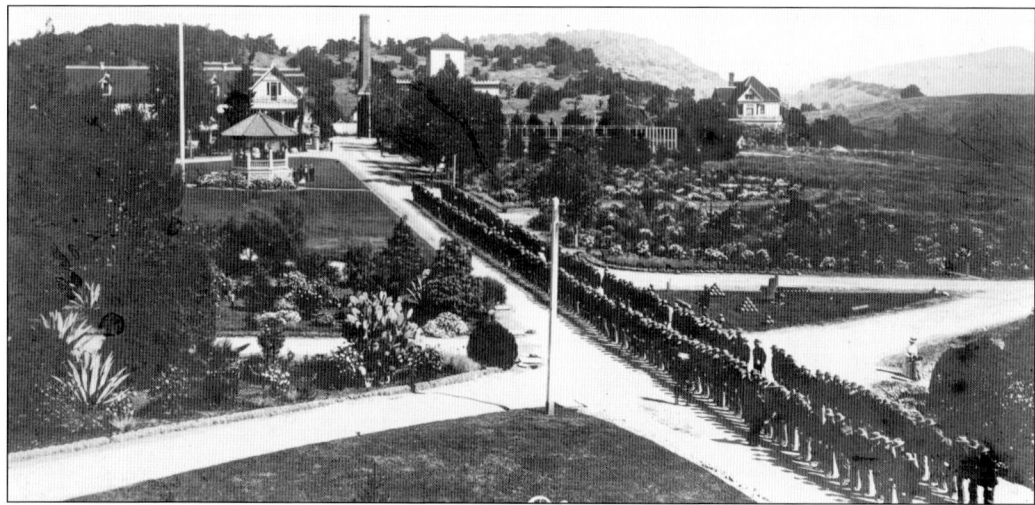

The Veterans Home was operated under the direction of a military commandant by the California Military Department until 1955, when the Department of Veterans Affairs was established. Prior to 1955, veterans were called to assemble in full military uniform for marching drills. In later years, the Department of Veterans Affairs appointed a state administrator to lead the Veterans Home, and residents transitioned to a more civilian lifestyle and attire. (Information taken from the 2009 Veterans Home Brochure; photograph courtesy of the archives of the Veterans Home-Yountville.)

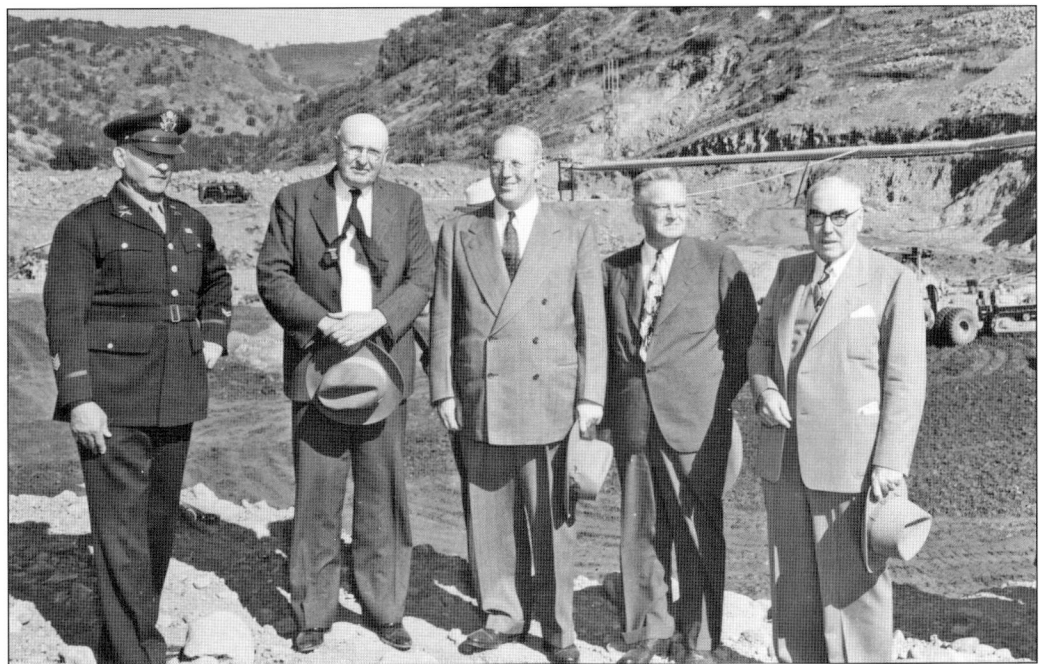

As a Congressional Medal of Honor recipient, Colonel Holderman brought recognition and prestige to the Veterans Home. He frequently invited state and national dignitaries to visit the Veterans Home. Pictured here in the early 1950s, from left to right are Col. Nelson Holderman, Owen Duffy, California governor Earl Warren, James Dean, and an unidentified gentleman. This photograph was taken at the construction site of the Veterans Home–operated Rector Dam. (Courtesy of the Napa Historical Society.)

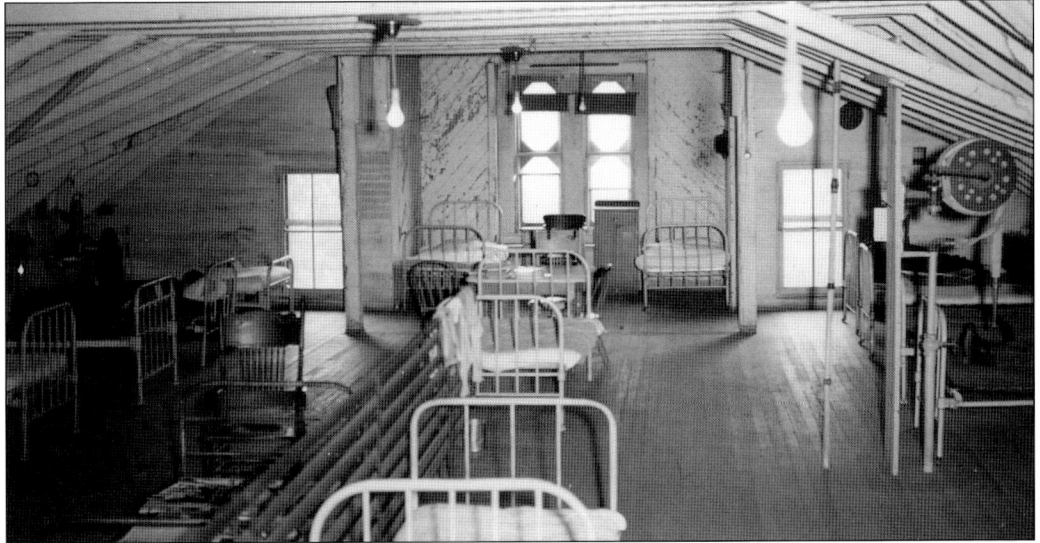

This rare c. 1919 photograph shows the men's dormitories located in the attic of the Grand Mark Administration Building. As demand for residence grew in the early years, regular dormitories quickly became crowded and attic dormitories were added. Once ownership of the Veterans Home transferred to the State of California, more dormitories were built to relieve the overcrowded conditions. (Courtesy of the archives of the Veterans Home of California-Yountville.)

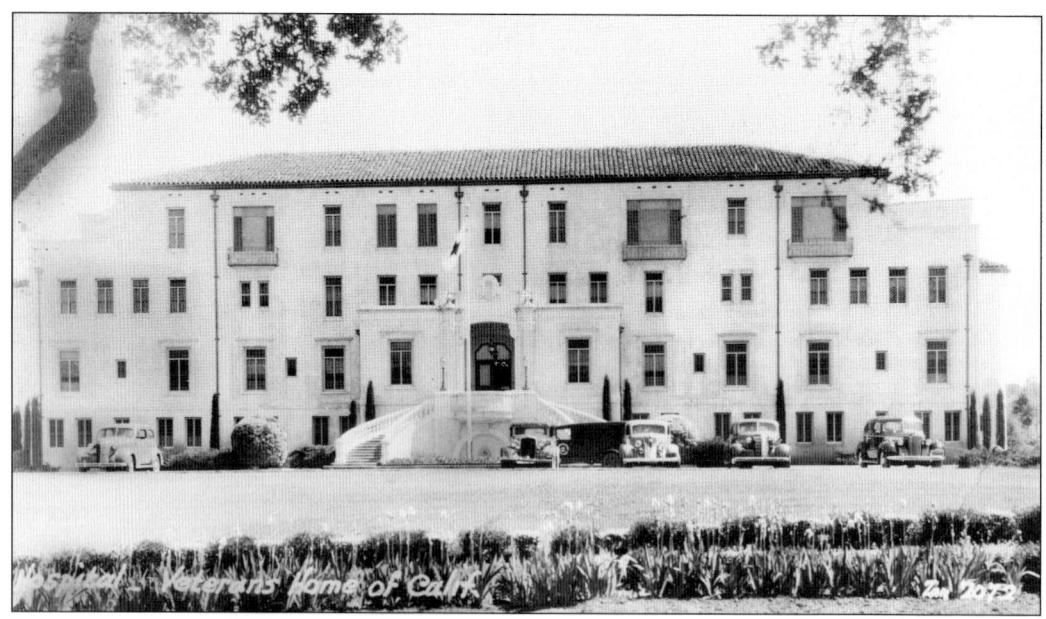

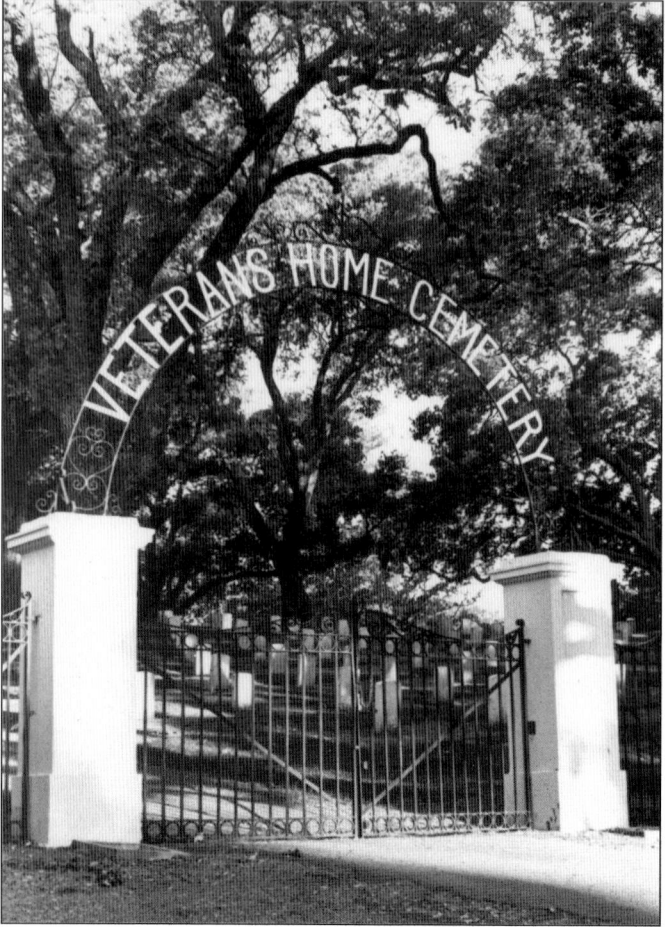

Throughout his tenure, Colonel Holderman worked ceaselessly to improve the physical and social lives of the Veterans Home residents. He lobbied for funds to improve the power plant at the Veterans Home as well as to repair old and dilapidated buildings. He was responsible for the construction of a 500-bed hospital facility on the grounds. In 1932, the hospital which bears his name opened its doors for the first time. During the construction of the hospital, construction workers unearthed the remains of a uniformed soldier in an unmarked grave. This veteran was laid to rest in a place of honor at the top of the current Veterans Cemetery (pictured below around 1980) and has become the Veterans Home "Unknown Soldier." (Above photograph courtesy of Phyllis Vallerga; below photograph courtesy of the archives of the Veterans Home of California-Yountville.)

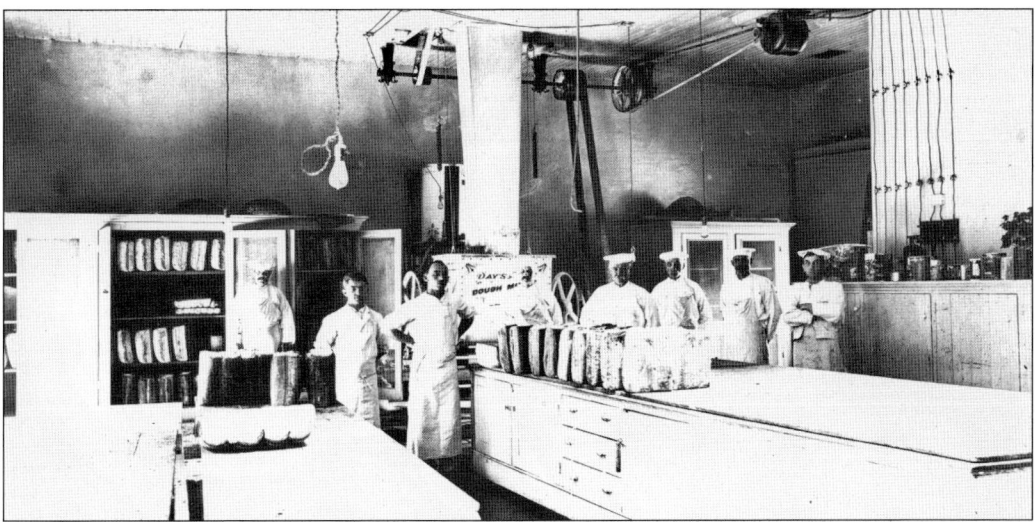

When the State of California took over control, the grounds of the Veterans Home consisted of 910 acres of land, numerous buildings, a dairy herd, chicken hatchery, and a hog farm. This early 1900s photograph shows several unidentified bakers in a kitchen at the Veterans Home. Outside workers were employed on the Veterans Home staff, and veterans were also encouraged to work and contribute to the operation of the home. (Courtesy of the Napa Historical Society.)

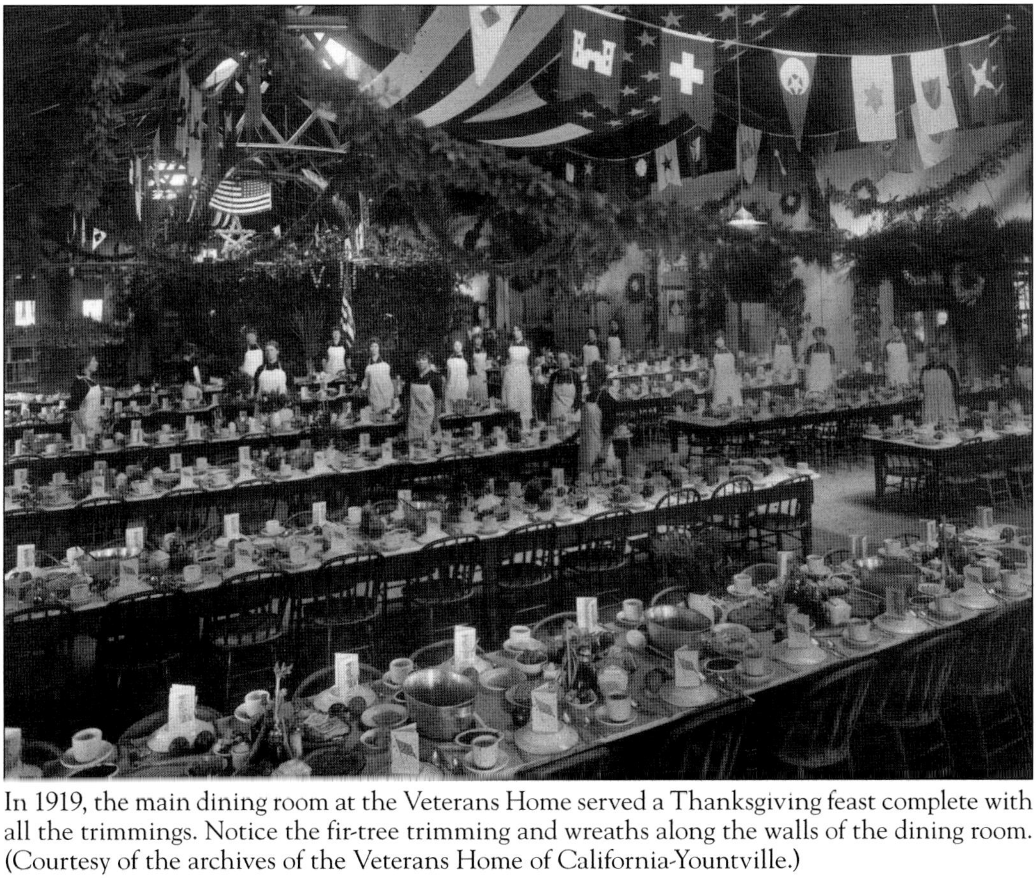

In 1919, the main dining room at the Veterans Home served a Thanksgiving feast complete with all the trimmings. Notice the fir-tree trimming and wreaths along the walls of the dining room. (Courtesy of the archives of the Veterans Home of California-Yountville.)

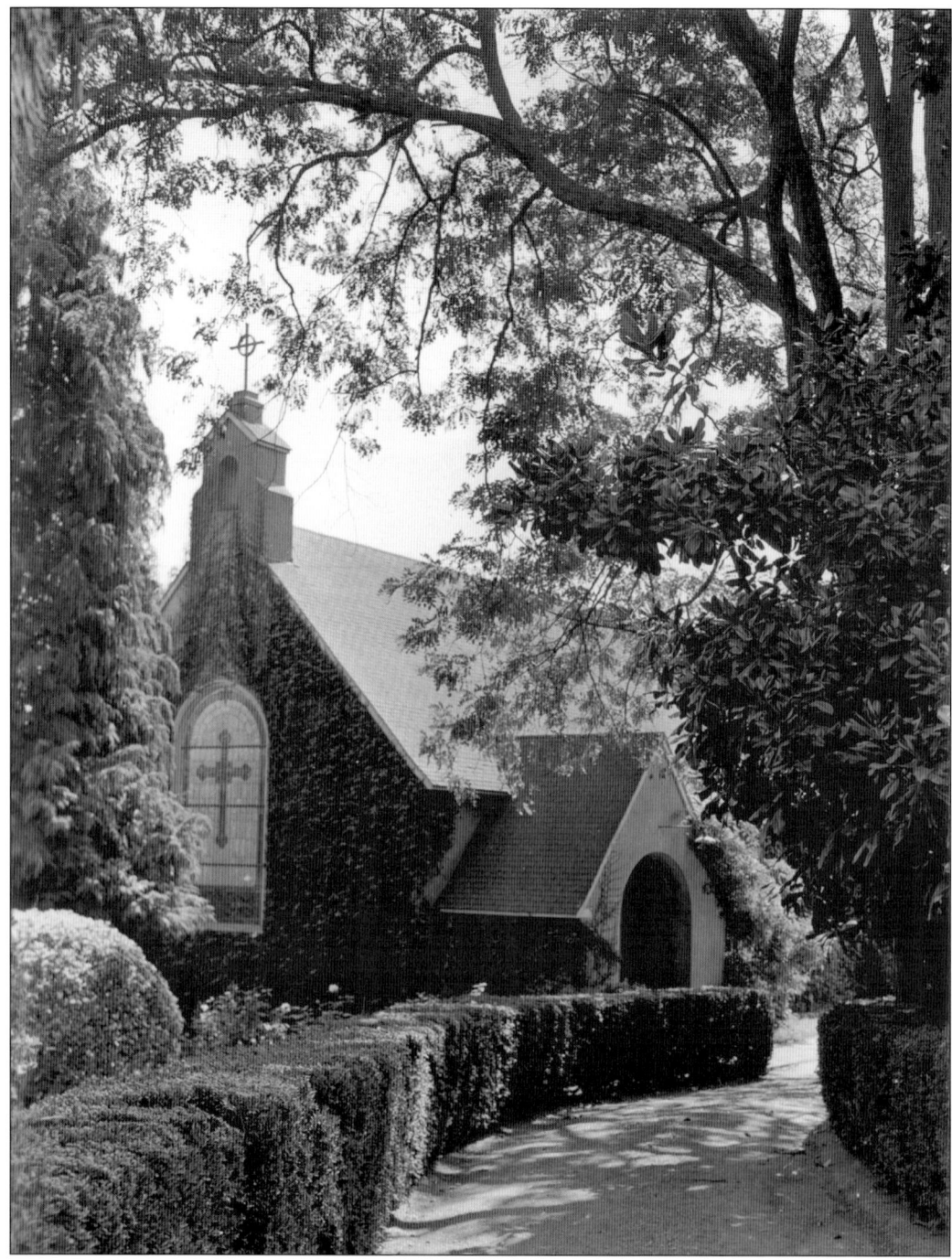

Built in 1918, the Veterans Home Armistice Chapel is an all-faith chapel designed in late Gothic Revival–style architecture by George MacDougall. The landscaping around this historic building was designed in part by John McLaren, who was the landscape designer of Golden Gate Park in San Francisco, and Cleve Borman, for whom the veteran's baseball field is named. The Armistice Chapel is on the National Register of Historic Places, No. 79000510. (Courtesy of Barbara Dulinsky.)

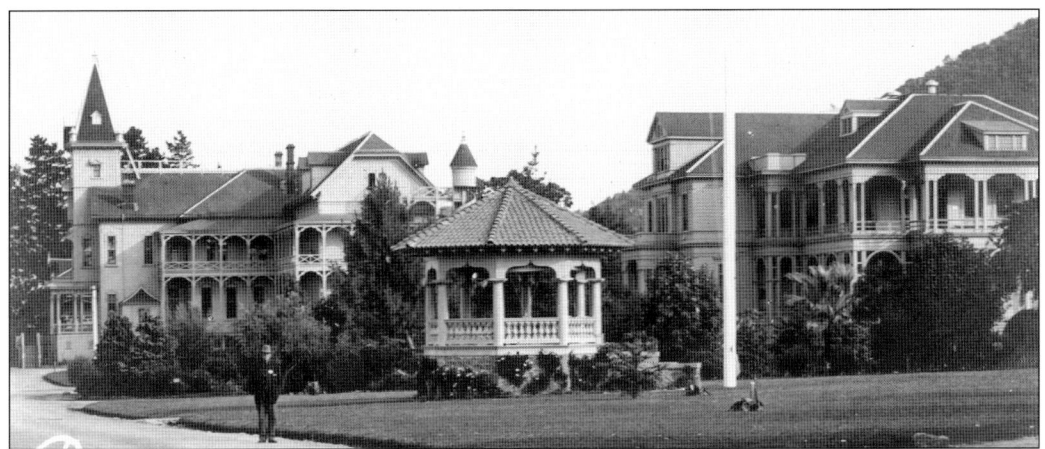

The Veterans Home bandstand was built in the early 1900s and is presently the oldest remaining structure on the Veterans Home grounds. Known for its many parades, marching bands, and civic celebrations, the Veterans Home has served not only Veterans Home residents but also the greater community. During the Depression, local families came to the Veterans Home for food and support and were never turned away by Colonel Holderman and his staff. (Courtesy of Barbara Dulinsky.)

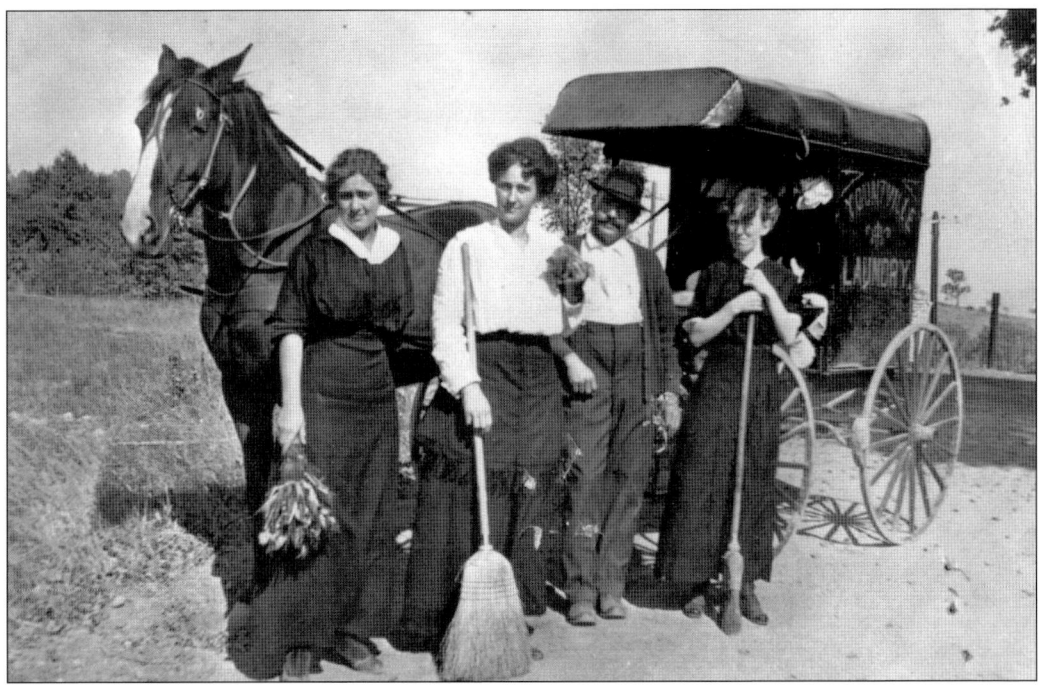

The Veterans Home provided opportunities for employment for many residents living in Yountville. In this c. 1910 photograph, the side of the wagon reads, "Yountville Laundry." The inscription on the back of the photograph reads, "Yountville residents John Landers family." The author wonders if this is actually referring to the members of the John Lande family, proprietors and owners of the now famous historic building the French Laundry. (Courtesy of the archives of the Veterans Home of California-Yountville.)

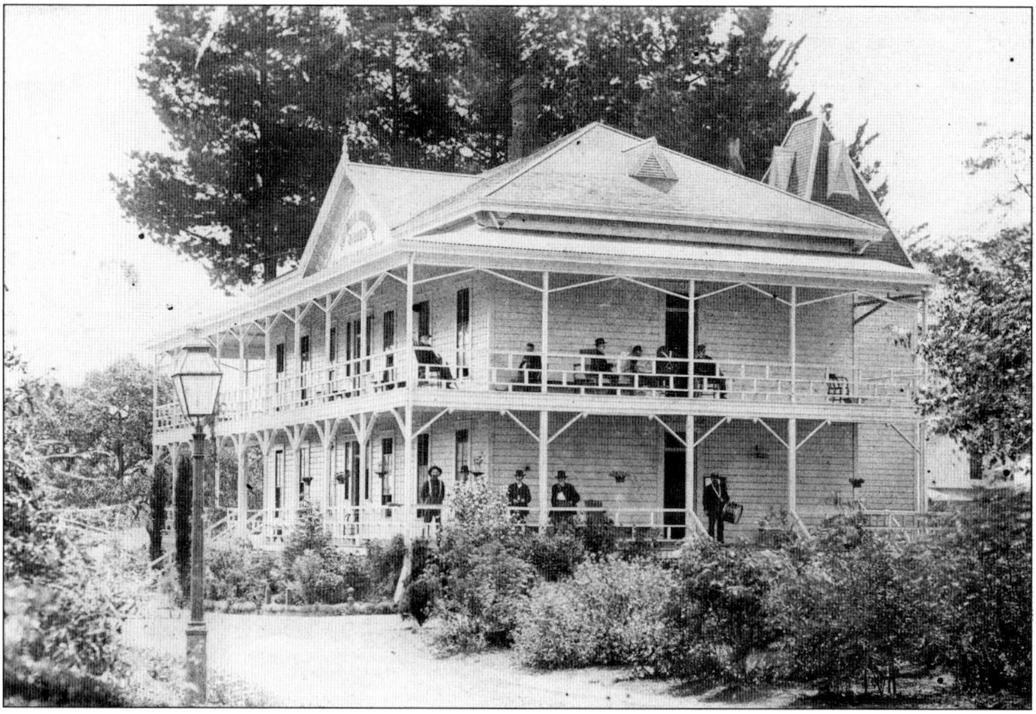

This photograph of the early barracks near the administration building shows veterans relaxing on the porch. When the doors first opened in 1884, the Veterans Home was open to all veterans west of the Rocky Mountains. Original admission logs showed that many men served in the Civil War, the Mexican-American War, and the Indian Wars. Today the Veterans Home is focused on meeting the needs of "aged and disabled" California veterans and has added a short-term assistance program for Iraq and Afghanistan veterans called "The Pathway Home." (Courtesy of Phyllis Vallerga.)

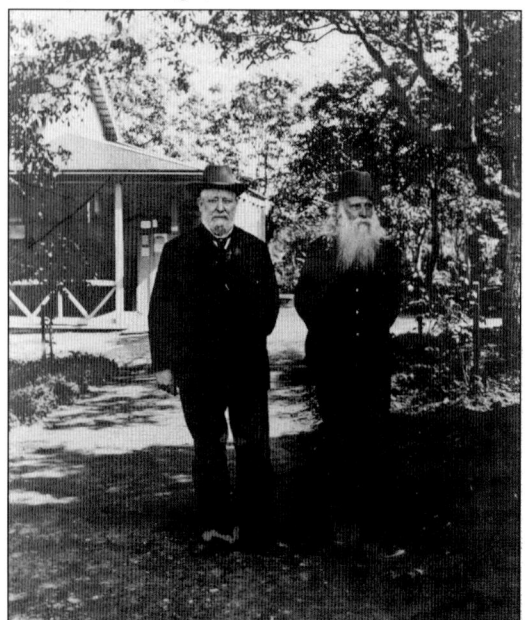

This historic photograph depicts two unidentified veterans strolling around the grounds of the Veterans Home. In earlier years, the grounds of the Veterans Home boasted of manicured Mediterranean gardens and landscaping, held numerous parades and civic celebrations, and entertained distinguished visitors and dignitaries. In 2009, the Veterans Home of Yountville offers residents proximity to scenic hiking trails, use of a newly renovated swim center, access to world-famous performances at the Lincoln Theater, and a warm welcoming membership to the Napa Valley Museum. (Courtesy of the Napa Valley Museum.)

Four
EARLY 20TH CENTURY

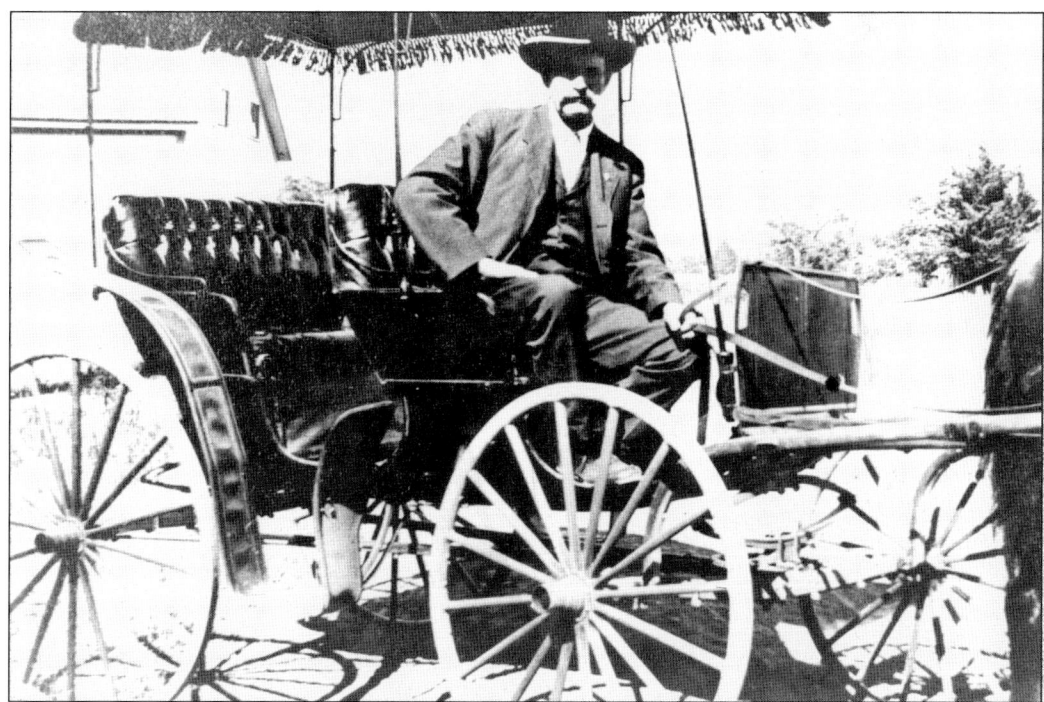

Posing for this picture in 1910, John Lee Webber sits atop his horse-drawn carriage. Transportation by carriage in early times was sometimes difficult and often uncomfortable. Protection from the elements came in the form of an overhead canvas carriage top and required carriage riders to wear hats. Unfortunately, protection from the dusty roads carried few remedies. John L. Webber was a Napa County supervisor for many years and was responsible for much of the county's efforts to improve the dirt roads by surfacing them with "macadamized" rock. In this procedure, Napa County roads were "paved" by layering a mixture of oil and gravel over the surface of the road to reduce the disturbance of dust and grime. (Courtesy of Barbara and Bud Dulinsky.)

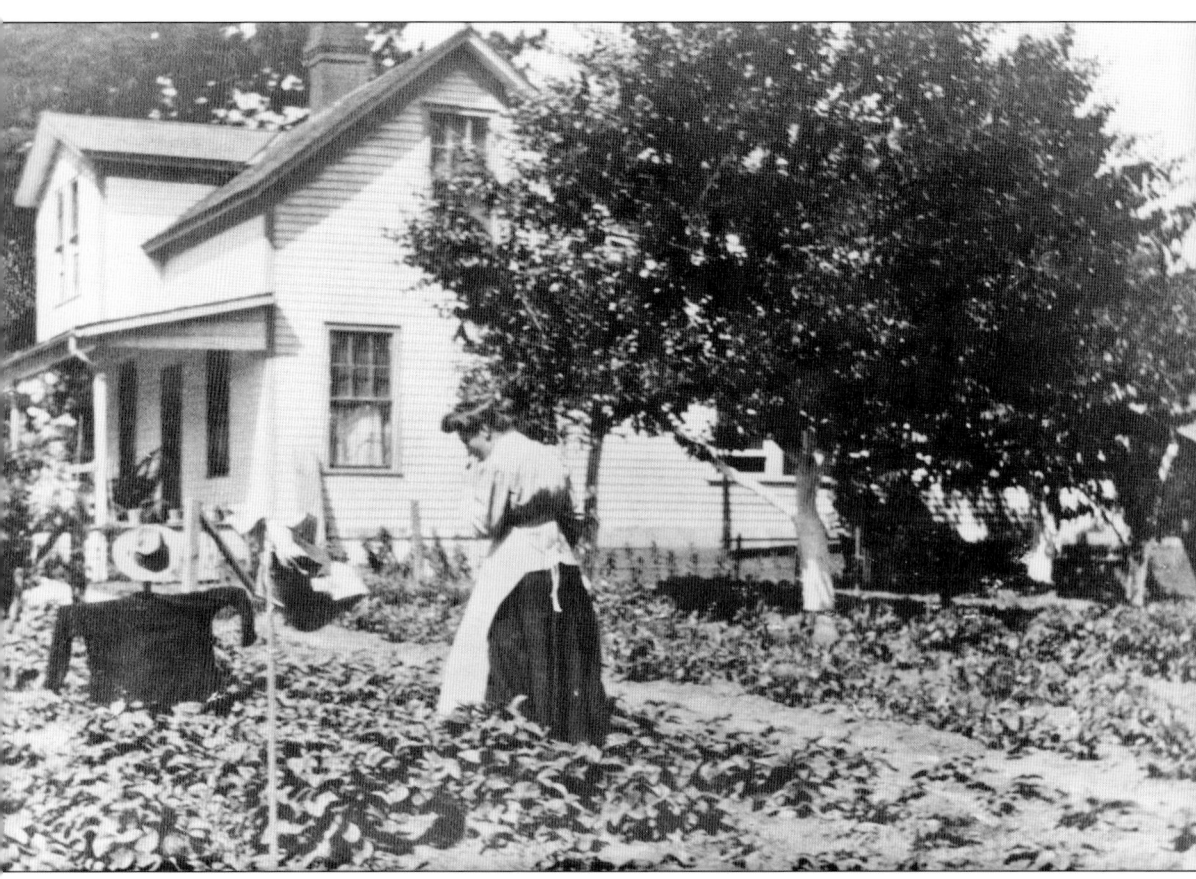

The Webber House is a two-story frame farmhouse and barn located on the corner of Webber Avenue and Jefferson Street. Originally this building stood on the ranch of Capt. John Grigsby, located southeast of Yountville. John Grigsby is remembered today as one of the key players in the formation of the Bear Flag Revolt. According to Napa historian Floyd Stone in his extensive research on the chain of land titles in Yountville, Capt. John Grigsby once owned much of the land currently occupied by present-day Yountville and the grounds of the Veterans Home. The famous historic farmhouse was moved to its present location in the 1890s. This 1901 photograph shows Nancy (Grigsby) Webber at work in her garden. In 2008, the historic Webber House is operated as the Lavender Bed and Breakfast Inn. (Courtesy of Barbara and Bud Dulinsky.)

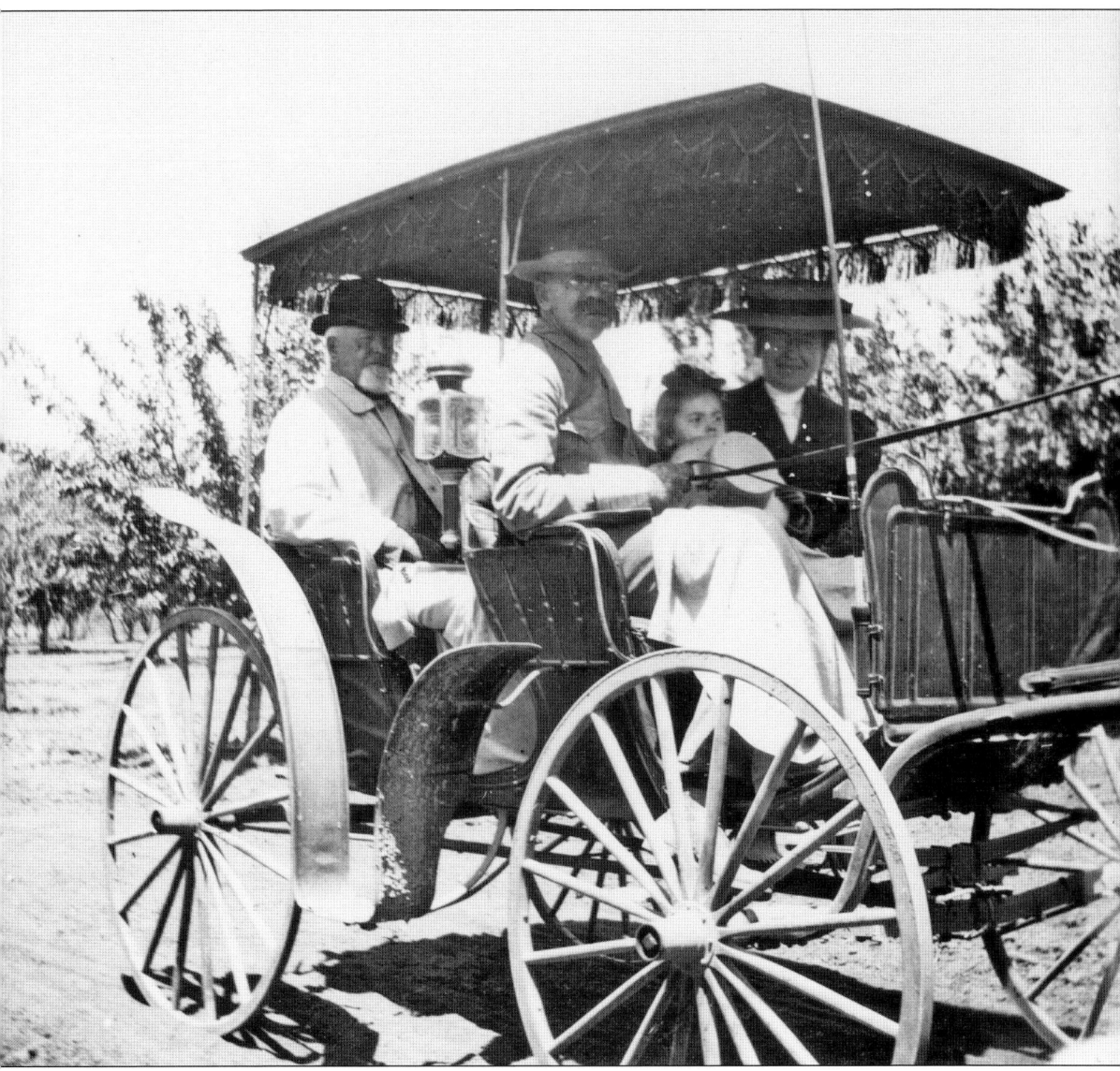

In 1910, U.S. District Judge John J. DeHaven purchased 25 acres of land located on the current site of Rancho De Napa mobile home park. Posing in 1912 for a photograph on the DeHaven Acres Estate are, from left to right, the Honorable John J. DeHaven, his son Jo J. DeHaven, granddaughter Lee DeHaven (Atwood), and daughter Sarah L. DeHaven. Notice the mud flaps on the horse-drawn carriage, as well as the carriage lantern. (Courtesy of Dr. James Atwood.)

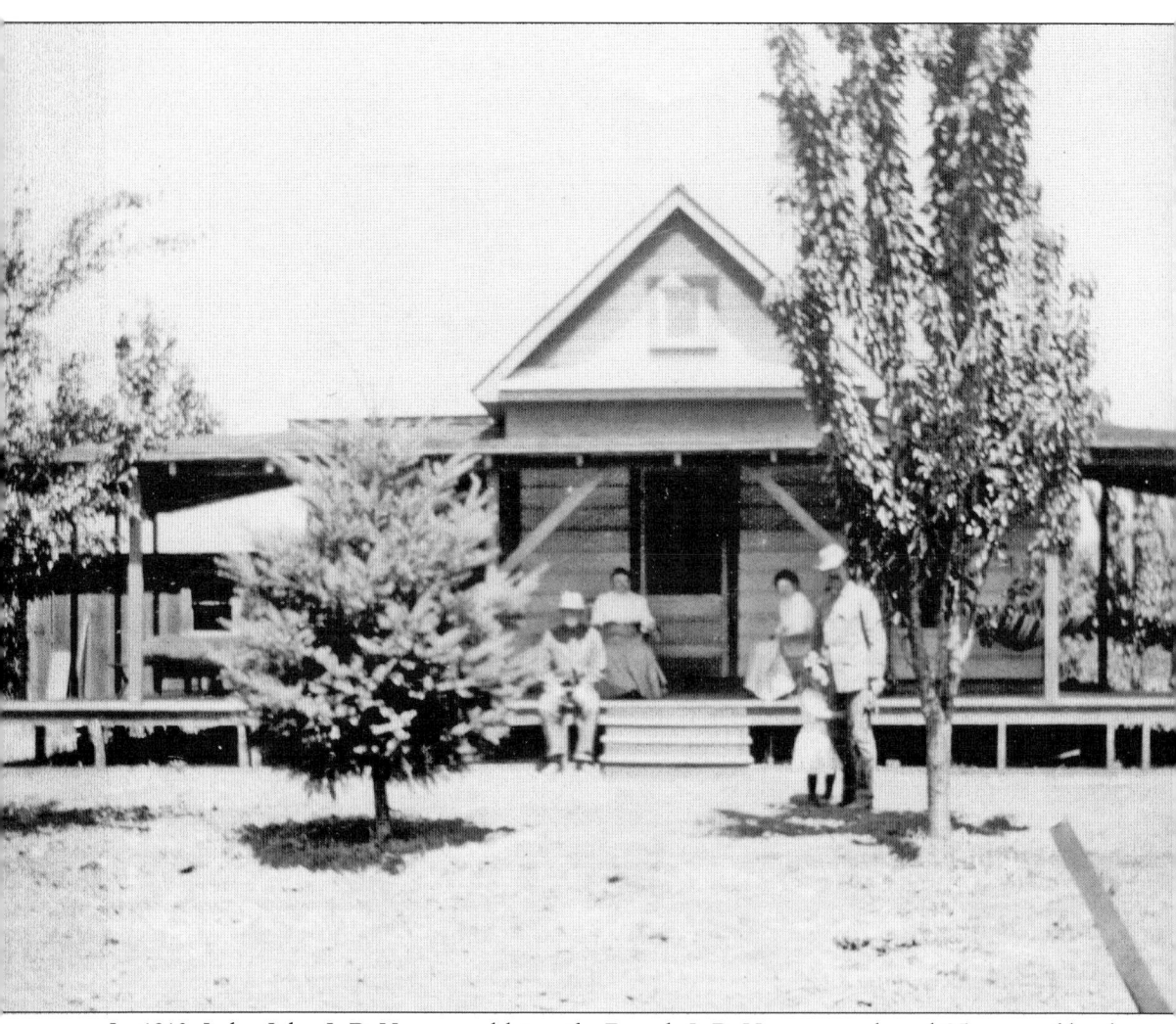

In 1910, Judge John J. DeHaven and his wife, Zeruah J. DeHaven, purchased 25 acres of land originally owned by Salvador Vallejo. The estate included a four-room house (pictured above in 1912) originally built in 1896. In 1927, the DeHavens' son and daughter purchased an additional 10 acres north of the property and called the estate DeHaven Acres. Featured in this photograph are Judge John J. DeHaven, Zeruah J. DeHaven, daughter Sarah L. DeHaven, granddaughter Lee DeHaven Atwood, and son Joe J. DeHaven. (Courtesy of Dr. Jim Atwood.)

Yountville residents Mathias Van de Leur and his granddaughter, Martha, posed for this photograph in 1921. Mathias owned and operated the White House Hotel located on the southwest corner of Adams and Yount Street. In his many years as a public servant, Mathias was a Napa County supervisor as well as the superintendant of the Yountville School District. Known throughout the county as a master stonemason, Mathias' work included the stone construction of the Hatt Building in Napa, the first stone bridge over the Napa River at the Yountville Crossroads, and the construction of the Catholic church in St. Helena. (Courtesy of Lee Hart.)

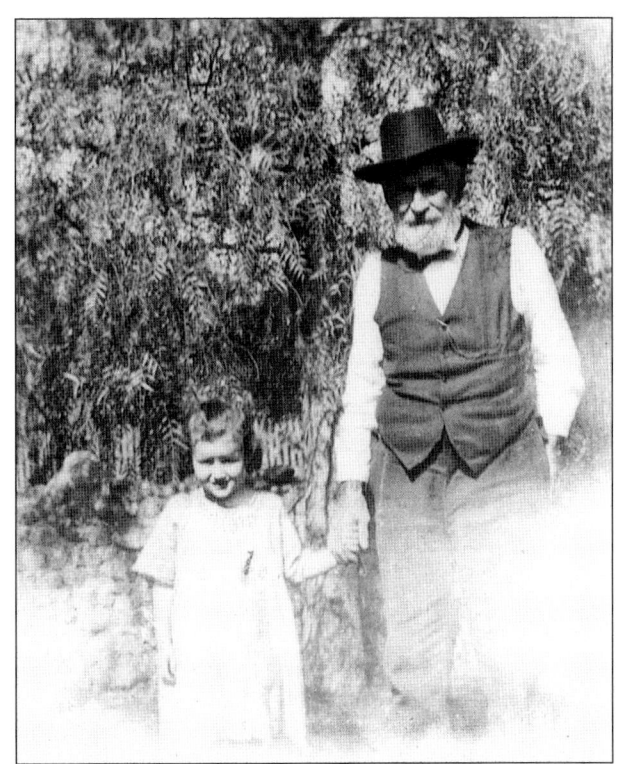

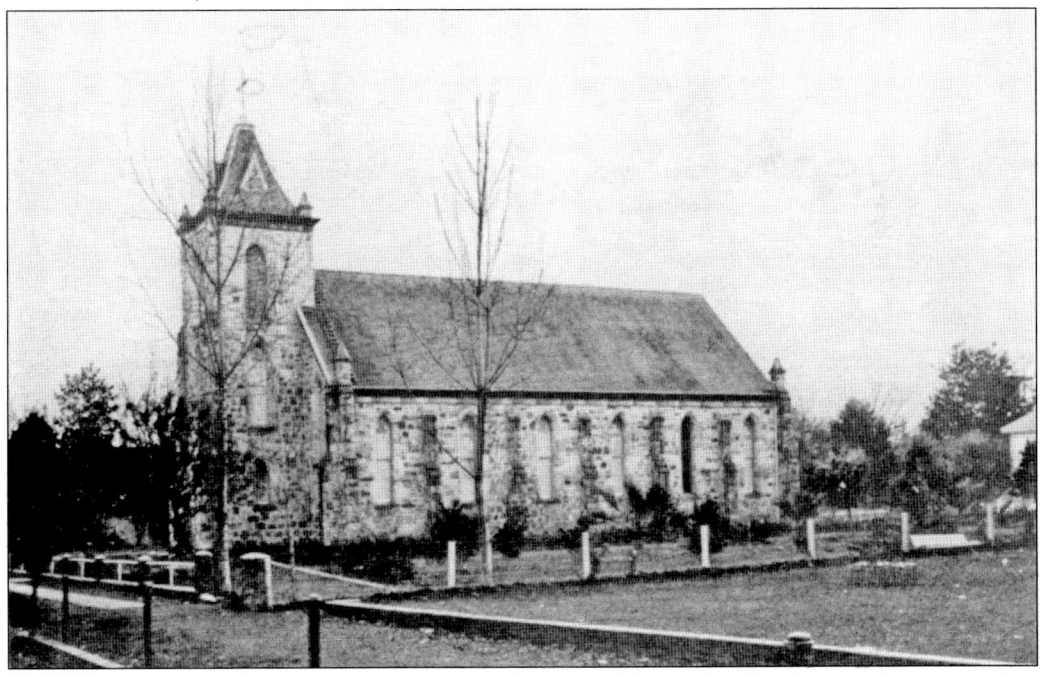

Shown here around 1907 is the Catholic church in St. Helena. The St. Helena Church was first conceived by the efforts and vision of Fr. Michael Mulvihille in 1877. After Father Mulvihille passed away, Rev. Maurice Slattery oversaw the completion of the St. Helena Catholic Church. The church was dedicated on March 28, 1878. (Courtesy of the Napa Valley Museum.)

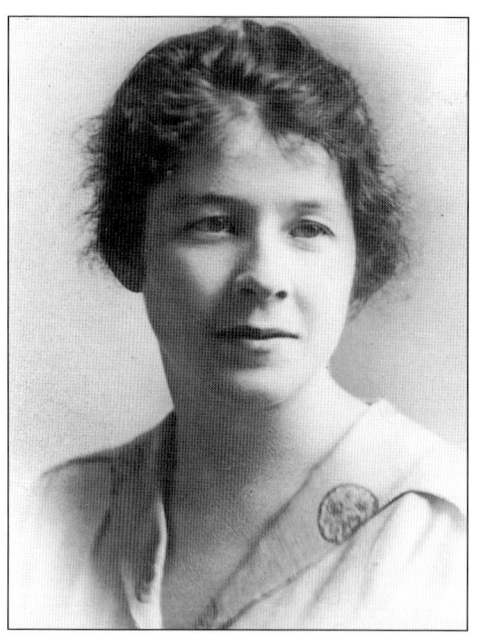

Martha Van De Leur continued the public service of her grandfather in her employment at the Yountville Grammar School. For 23 years, she was the principal of the Yountville School and then took over as principal of the Salvador School. Martha had a passion for roses and was responsible for the first planting of roses at both schools. She also planted the roses at the Van de Leur Park in Yountville, which was named in her honor in 2004. (Courtesy of Lee Hart.)

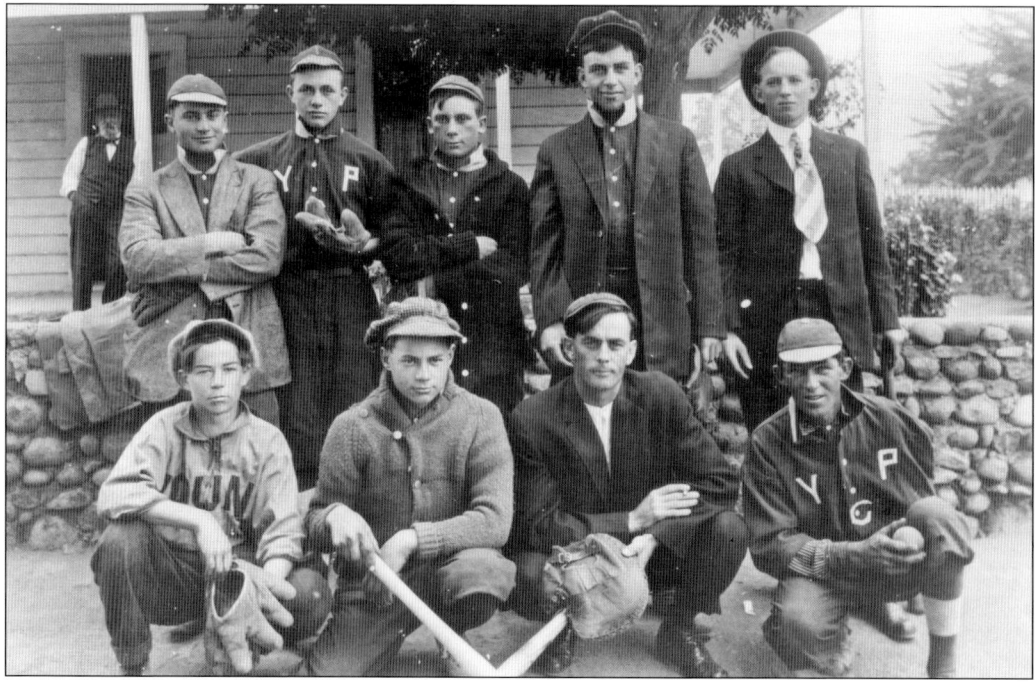

Carrying on the early 20th century's national passion for baseball, these young men took up their bats and gloves to represent Yountville in local games. Photographed c. 1915, three of these baseball players have recently been identified by current Yountville residents. From left to right are (kneeling) Bill Dutton, Sylvio Tonascia, an unidentified player, and John Van De Leur. Note the missing arm of young John. In spite of losing his arm, he was active in several stonework projects, including the stone fence pictured here at the Van de Leur home on the southwest corner of Jefferson and Monroe Streets. Overlooking the team on the left side of the picture is Mathias Van de Leur. The men in the second row are unidentified. (Courtesy of Lee Hart.)

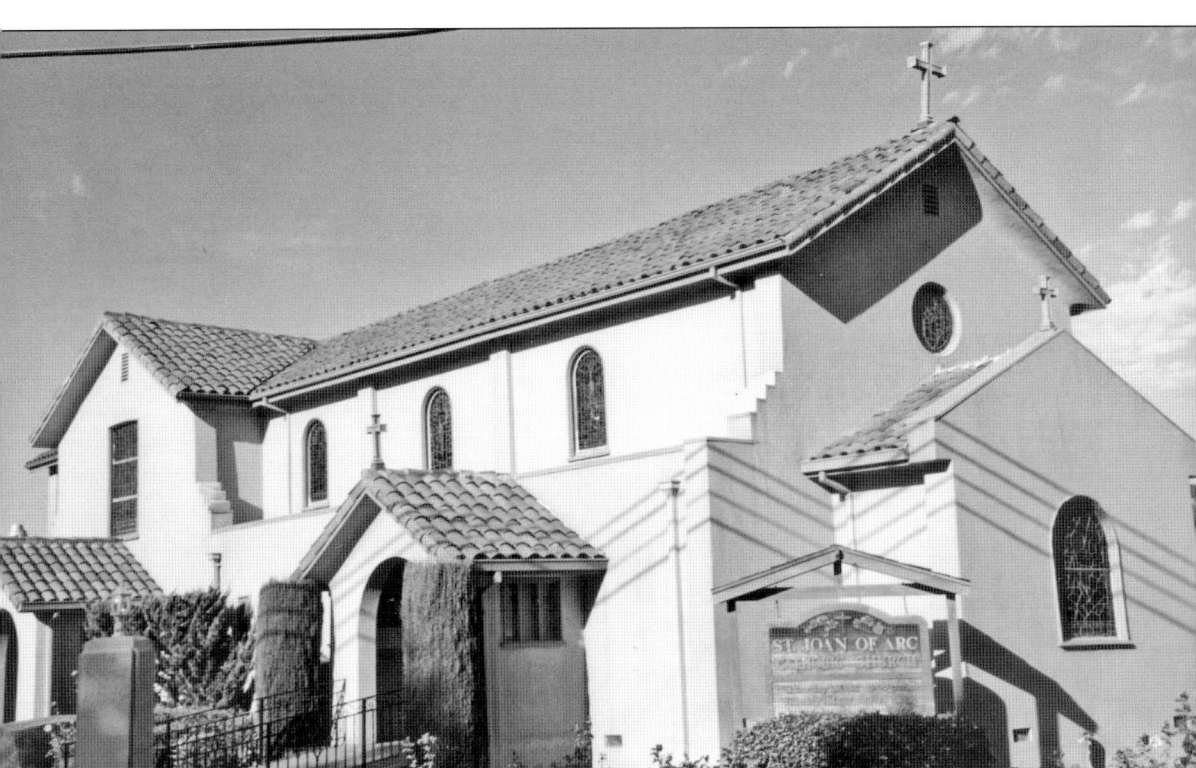

Fr. Francis McCarthy was first assigned to assess the feasibility of a Catholic church in 1920. After working at the Veterans Home and with the parish at Rutherford, Father McCarthy determined that Yountville would be the site of a new Catholic church. Henry Grigsby, grandson of Bear Flagger John Grigsby, donated the lot of land upon which the St. Joan of Arc Catholic Church was built. Ground was broken in May 1921, due in part because of the hard work and fund-raising efforts of the local Yountville parishioners. The many fund-raising endeavors of the parishioners included a rodeo held at the Trubody Ranch, annual fairs, and biweekly card club sessions held in the Gibbs Hall throughout the year. (Courtesy of Lee Hart.)

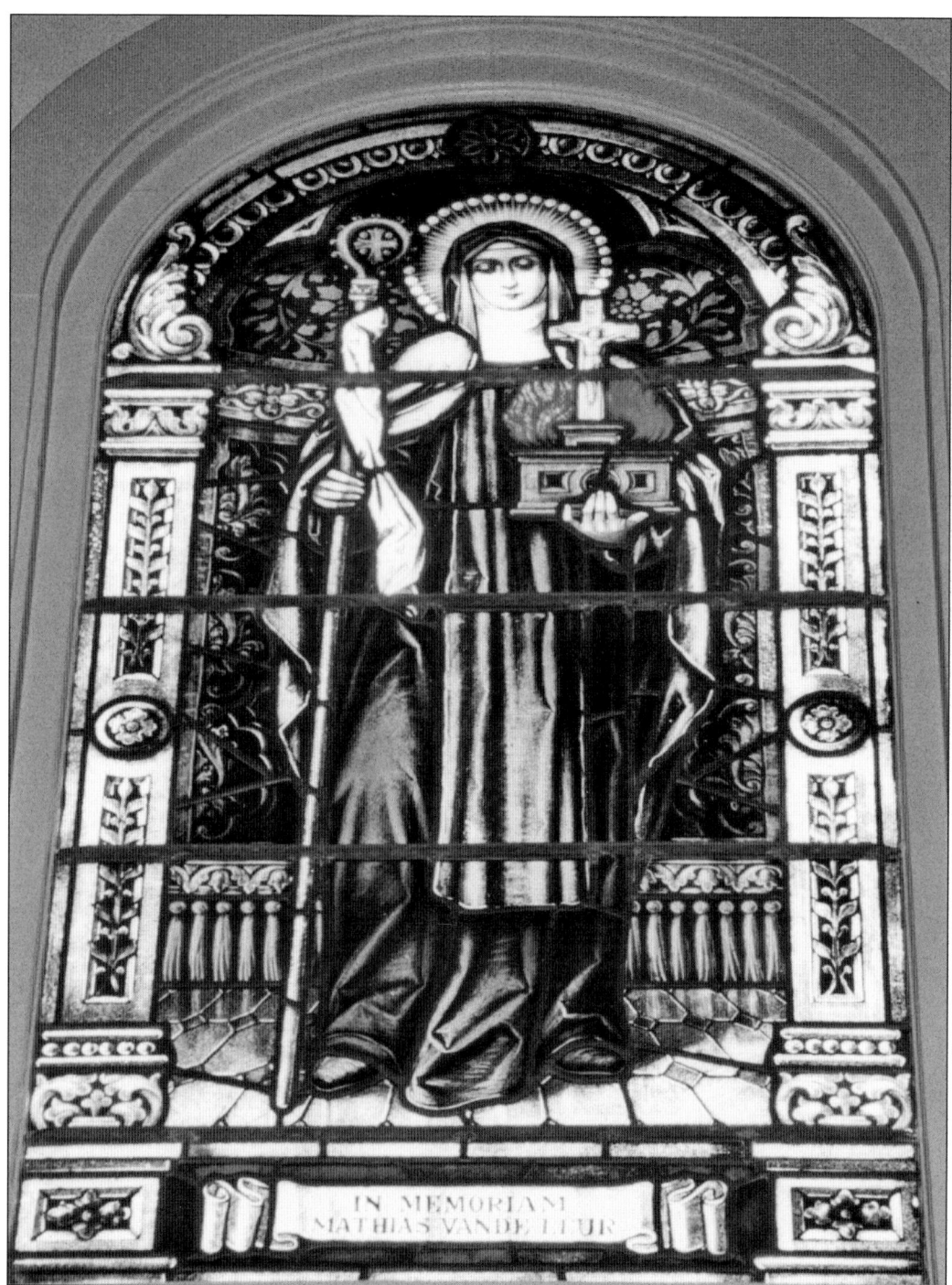

To honor the sacrifices of the men at the Veterans Home, Father McCarthy bestowed the name St. Joan of Arc upon the Catholic church in Yountville. The stained-glass photograph shown here depicts the image of St. Bridget of Ireland. This glass was installed in memory of well-loved Yountville resident and stonemason Mathias Van de Leur, who died in 1924. (Courtesy of Lee Hart.)

Featured in this picture are the Tonascia brothers, Joseph and Sylvio, who started Tonascia Market at the north end of Washington Street, which is now the site of Gordon's Café. For over 70 years, Tonascia Market was an integral part of the Yountville community, providing not only food and groceries to the citizenry but also providing many first jobs to Yountville's young people. The grocery store was operated by the family from 1916 to 1983. (Courtesy of Virginia Crowe.)

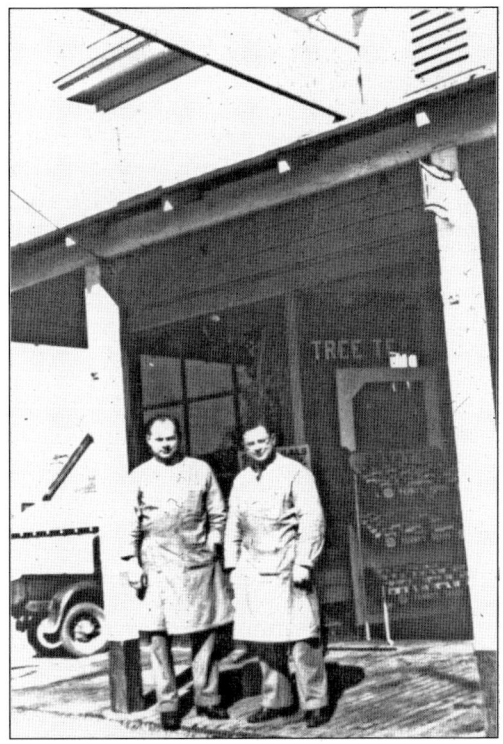

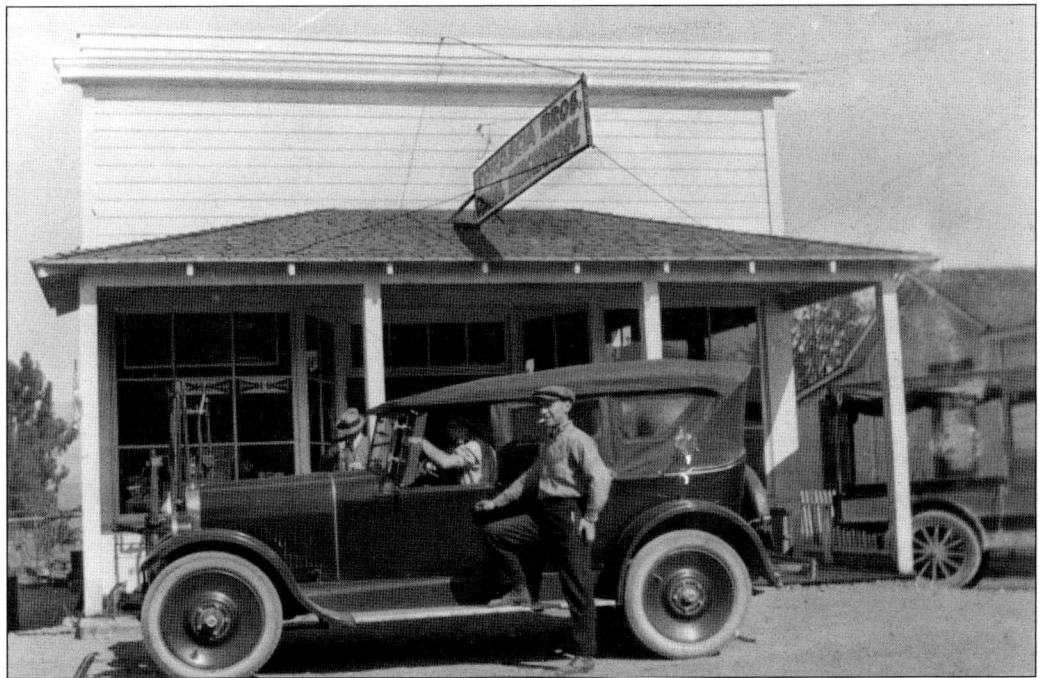

More than just a grocery store, Tonascia's Market had several community functions over the years: a gathering place to exchange community news, a telephone exchange office, and a last stop before heading up valley. In this c. 1920 image, two unidentified men pose in front of Tonascia's Market. (From the manuscripts of John Wichels; photograph courtesy of Edgar Beard.)

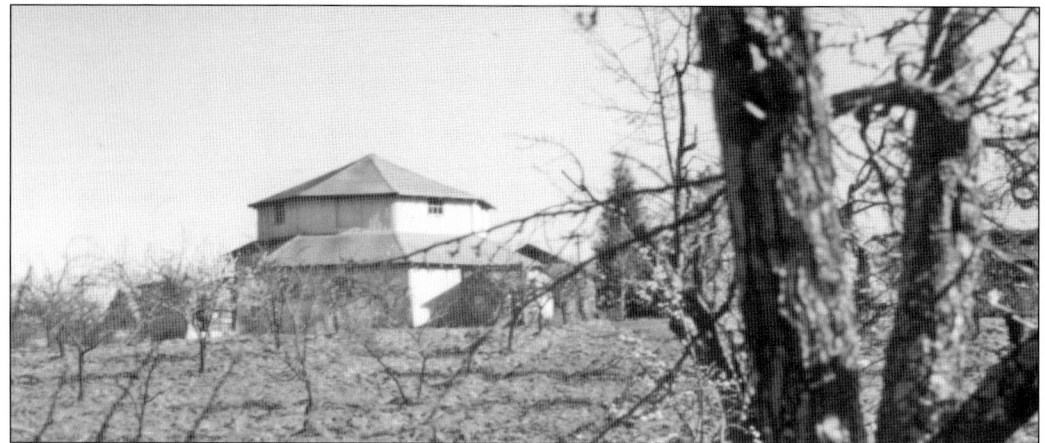

The Octagon Barn, built in the mid-1930s, was owned by Tonascia brother Sylvio and his wife, Marie. The Octagon Mode design was very popular in the 1930s because it allowed for a one-fifth greater floor area than a traditional square. Although this Depression-era architectural style was originally used in home designs, the Tonascia Family had it built as a barn for their horses. (Courtesy of Mindy Jordan.)

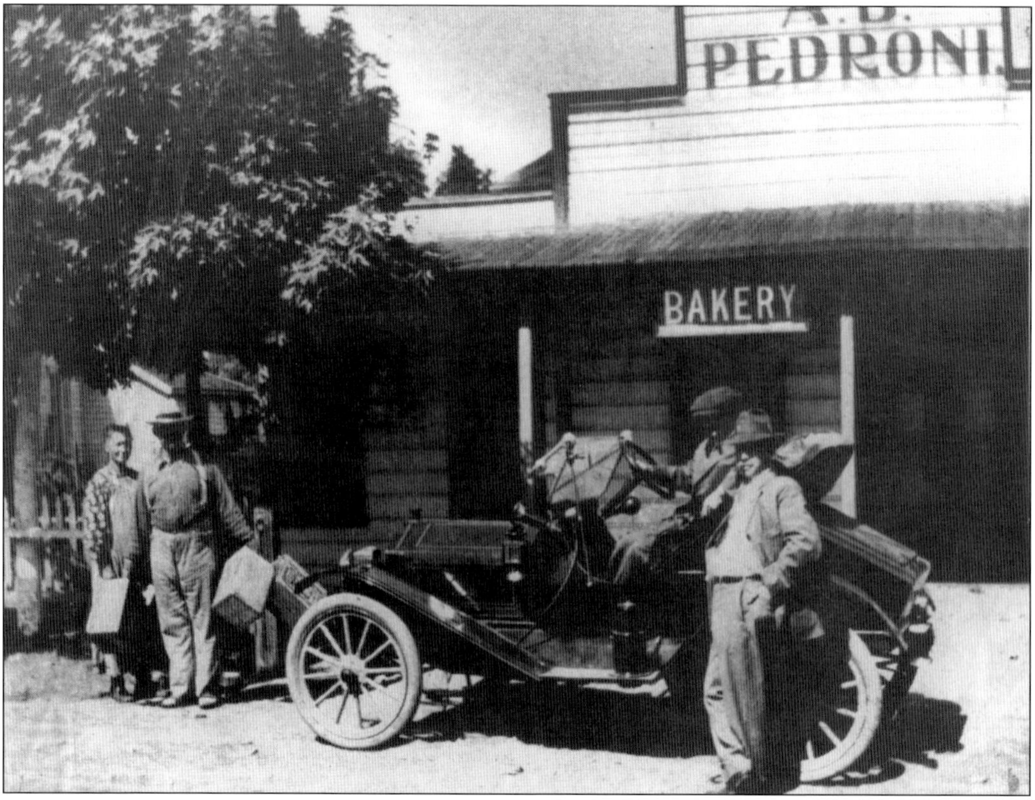

The unidentified men posing for this c. 1915 photograph are standing in front of a bakery belonging to Italian baker A. B. Pedroni. Pedroni Street in Yountville is named in honor of this resident, although the site of the Pedroni Bakery was believed to have been located near what is now the corner of Madison and Yount Streets. (From the manuscripts of John Wichels; photograph courtesy of Edgar Beard.)

Five
THE MID-20TH CENTURY

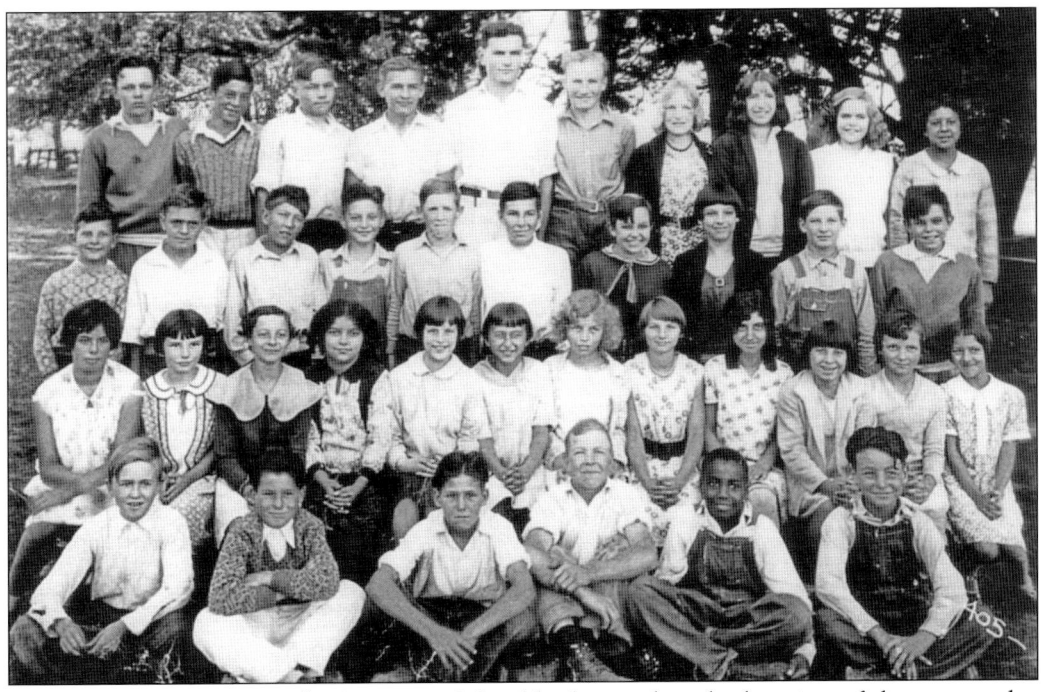

By the 1920s, the Yountville Grammar School had moved to the location of the present-day Yountville Town Hall. Many of these students' children and grandchildren would attend Yountville Elementary two generations later. This picture is c. 1936. Those identified include (first row) Clarence Han, Billy Johnstone, Ben Barboza, Charlie Farris, Harry Drinkwater, and Joe Tonascia; (second row) Mildred Johnstone, Marcia Viney, Betty ?, Madeline Mesquita, Betsy ?, Evelyn Ghirardi, Maxine Tower, Irene Noris, Marie Quadrado, Mary Bardessono, Lois Morgan, and June Borman; (third row) Melvin Boybosa, Joey Cavalli, Wayne Wheeler, Jimmy Tonascia, Dave Hahn, Tony Quadrado, Ellen Filmer, Cuina Bardessono, Gwenith Flock, and Tommy Filmer; (fourth row) Edward Filmer, Harold Johnstone, Thomas ?, Howard Crouse, Bert Tarrizo, Robert Tawer, Beatrice Lee, Emma Borelli, Mary Jane ?, and Carmen Rodoni. (Courtesy of John Callison.)

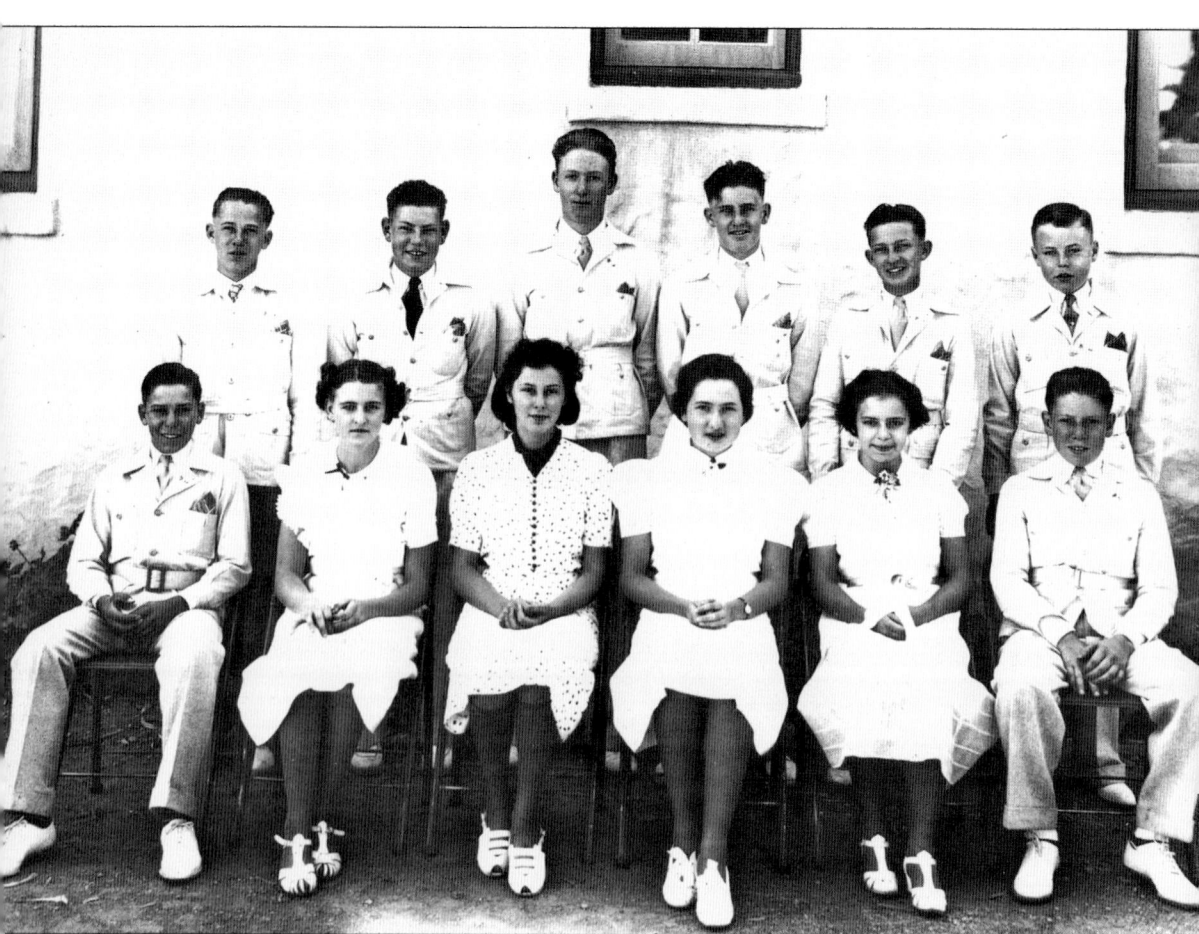

In 1937, the Yountville Grammar School went up to eighth grade. Notice the uniforms of the graduating class of 1937. Pictured from left to right are (first row) Pete Bardessono, unidentified, Zizi Montelli, Marie Vallerga, Betty Ann Hattler, Bob Massoni; (second row) Bill Lilienthal, Les Hein, Edgar Beard, Don Anderson, Jim Forrester, and Joe Hahn. (Courtesy of Maxine Bardessono and John Callison.)

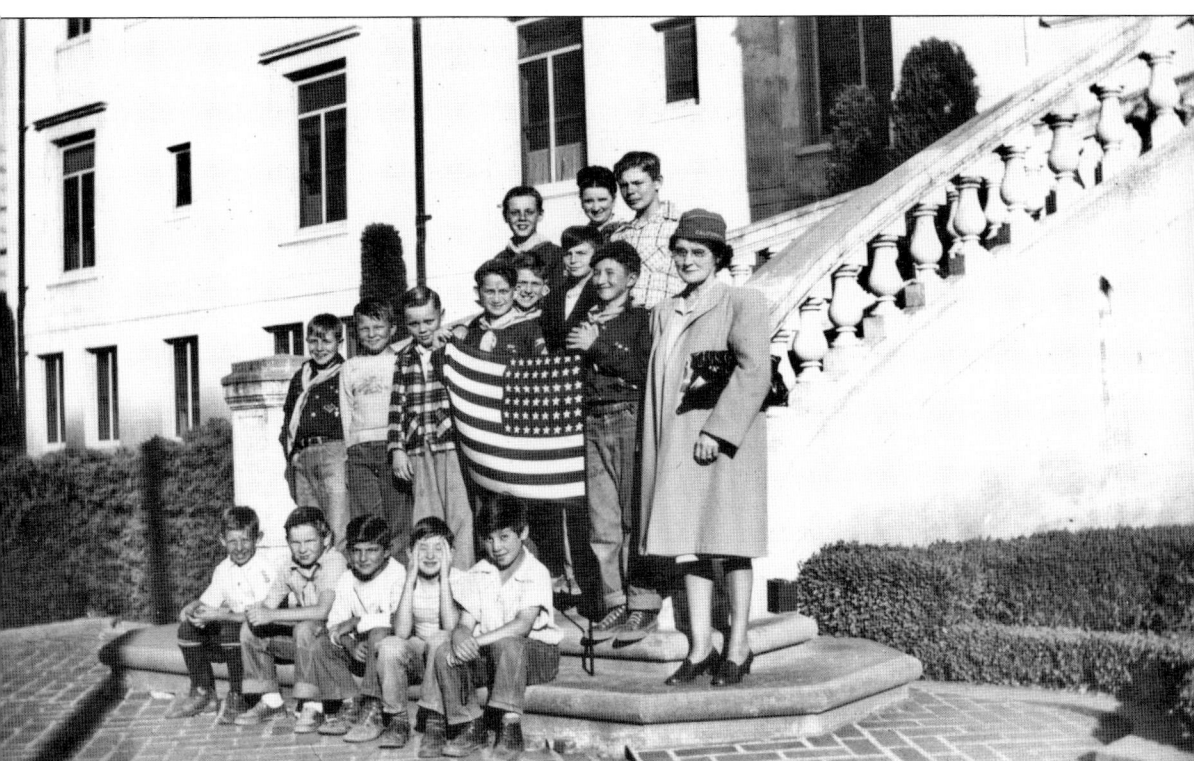

Since the 1930s, many of Yountville's young men have been associated with the Boy Scouts of America. Pictured in 1946, the following young men posed for this picture on the steps of the Holderman Hospital at the Veterans Home. From left to right are (first row) Darrel Martin, Johnny Marquez, Vernon Flock, unidentified, Carlos Robles; (second row) David Martin, Ray Standridge, Bob Carrol, Donald Martin, Junior Bradley, John Callison, Mrs. Cook; (third row) Eddie Schultz, Muriel Callison, and Bob Lilienthal. (Courtesy of John Callison.)

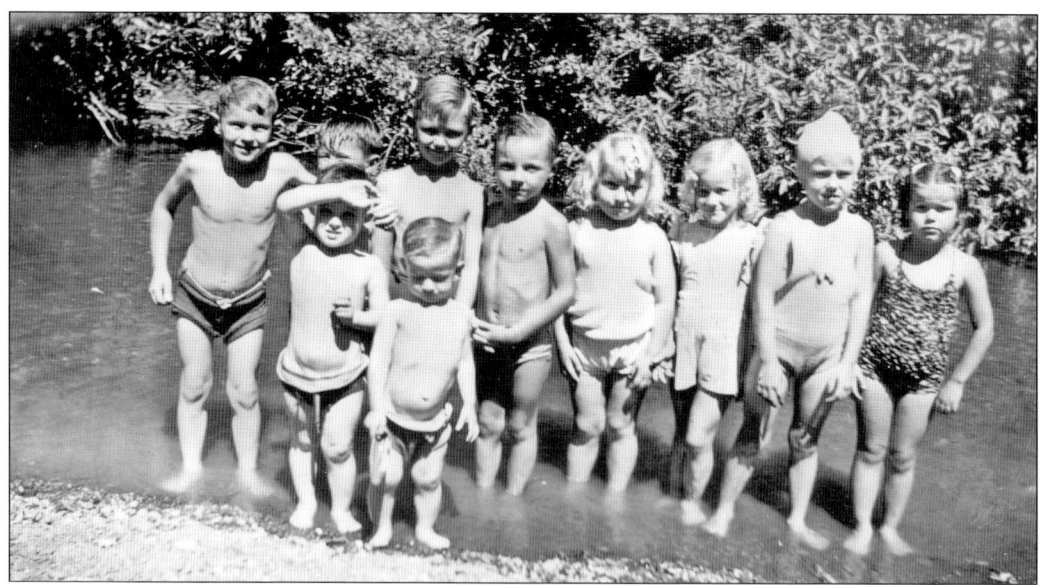

Since the time of the Caymus Indians, children have played in the Napa River. In 1942, young John Callison celebrated his sixth birthday with his friends in the "scout hole." The children standing in the river are (first row) Vern and Ron Flock; (second row) Jim Duff, John Callison, Dwane Hudson, Eddie Shultz, Wynema Lollis, Robin Phophet, Colleen Anderson, and Mona Shultz. (Courtesy of John Callison.)

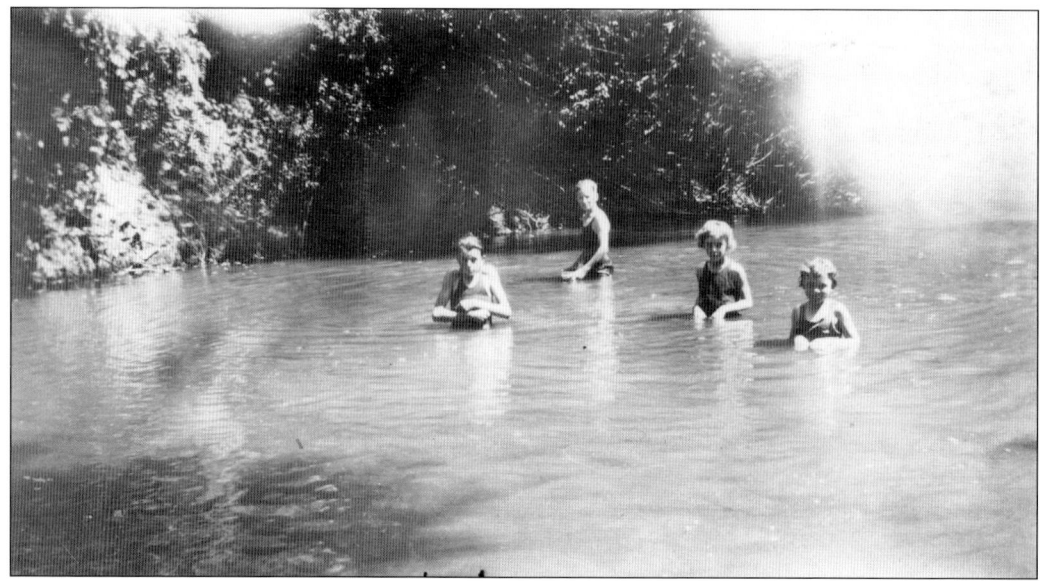

The unidentified children swimming in the Napa River's "scout hole" posed for this 1928 photograph. (Courtesy of Barbara and Bud Dulinsky.)

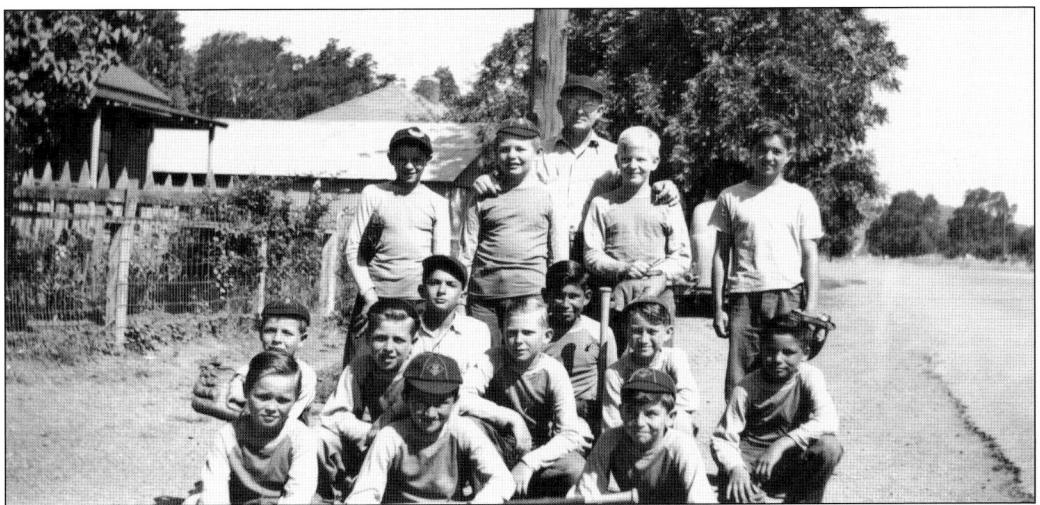

The boys in this picture are preparing for a baseball game in the early 1950s. Note the location of the boys on Yount Street. To the north and across the dirt road is the Yountville Grammar School. Pictured from left to right are (first row) Ken Landay, John Callison, and Harold Bradley; (second row) David Martin, Donald Martin, Irving Land, Bob Carrell, and Angel Robles; (third row) Tony Marquez and Alfred Rodriguez; (fourth row) Jim Duff, Bob Lilienthal, Gilbert Williamson, and Deramus Tallent; (fifth row) Oscar Martin. (Courtesy of John Callison.)

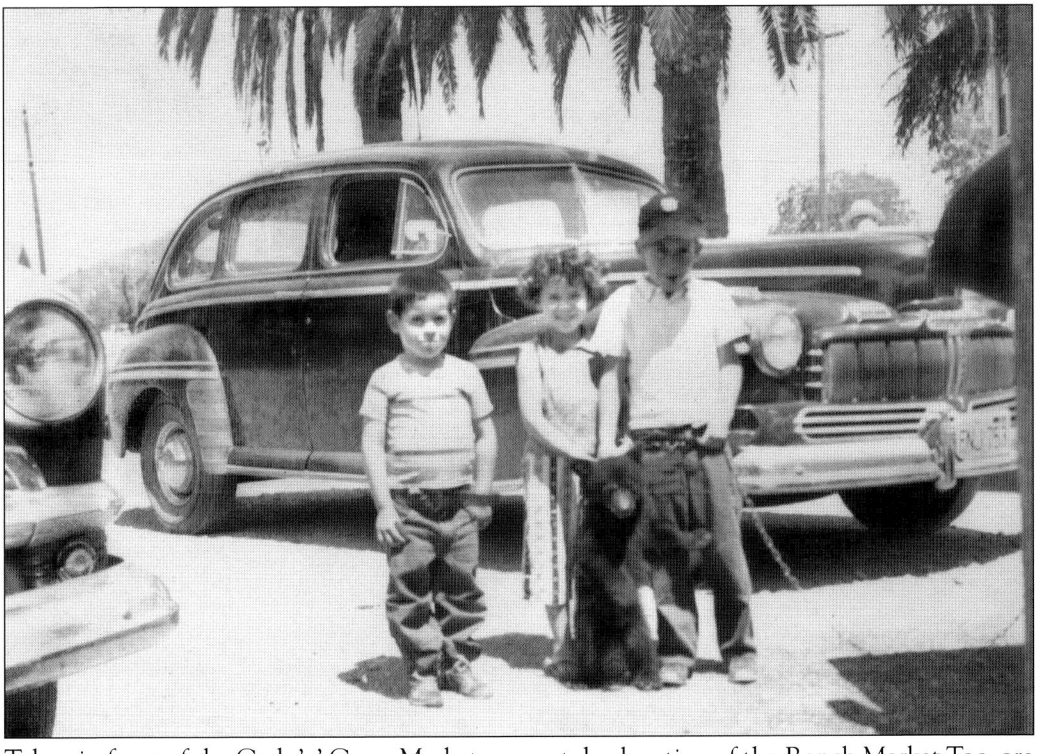

Taken in front of the Cash 'n' Carry Market, present-day location of the Ranch Market Too, are three of the Bardessono children. From left to right are John, Bonnie, and Bruce. The pet bear was one of several exotic animals kept in Yountville, and it later became one of the bears that starred in the 1960s television series *Gentle Ben*. (Courtesy of Maxine Bardessono.)

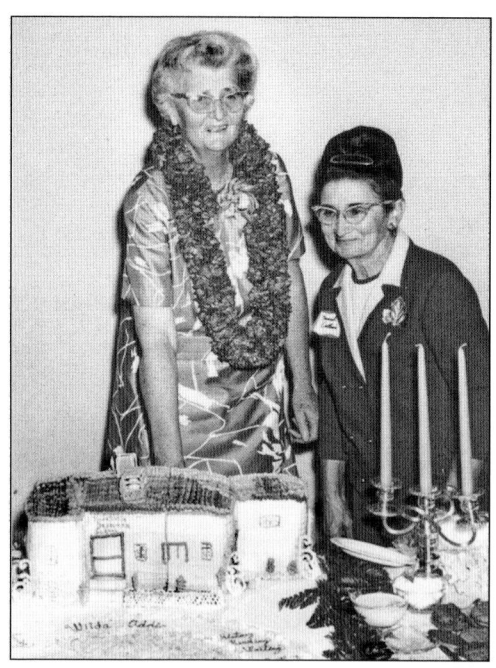

Wilda Addis (left), a legendary Yountville teacher, began her career at Yountville Grammar School in 1923. For over 40 years, she maintained strict classroom discipline as she educated several generations of Yountville children. Muriel Callison (right), Wilda Addis's friend and coworker, began the first hot lunch program at Yountville Grammar School in 1933. She fed countless Yountville children for 30 years without missing a day. Taken during her retirement party in 1967, this photograph shows Wilda Addis posing with Muriel Callison. The cake, baked by Muriel Callison, was made in the shape of the Yountville School. (Courtesy of John Callison.)

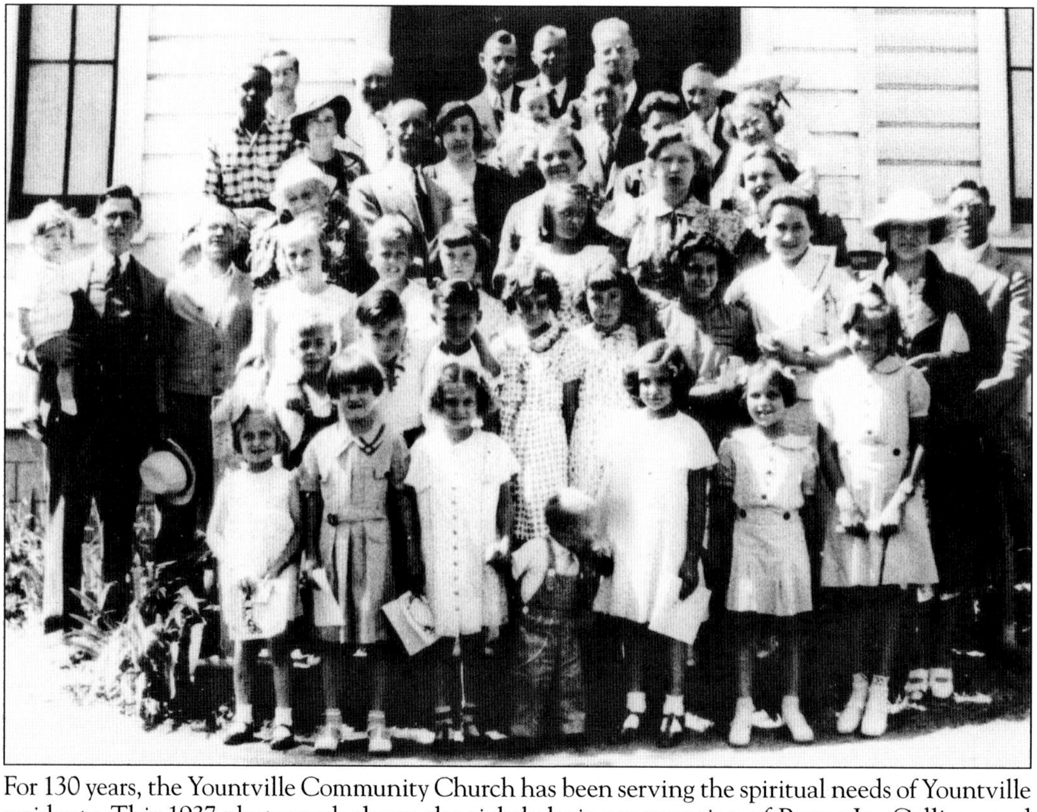

For 130 years, the Yountville Community Church has been serving the spiritual needs of Yountville residents. This 1937 photograph shows the tightly knit congregation of Pastor Jay Callison and his wife, Muriel. In the first row, notice little Jim Duff (fourth from the left) biting the hand of his sister, Velda. (Courtesy of Jim Duff.)

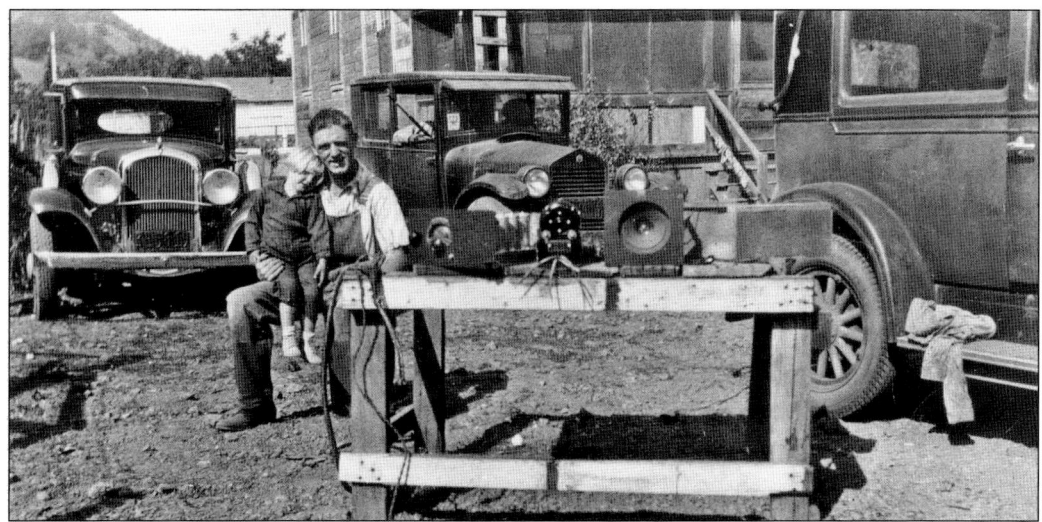

This early 1930s photograph shows Rudy Bauman and his daughter Lois in front of their family house on Madison Street. Lois Bauman Bishop and her sister Phyllis Bauman Vallerga are the descendants of the Volz family, the early Yountville pioneers featured on page 35. (Courtesy of Phyllis Vallerga.)

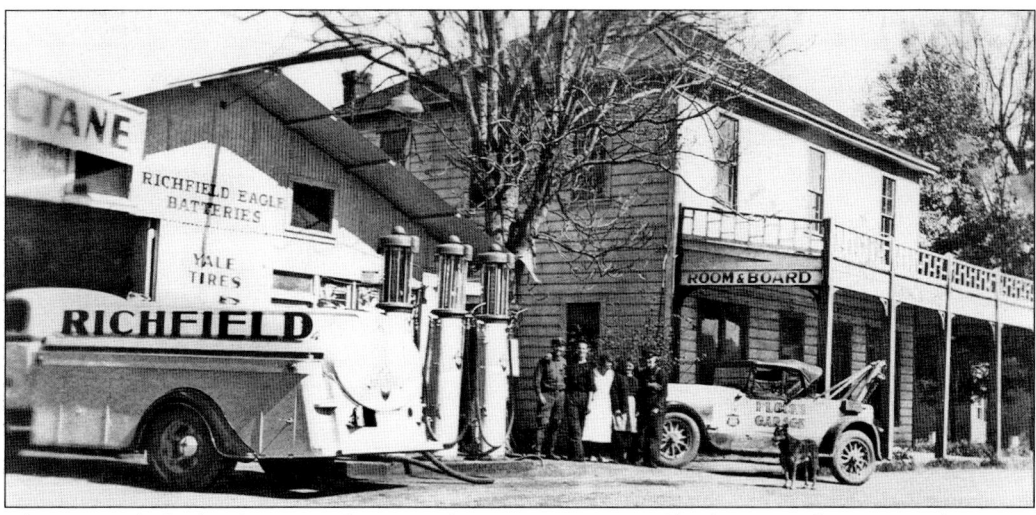

The original Flock's Garage, a longtime business in Yountville that is no longer standing, was located just north of the St. Joan of Arc Catholic Church on Highway 29. Millard Flock started the repair shop seen on the left in 1929, shortly after he arrived in Yountville from Orosi, California (near Fresno). The construction of the shop and gasoline station was completed in 1932. The two-story building on the right was built in 1890 and was originally the Columbia Hotel. Later it became a dentist's home and office, followed by a saloon and dance hall. In 1939, the second floor of the old hotel was removed, and the building became the home of Millard and Evalyn Flock, as well as a business office and small grocery store. The grocery store was located in the right front corner of the building, and the gasoline pumps were moved from the front of the shop to in front of the office. In the late 1940s, the repair shop was expanded to the rear, doubling its size. (Courtesy of Vernon Flock.)

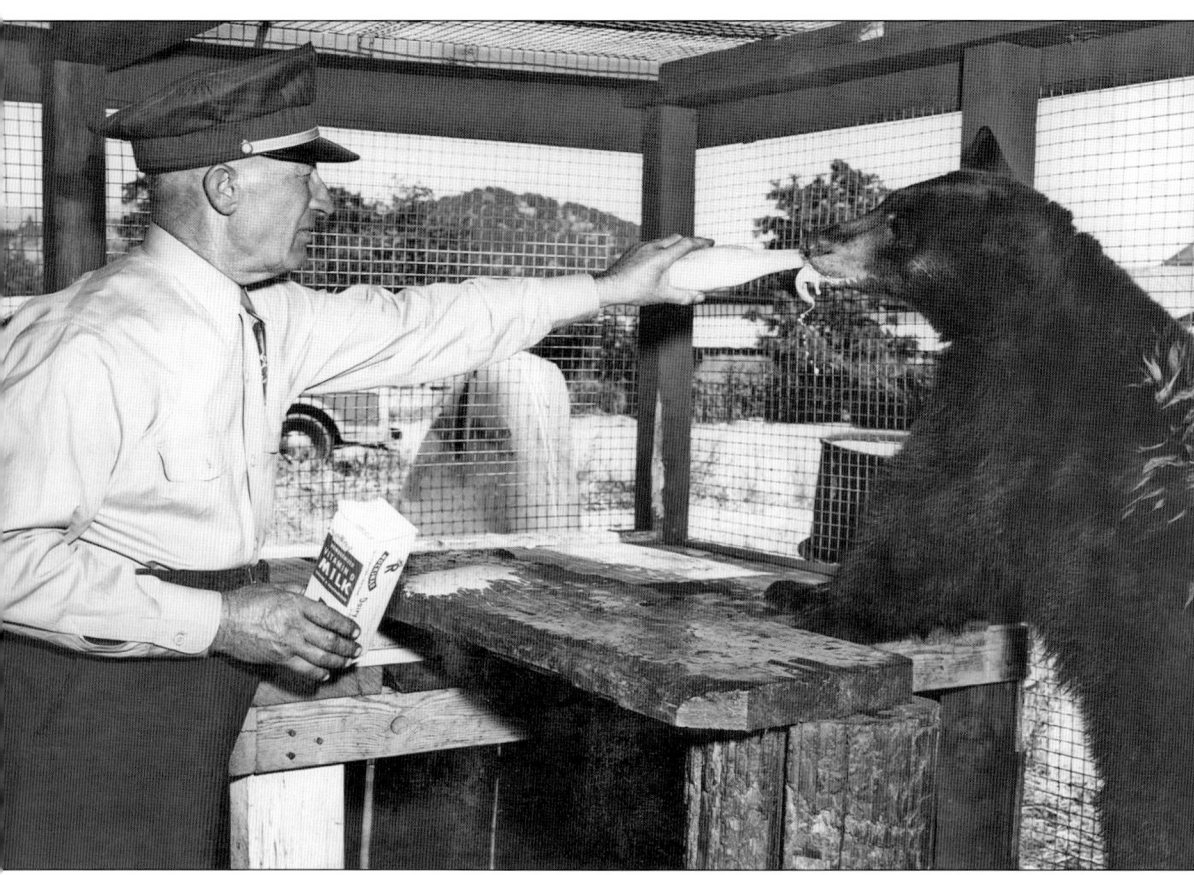
This photograph was taken in the late 1940s and shows Millard Flock with his pet bear, Coco. Flock had an exotic pet menagerie that was the delight of the neighborhood. (Courtesy of Vernon Flock.)

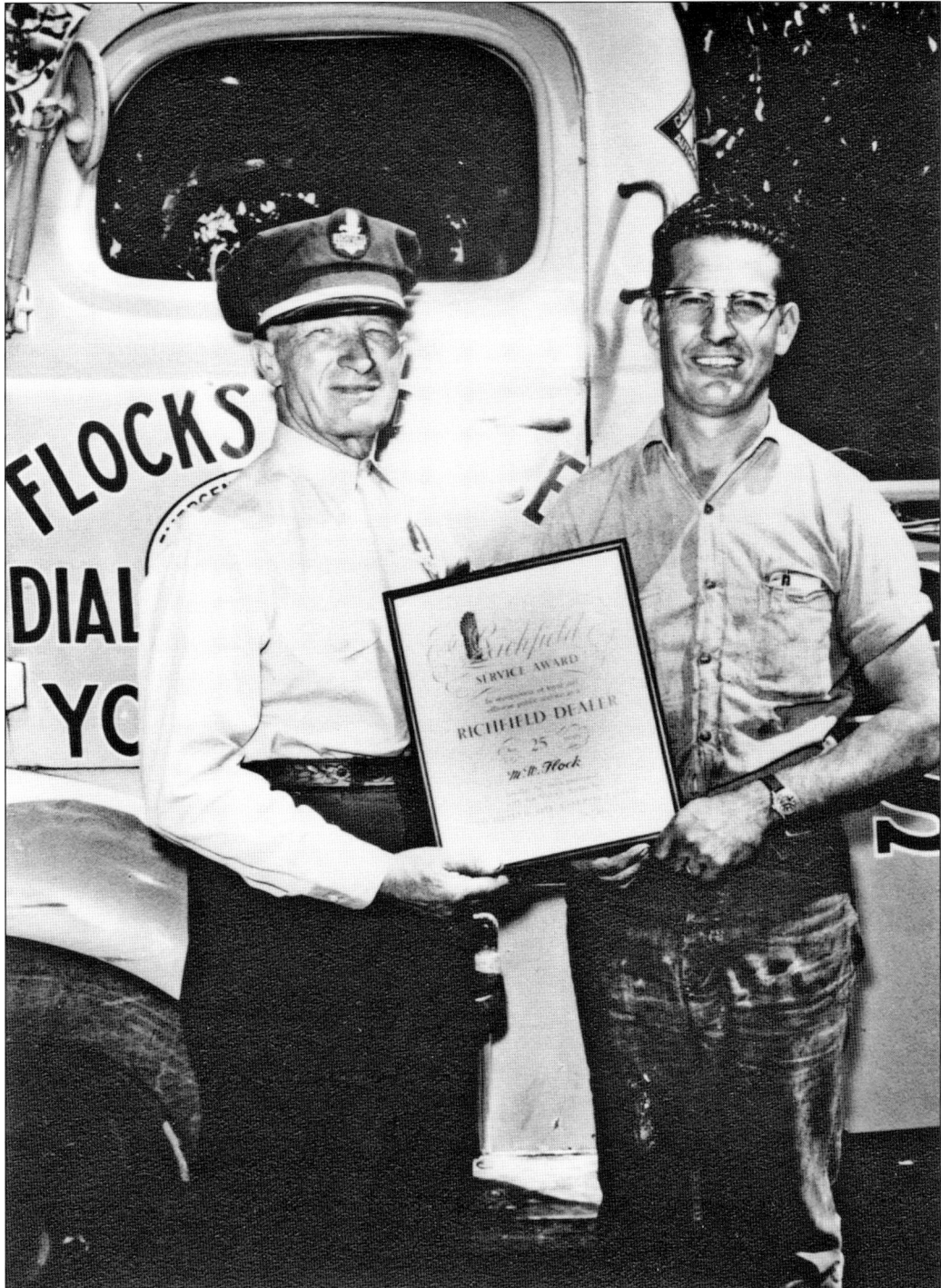

This photograph of Millard Flock and his son Gwen (G. B.) was taken in the mid 1950s. Both Flock men proudly display an outstanding service station award by the Richfield Oil Company. Unlike many gas stations in 2009, service stations in the past provided not only a gasoline fill-up but also an oil check, windshield washing, and a tire check. (Courtesy of Vernon Flock.)

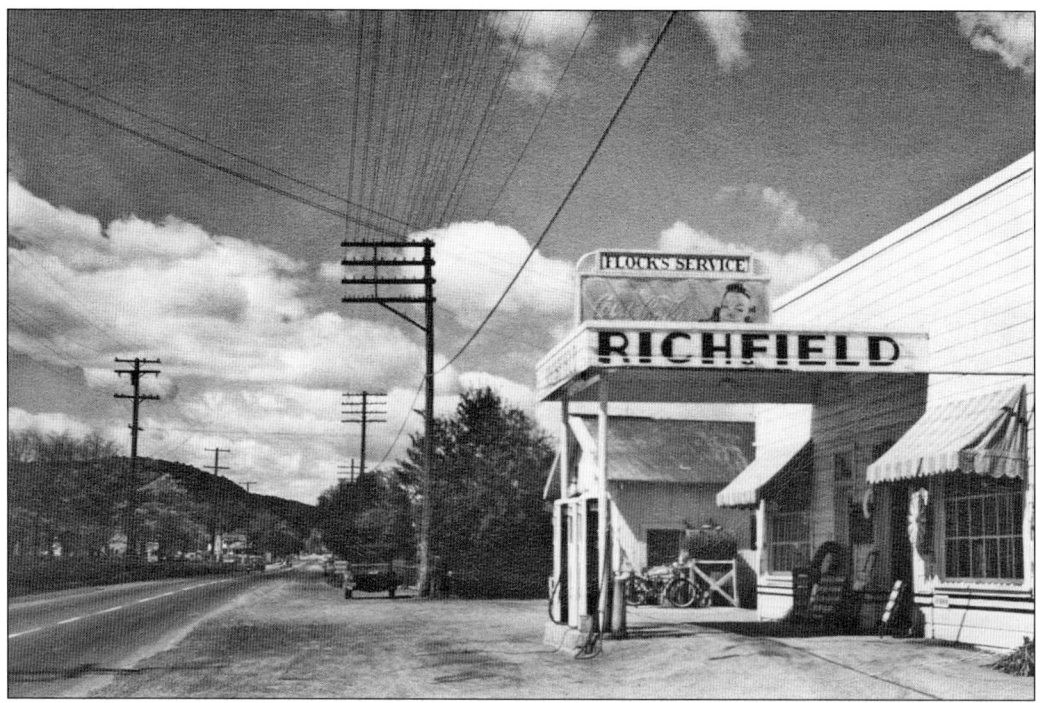

This mid-1940s photograph of Flock's Garage shows Washington Street to the north. Known then as County Highway 29, Washington Street was the main thoroughfare through Yountville. (Courtesy of Vernon Flock.)

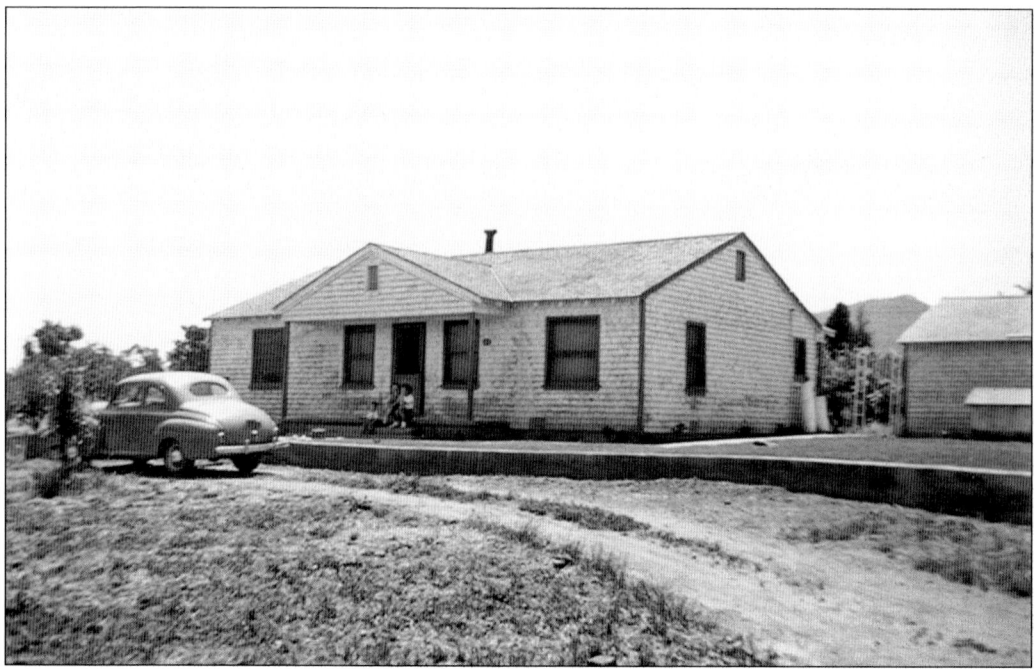

The Flock family moved from Washington Street to Talent Lane in the mid-1950s. In the background of this 1948 photograph, Veteran's Peak can be seen. Not visible are the numerous large trees that dominate the area in 2008. (Courtesy of Vernon Flock.)

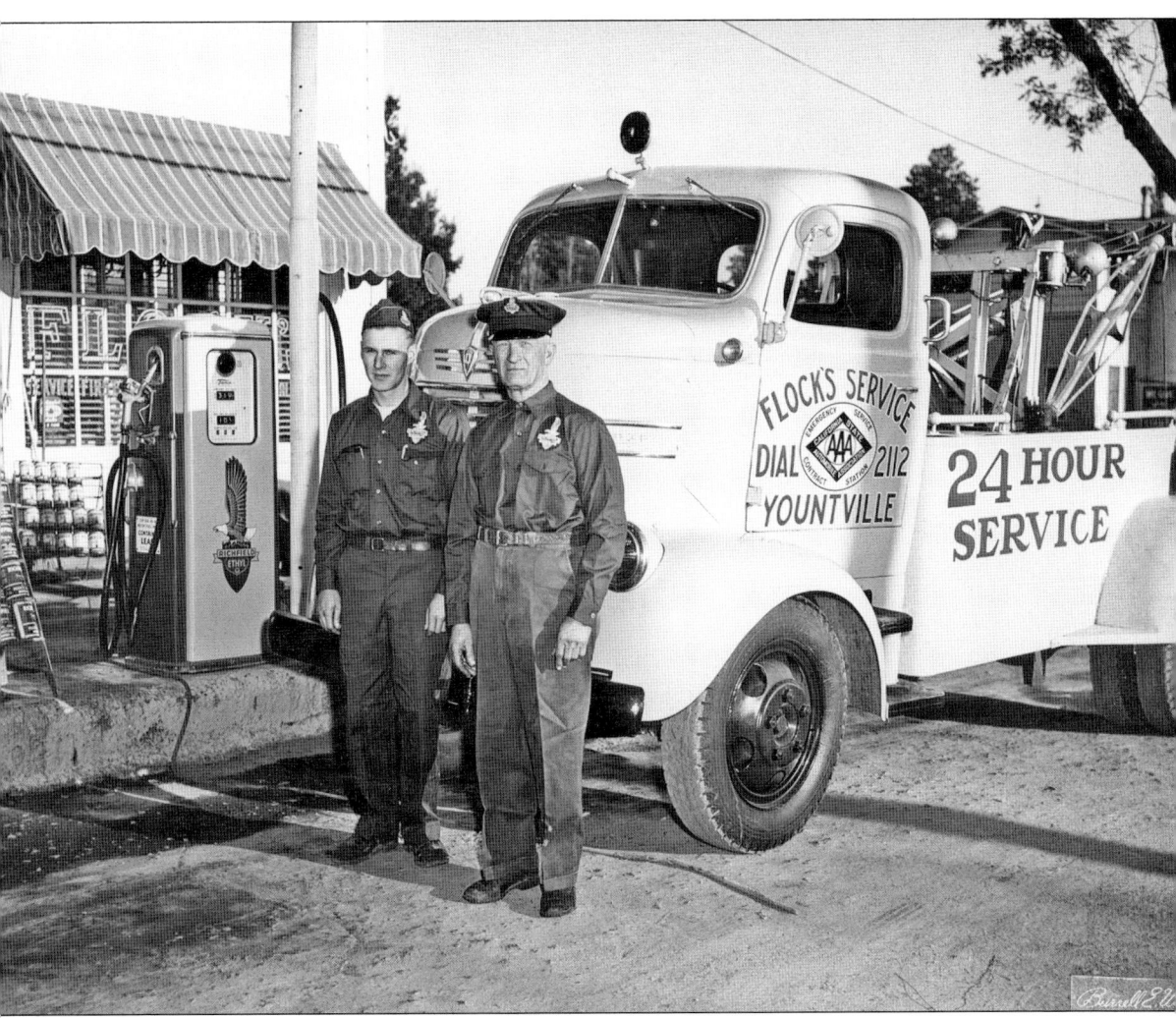

Dressed in uniforms of the day, Millard Flock (right) and service station attendant Paul Chastain pose in this 1940s photograph. Vernon Flock, Millard's grandson, recalled his early years of employment at his grandfather's service station, including the memory of a large pit in the ground of Flock's Garage where automobiles received oil changes. In the days before service station hydraulic lifts, attendants would drive the vehicle over a recessed pit in the ground. The attendant would then descend a ladder into the pit in order to drain the oil from the bottom of the car. No matter how careful the attendant was, oil stains were sure to follow. (Courtesy of Vernon Flock.)

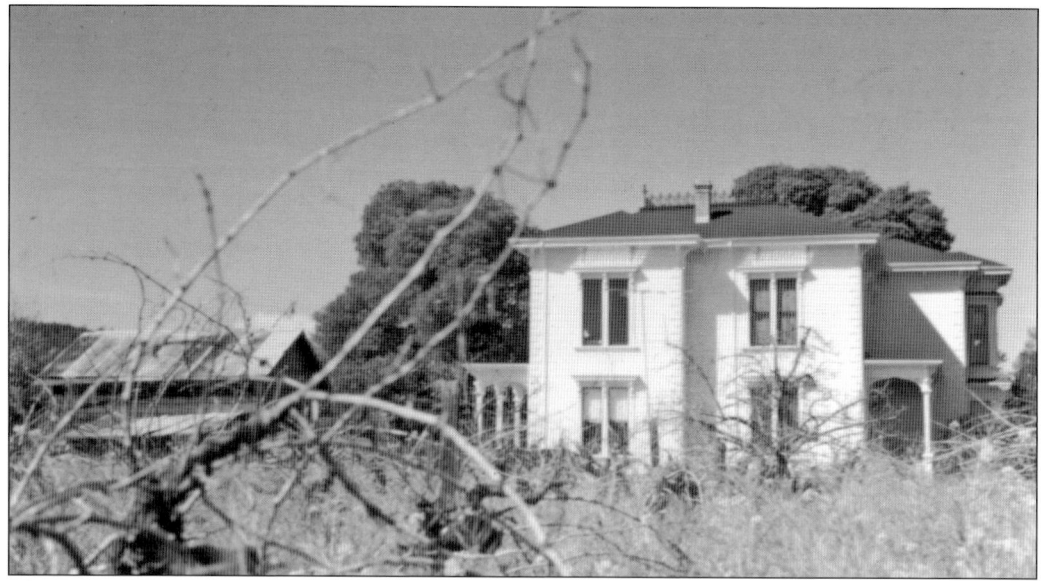

This c. 1973 photograph shows the Fawver House in the mid-1970s. In 1863, pioneer Thomas Fawver left Missouri. After traveling extensively throughout the United States and Oregon, the Fawver family finally settled in the Napa Valley in 1871. Fawver and his extended family purchased land and eventually constructed a 91-acre ranch and winery located on Washington Street, approximately one mile north of Yountville. In 1895, Thomas Fawver's son J. Clark Fawver decided to expand the winery operation and relocate the business south to the then-vacant Eschol Winery, located at the present-day location of Highway 29 and Oak Knoll Road. After leasing the winery for a period of approximately 10 years, J. Clark Fawver closed the winery operations in Yountville and was able to purchase the Eschol winery estate from brothers James and George Goodman. In 2008, the only remnant of the winery and estate is the beautifully restored Fawver House. (Courtesy of Mindy Jordan.)

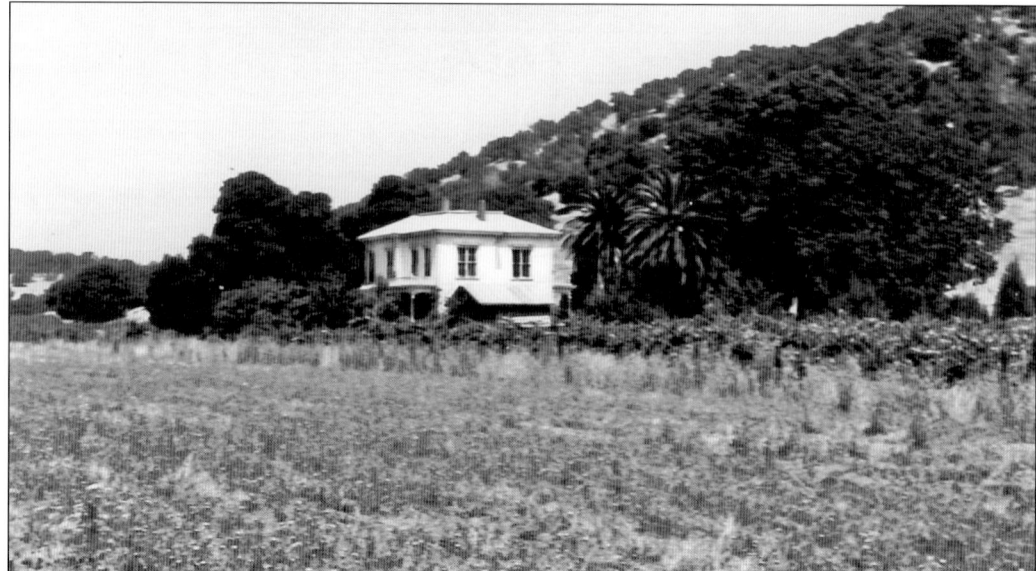

As seen in an early 20th century photograph, the Fawver House architecture has remained relatively unchanged over the years. (Courtesy of the Napa Historical Society.)

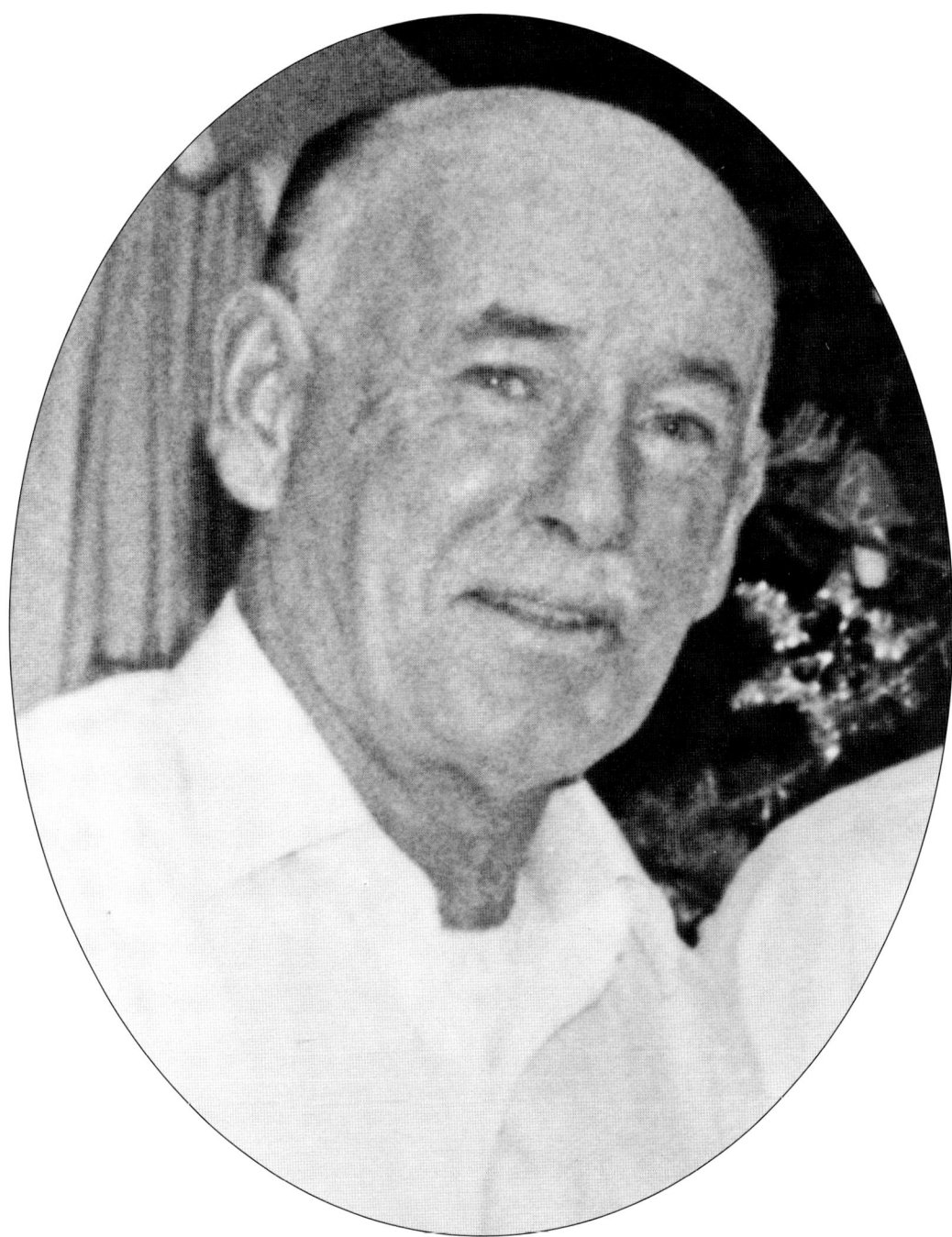

Jack Forrester, the son of James and Mary Forrester, lived in Yountville his entire life. He owned a bar in Oakville, as well as several commercial and residential properties, including the Rex Hotel located on Washington Street. Jack and his wife also owned a 17-acre prune orchard, which offered several Yountville young people their first jobs. Jack Forrester was friend to well-known Yountville resident Jim Ghirardi. Throughout their lifelong friendship, the two men spent many hours hunting quail and deer. In later years, the Forrester property estate was developed as the Washington Park subdivision. (Courtesy of Lee Hart.)

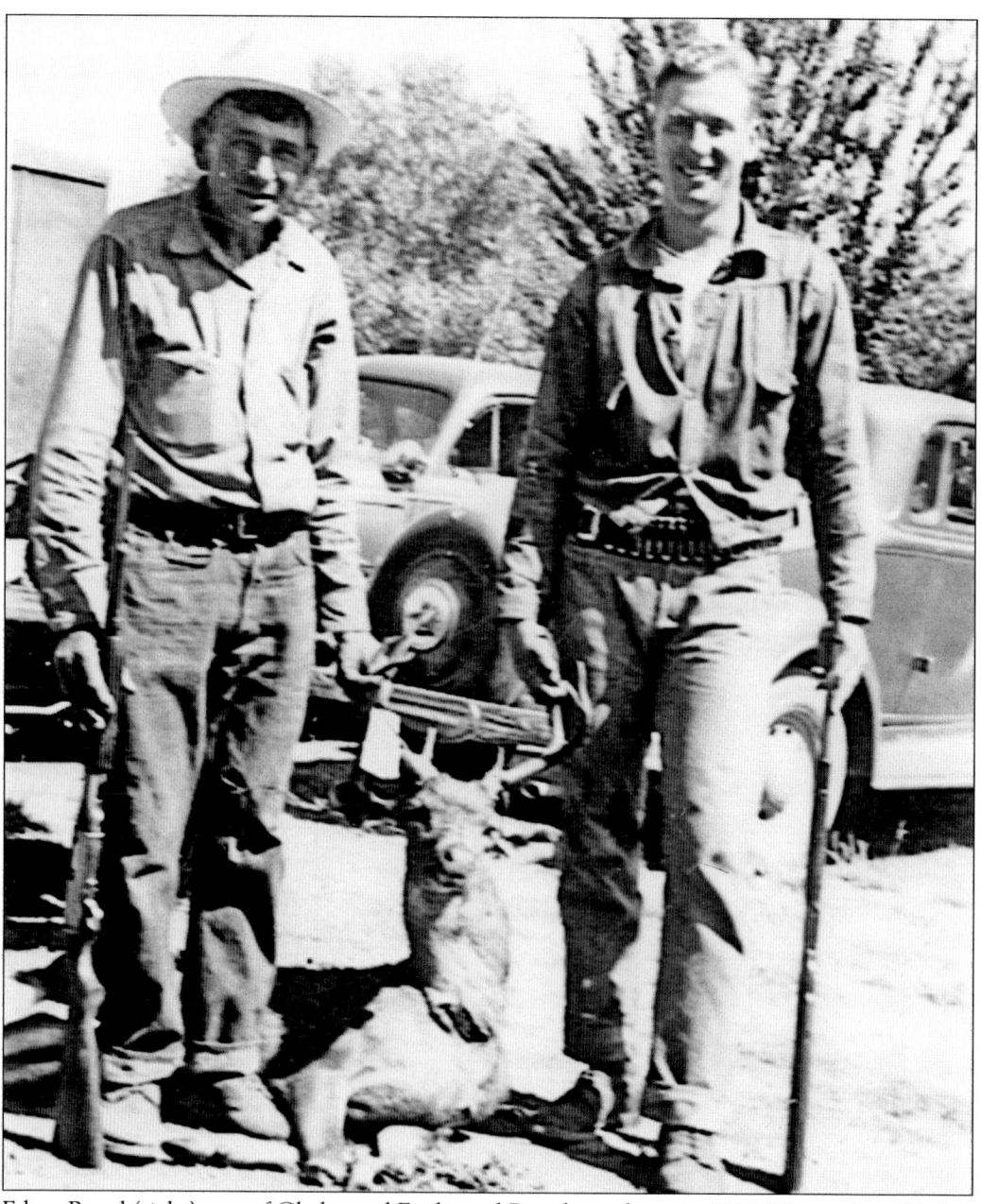

Edgar Beard (right), son of Gladys and Ferdinand Beard, was born in 1924. His mother, Gladys, was the postmaster of Yountville and later the postmaster of the Veterans Home for over 42 years. He spent his childhood exploring the banks of Hopper Creek, shooting baskets on the dirt basketball courts of Yountville Grammar School, and playing with his friends. On reflection of his childhood spent in Yountville, Edgar never forgot the adventures and skills he learned in Boy Scout Troop 36, sponsored by the Veterans Home of California-Yountville. Growing up in Yountville, Edgar and his friends Pete Bardessono, Joe Hahn, Dick and Eugene Tonascia never failed to mind their manners in the classroom of Wilda Addis, teacher at the Yountville Grammar School. This 1950s photograph shows Edgar Beard with his friend Jim Ghirardi after a successful deer hunt. (Courtesy of Lee Hart.)

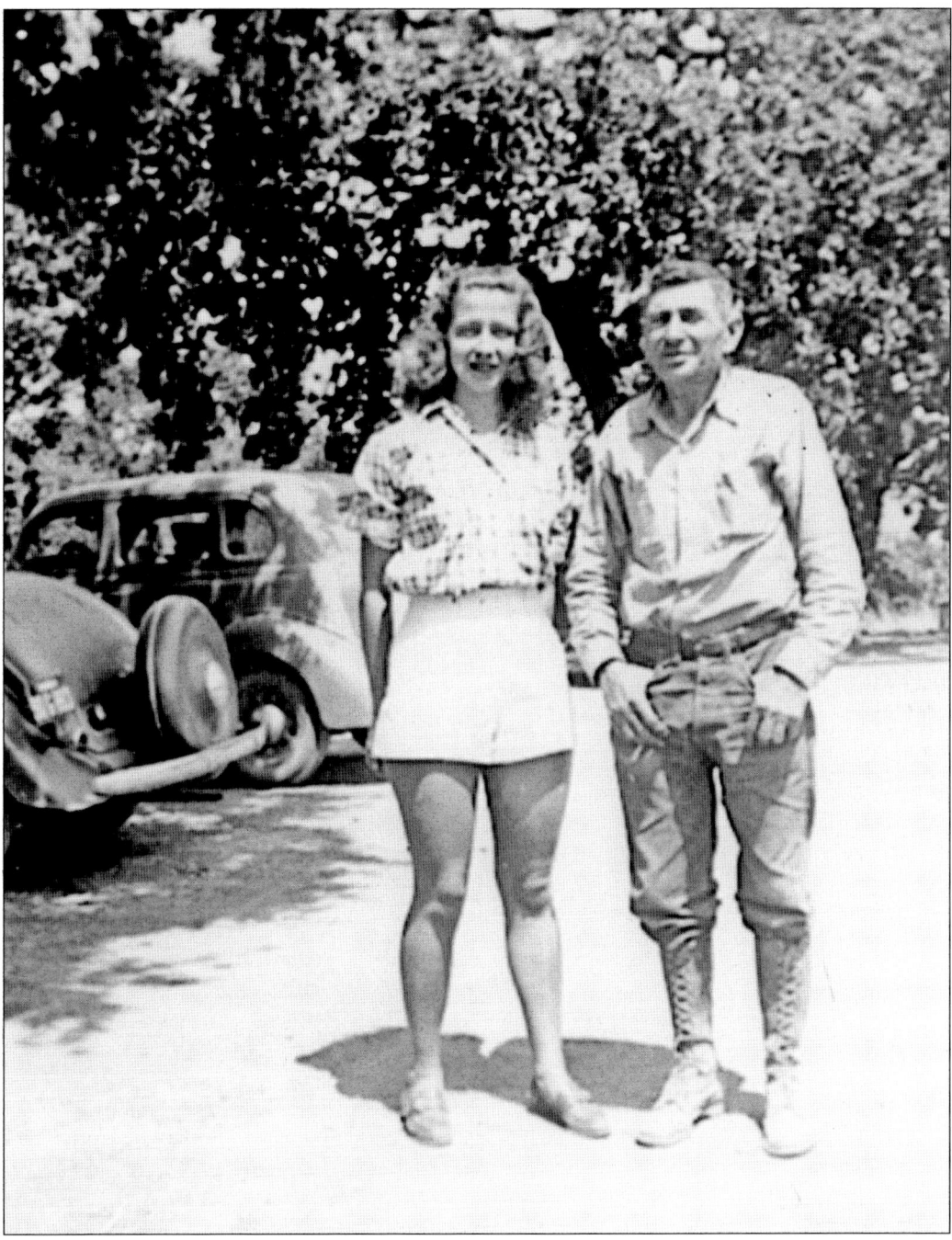

James Ghirardi, a longtime Yountville citizen, was born in 1888 to the parents of Antone and Maria Ghilardi (note the spelling change). The Ghirardi family settled in Yountville in 1890 and owned approximately 200 acres west of the town of Yountville. Taken in the 1930s, this photograph shows James with his daughter Mabel. The Ghirardi family spans six generations of Yountville citizens. The genealogical line is: Antone Ghilardi, James Ghirardi, Mabel (Ghirardi) Tiedemann, Donna (Tiedemann) Janes, Jason Janes, and Jason's two children, Tristan and Serafina. (Courtesy of Lee Hart.)

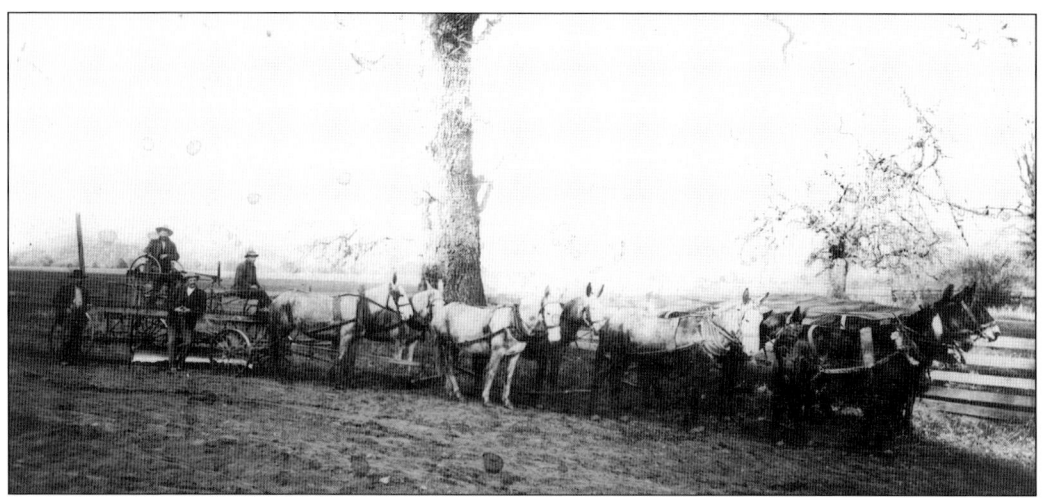

The unidentified men in this 1900s photograph are posing in front of an eight-mule team owned by the Viney Ranch. According to John Callison, who was born and raised in Yountville, "Mr. Ghirardi was the last man in the valley to farm with mule teams. You could hear his mules all over town when they started braying. . . . He plowed, disked, harrowed, planted, and harvested with his mules. He took the hay to his farm northwest of town and stored it in his barn. He also pruned and burned Bardessono's vineyard next to the school. He used a burn wagon after pruning the vines. It was quite a sight to see the wagon with flames shooting out and smoke billowing up moving around the vineyard. It never seemed to bother his mules, however." (Courtesy of Lee Hart.)

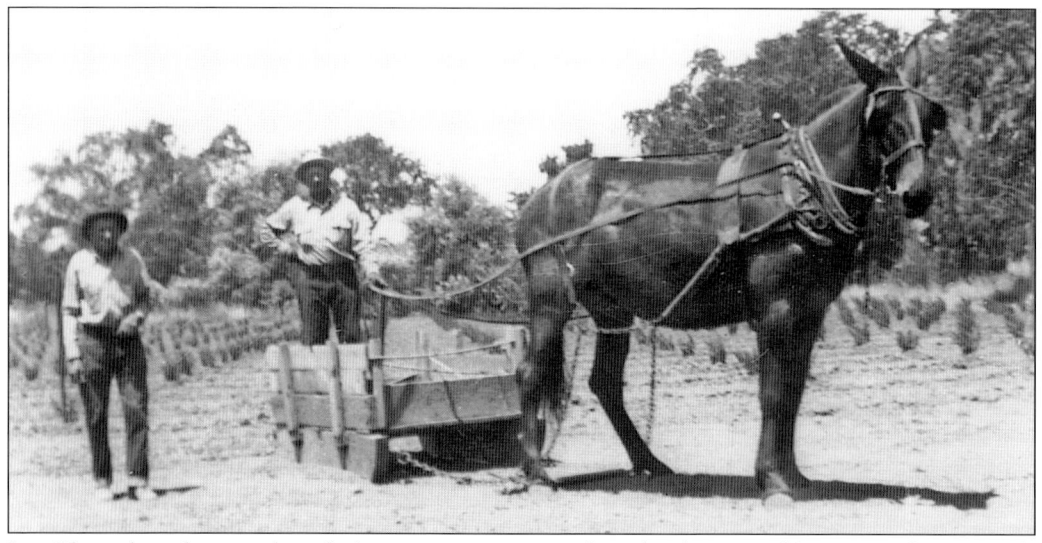

Jim Ghirardi and an unidentified man are getting ready to haul grapes. (Courtesy of Lee Hart.)

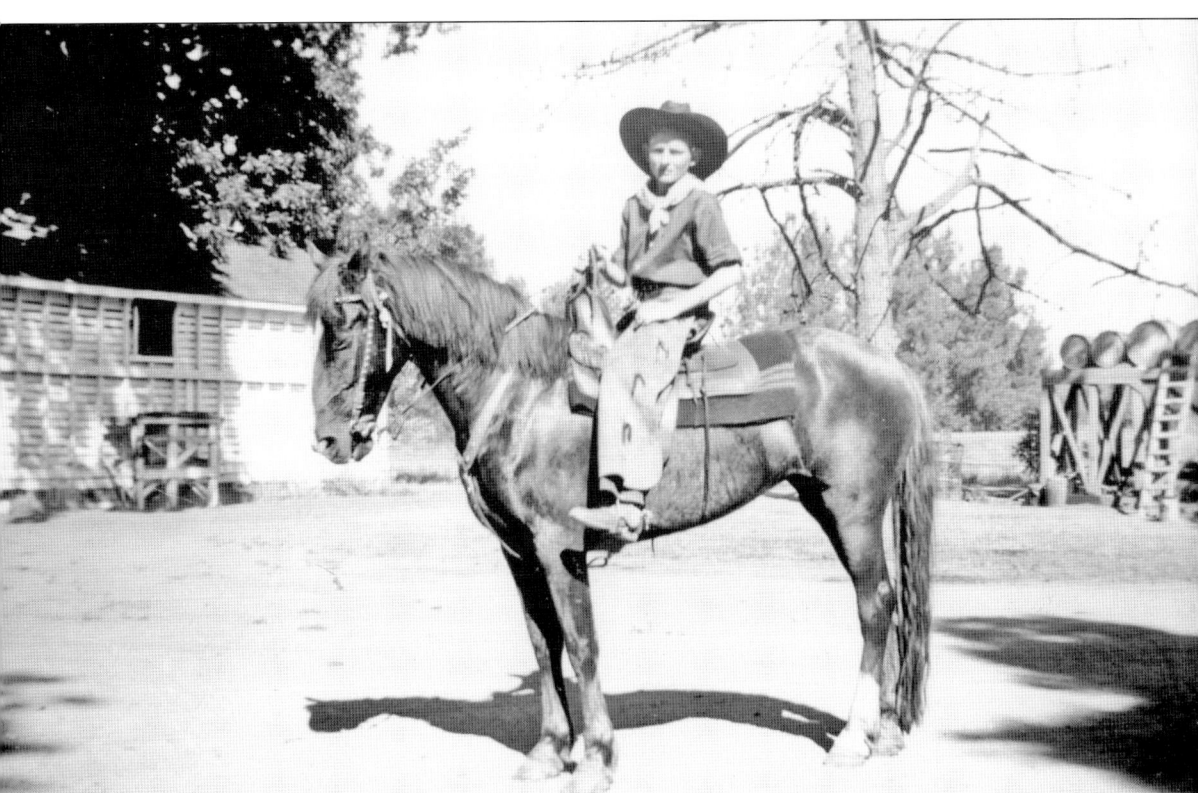

Prior to the 21st-century influx of high-end hotels, four-star restaurants, and tourist destinations, Yountville was primarily a community of family-run farms, ranches, and vineyards. Many Yountville children learned early on to hunt game, drive tractors, shovel hay, and ride horses. Pictured riding his horse on the Viney Ranch in 1936 is Yountville resident Edward Van de Leur. The Viney Ranch is located south of the St. Joan of Arc Catholic Church on Washington Street. (Courtesy of Lee Hart.)

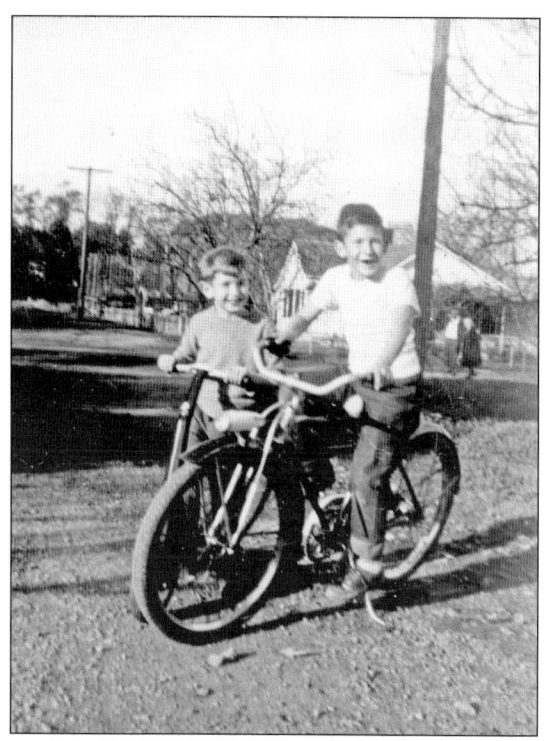

Posing for the camera in 1947 are two Yountville boys, Bill (left) and Lee Hart. They are in front of their home, located on the southwest corner of Jefferson and Monroe Streets, which is the old Mathias Van de Leur House. Lee Hart later grew up to become a distinguished law enforcement officer and George Yount historian. Each year, Lee Hart portrays George Yount in the Yountville Days Parade and Festival. (Courtesy of Lee Hart.)

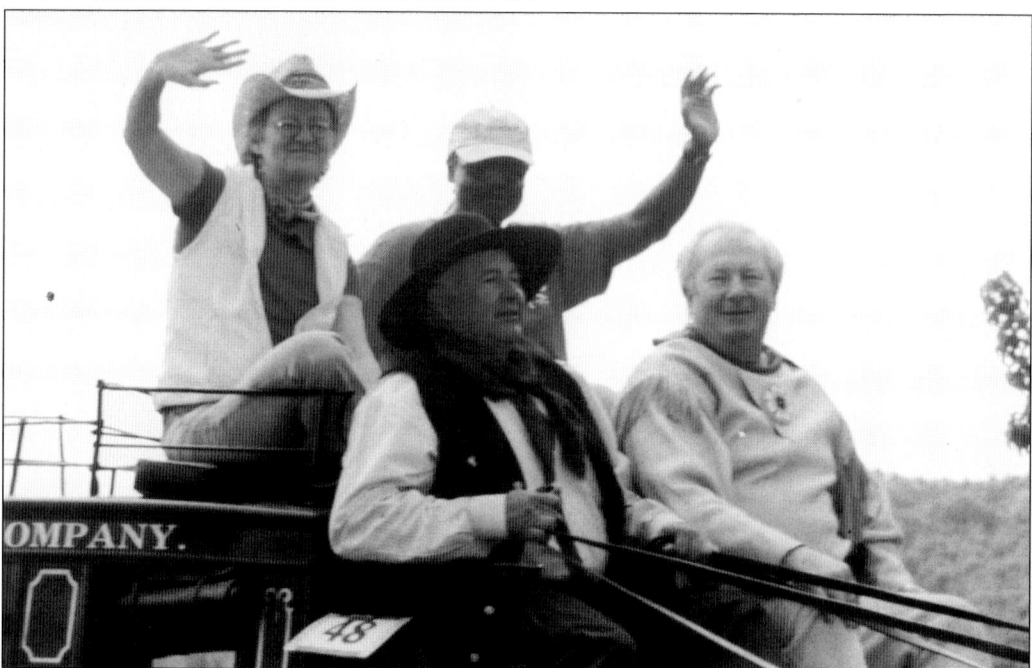

Representing his town 61 years later, this photograph features Lee Hart as George Yount riding on the Wells Fargo stagecoach. Featured in this Yountville Days and Parade Festival from left to right are (first row) an unidentified longtime Wells Fargo stagecoach driver, Lee Hart as George Yount; (second row) an unidentified longtime Wells Fargo bank manager, and Town of Yountville recreation director Kenneth Leary. (Courtesy of Lee Hart.)

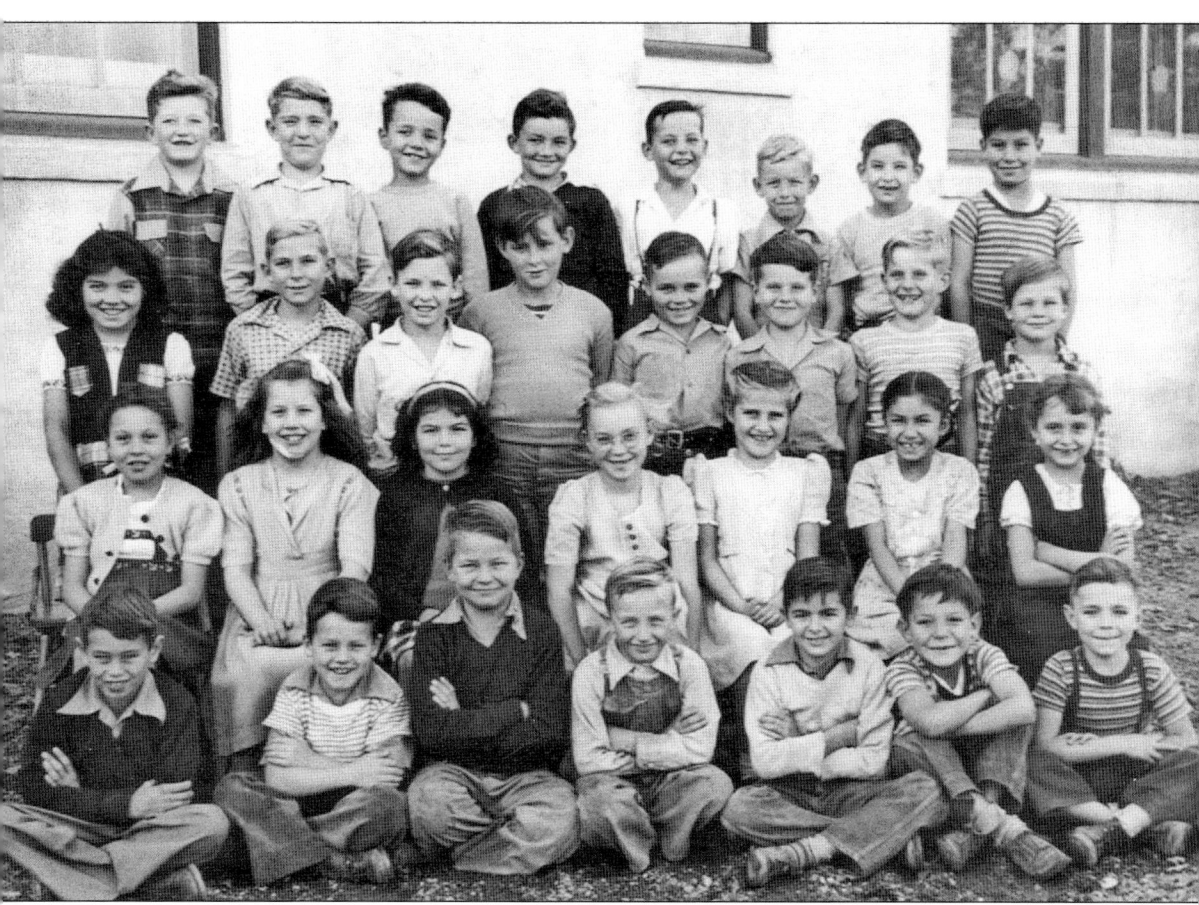

This photograph of Yountville Grammar School students was taken in the spring of 1947. Pictured from left to right are (first row) Bobby Silveira, Jerry Capito, Gilbert Williamson, Donald Standridge, unidentified student, Jim Robles, and Hugh Laney; (second row) Nona Grisel, Edna Mae Risley, Margaret Azavedo, Bernice Lloyd, Emily Olmstead, unidentified student, and Majorie Herrick; (third row) unidentified student, Irving Land, Gleason Sammons, unidentified student, Kenneth Laney, Roger Schulze, Ronald Cole, and Donald Cowan; (fourth row) Richard Ragatz, Ray Rhodes, Joe St. Clair, Larry Lloyd, Jerry Taylor, Darrell Martin, Vernon Flock, and Carlos Robles. (Courtesy of Vernon Flock.)

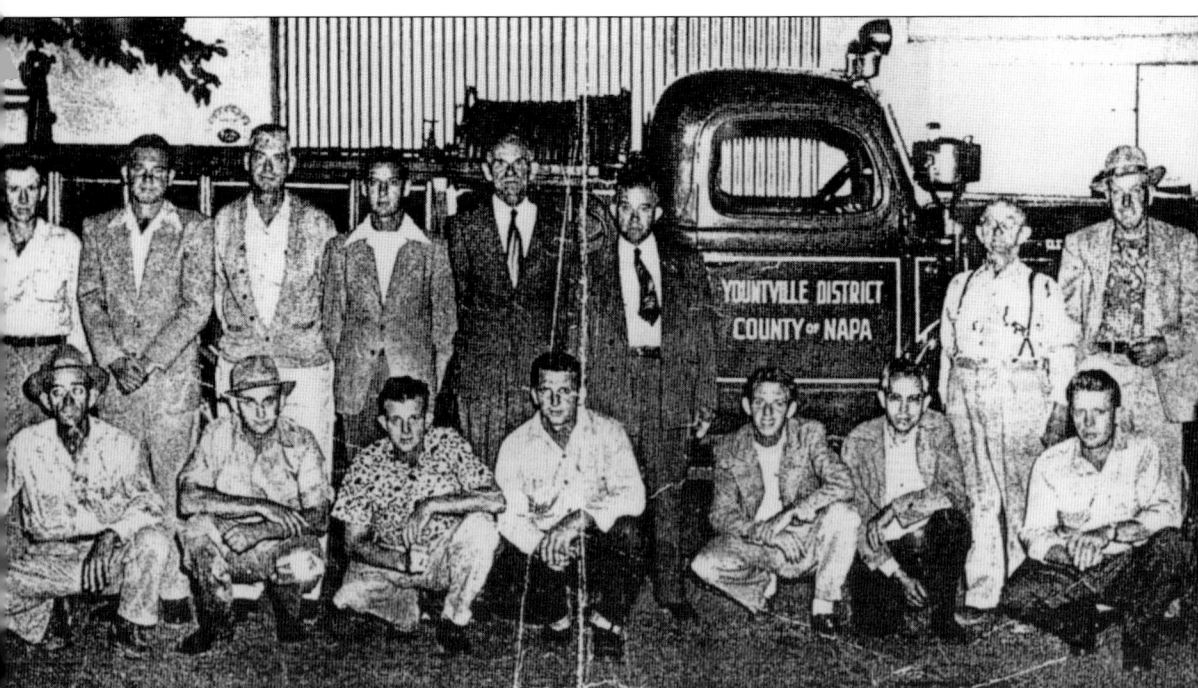

The volunteer Yountville Fire Department began with 13 members in 1917. Because many of Yountville's early structures were constructed with wood, a quick-responding fire suppression team was essential to the safety of both residents and structures. The first pieces of equipment, a hand pump and push cart, were obtained by the fund-raising efforts of the volunteer department. In 1929, a firehouse was constructed on the triangular portion of property now occupying the present-day location of VandeLeur Park. In this same year, a truck was purchased as well. This early 1940s newspaper reprint shows members of the Yountville Fire Department. From left to right are (first row) Cris Marquez, Henry Hill, Ed Lincoln, Jim Bresciani, George "Bud" Dulinski, Ben Arguello, Warren Lincoln; (second row) Robert E. Croxen, J. E. Lloyd Jr., J. C. Tyther, G. B. Flock, Morris Lilienthal, C. W. Johnson, Herman Dado, and N. P. Bartlow. (From the manuscripts of John Wichels; photograph courtesy of Edgar Beard.)

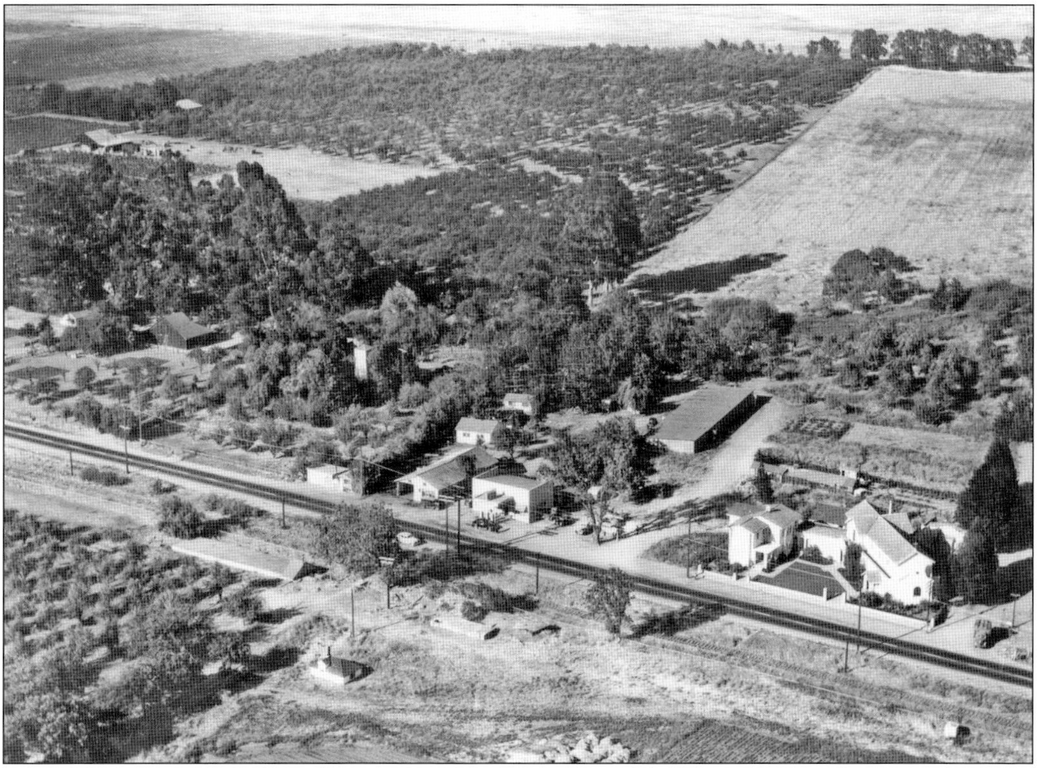

Flock's Garage and the Catholic church building are seen in this 1953 aerial view of Yountville. Note that the Highway 29 bypass of Yountville has not yet been constructed. (Courtesy of Vernon Flock.)

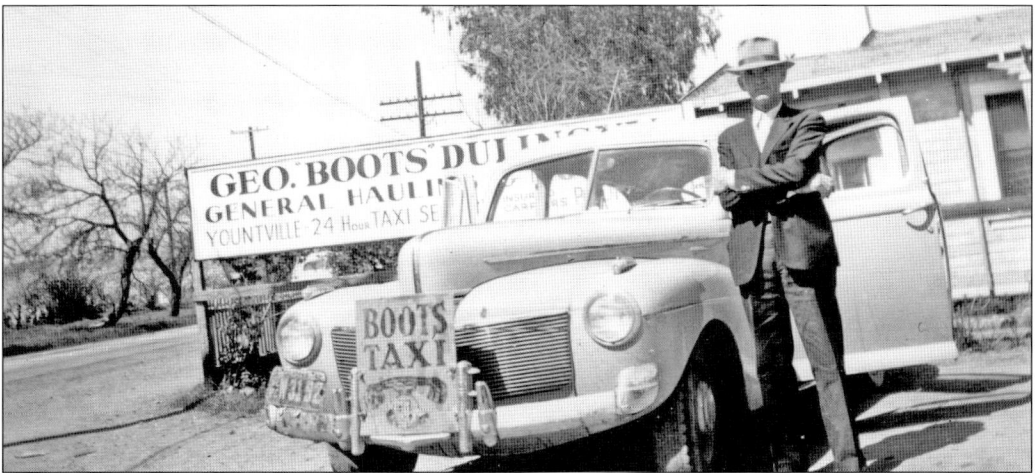

A state law, enacted in 1872 and amended with additions and several revisions in the early 1900s, restricted the sale of "any vinous, malt, or spirituous liquors" in excess of 3.2 percent alcohol by weight within 1.5 miles of any state prison and the Yountville Veterans Home. This law led to the development of a bustling taxi industry in Yountville during the early and mid-1900s that served residents of the Veterans Home by driving them to bars and liquor stores located outside the restricted area. In this c. 1944 photograph, George "Boots" Dulinsky poses with his taxi cab. (Courtesy of Barbara and Bud Dulinsky.)

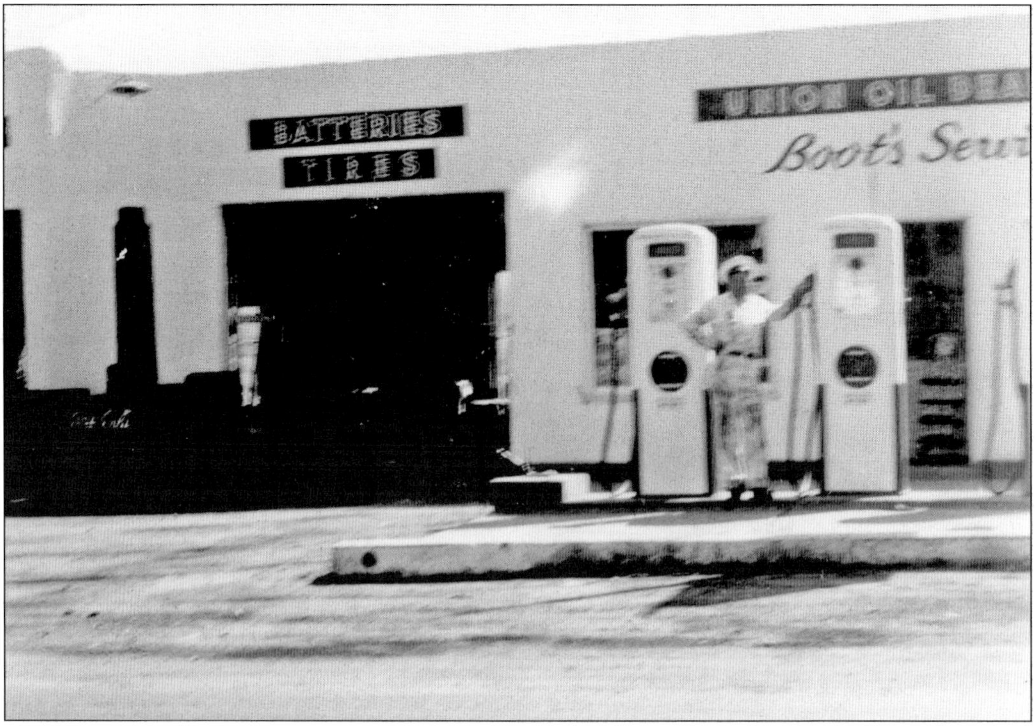

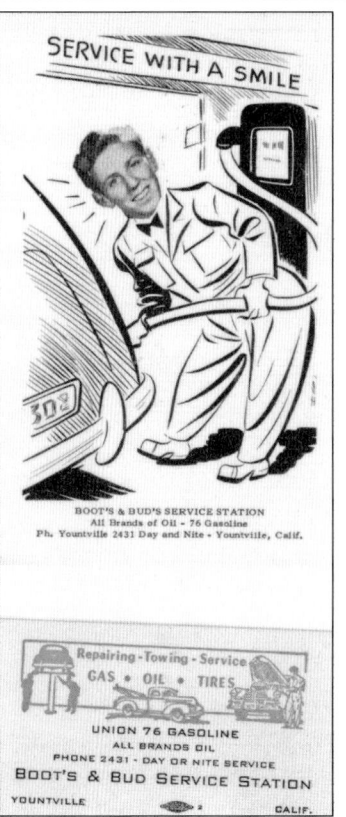

The Union Oil station, located on the current site of the V Marketplace parking lot, was built in 1947 by George "Boots" Dulinsky for his son Bud. When Bud returned from service in the air force, he came back to a service station complete with the business cards pictured to the left. Later on, the service station housed a gift store and secondhand shop. The Boots and Bud Service Station was torn down in the mid-1960s. The photograph and business card are both from around 1948. (Courtesy of Bud and Barbara Dulinsky.)

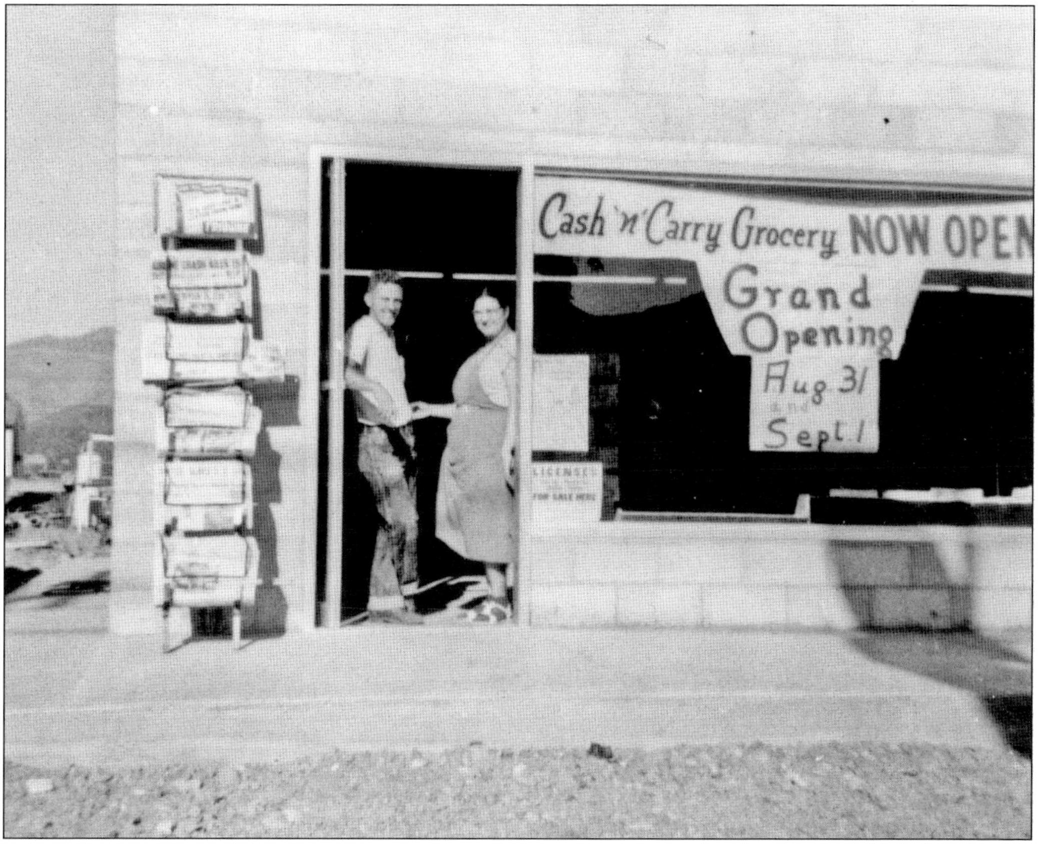

Yountville's Cash 'n' Carry, as it appeared in 1963, was owned and operated by Bud and Barbara Dulinsky. Years later, the building was enlarged and remodeled. Today Yountville residents know the site as Ranch Market Too. Note the large building to the left of the Cash 'n' Carry; this building was called the Castle Inn and was adjacent to the 2009 site of the Bistro Jeanty on Washington Street. (Both photographs courtesy of Barbara and Bud Dulinsky.)

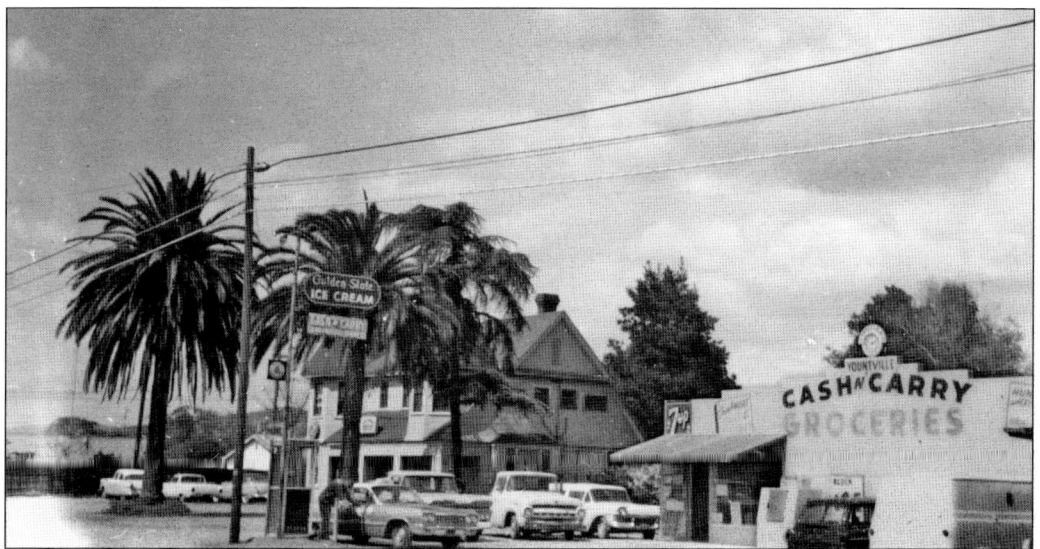

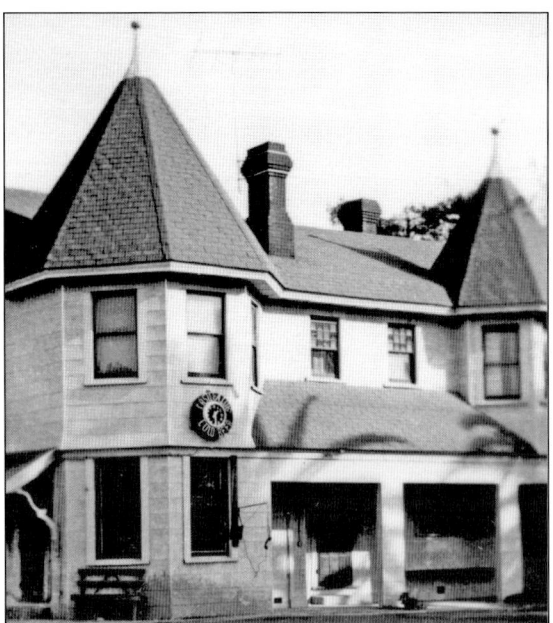

The Castle Inn, located near the current site of Bistro Jeanty, was built near the turn of the 20th century. The Queen Anne style of architecture was unusual for rural residences in the vicinity of Yountville. The property was first owned by William Gibbs, a prominent Yountville businessman and land owner. In addition to the Castle Inn, Gibbs owned large tracts of land from his purchase of the A. J. Clark property in 1883, which he sold to the Veterans Home nine months later. Gibbs also owned the Gibbs Dance Hall and the Gibbs Building on Washington Street. The Castle Inn caught fire in the mid-1960s and was demolished shortly afterward. (Courtesy of Barbara and Bud Dulinsky.)

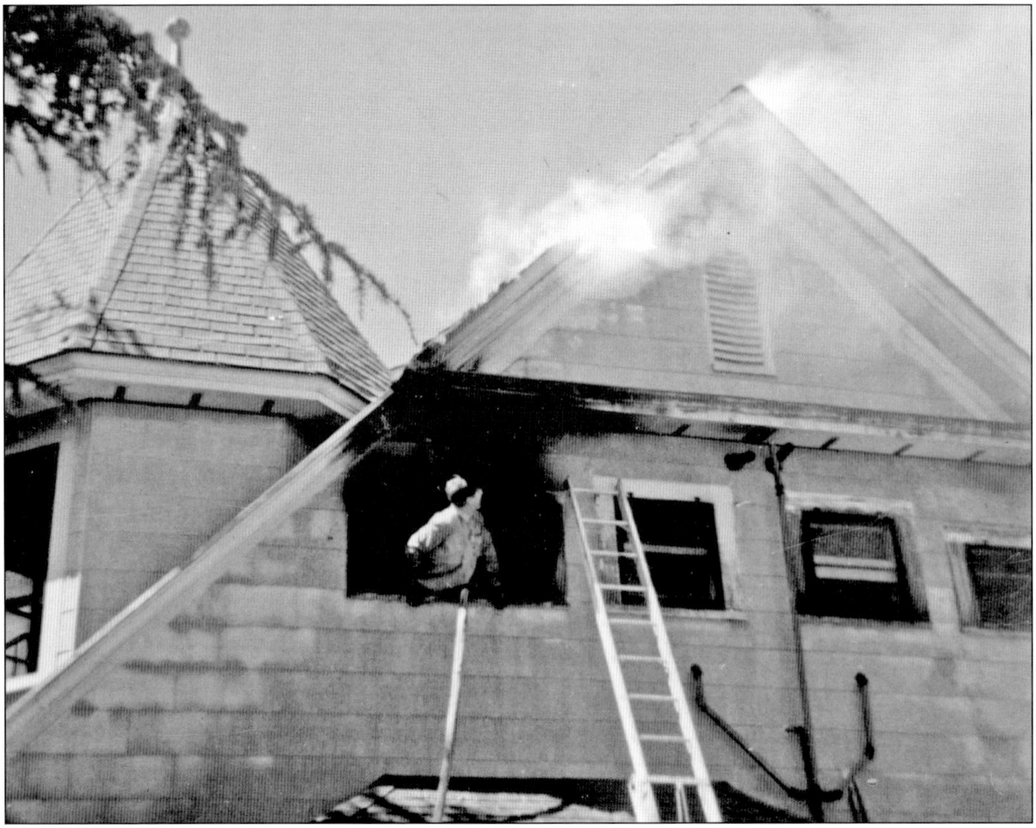

This c. 1965 photograph by George "Bud" Dulinsky captures the first few moments of a fire that eventually destroyed the Castle Inn. Due to irreparable damage, the Castle Inn was demolished in the mid-1960s. (Courtesy of Barbara and Bud Dulinsky.)

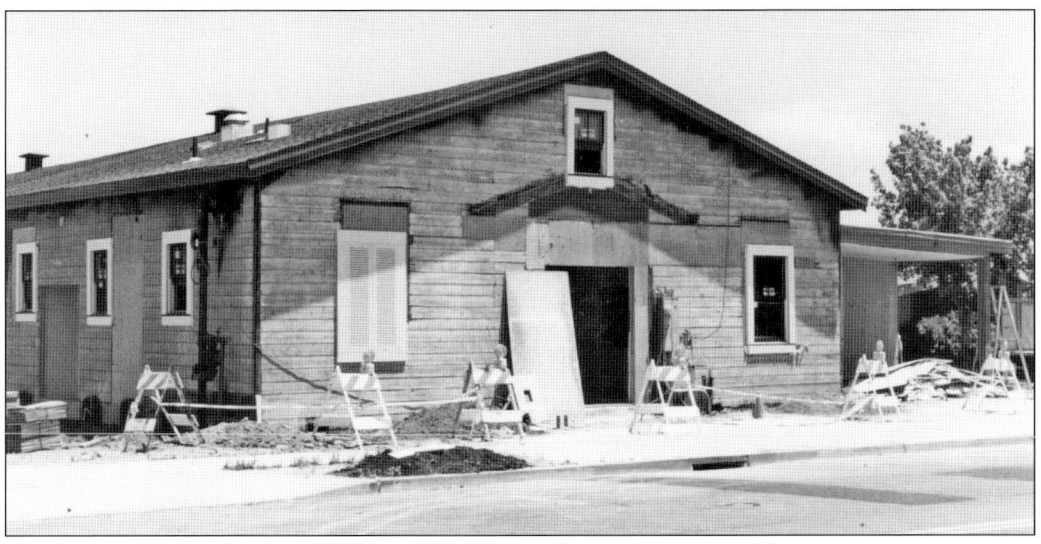

The Yountville Community Hall was originally built in 1926 and was designed as a community meeting place and dance hall. The *St. Helena Star* featured an article announcing the price of a dinner and dance at the grand opening celebration: 50¢. In 1982, Yountville town workers and residents joined together in efforts to remodel the historic structure. (Courtesy of Barbara and Bud Dulinsky.)

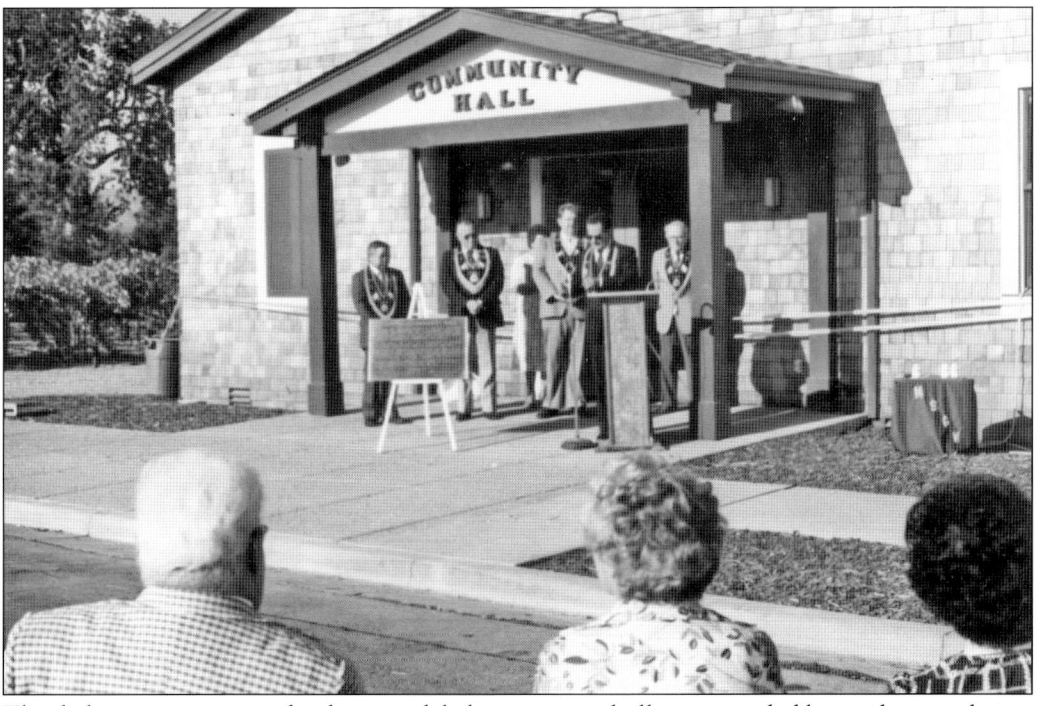

The dedication ceremony for the remodeled community hall was attended by residents and civic leaders. (Courtesy of Barbara and Bud Dulinsky.)

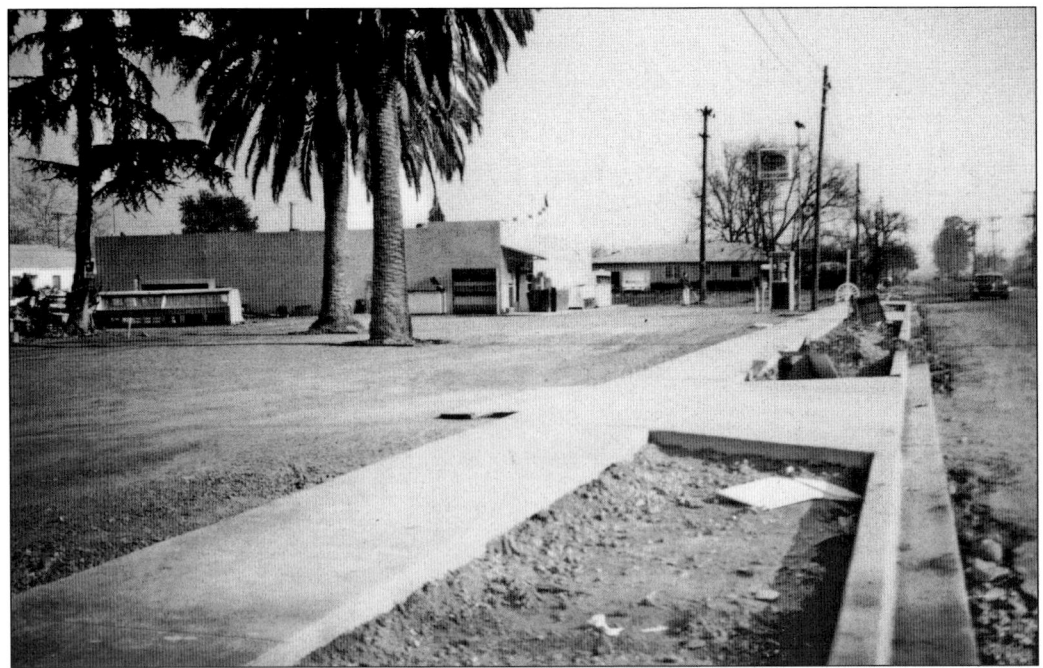

This photograph was taken in 1959 near the current location of Mulberry and Washington Streets, looking south. Notice the newly poured cement walkway along Washington Street. It will usher thousands of residents and tourists into the future businesses of the Yountville Bar and Grill, later to become the restaurant known today as the Bistro Jeanty. (Courtesy of Barbara and Bud Dulinsky.)

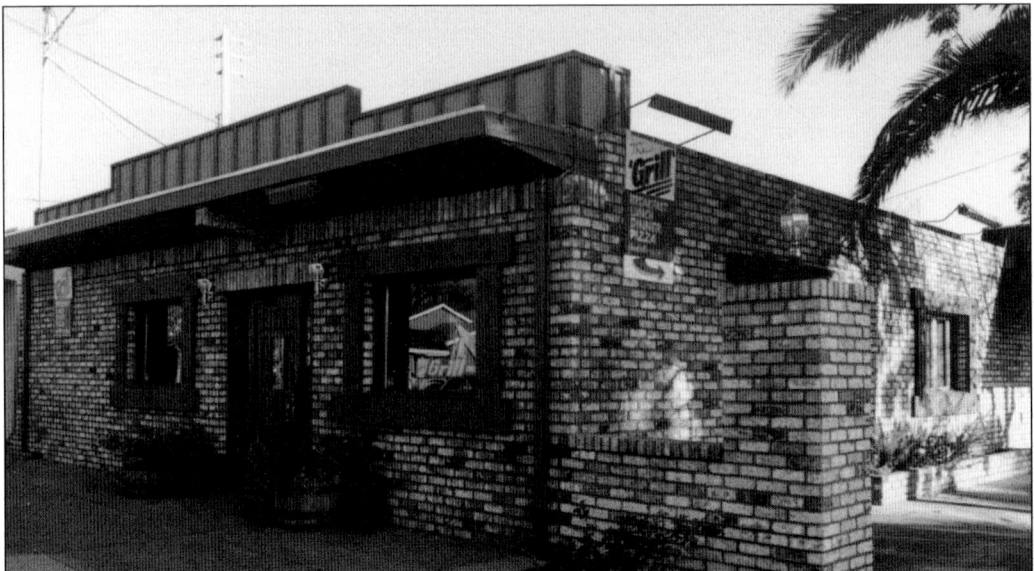

This 1991 photograph shows the exterior of The Grill, which was frequented by Yountville veterans and residents alike. Note the heritage palm trees in the upper right-hand corner. The historic palms were planted in the early 1900s as part of the landscaping of the Gibbs Mansion, later to be known as the Castle Club. (Photograph by Joe Gambatese, courtesy of the Town of Yountville.)

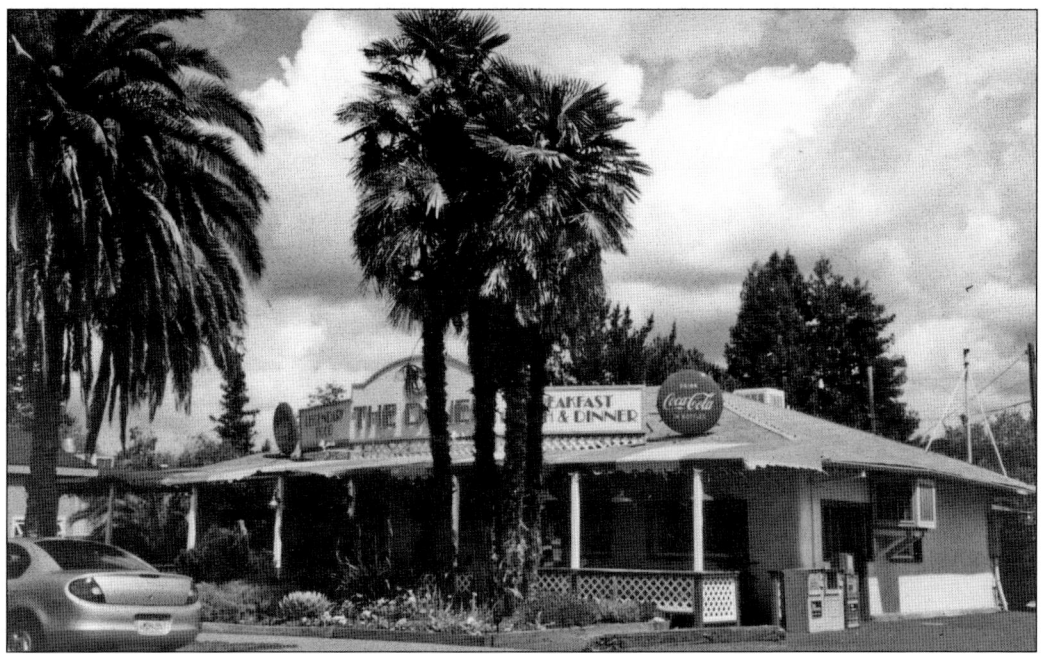

For many years, the Greyhound bus stop was a movable shelter that could be relocated from place to place. In the late 1940s, a permanent building was constructed on Highway 29, now called Washington Street. Originally operating as a Greyhound bus station for over 25 years, the business eventually closed. In 1976, under the management of Cassandra Mitchell, a new business reopened called The Diner. A favorite breakfast stop for many longtime Yountville residents, The Diner and was known for its outstanding omelets and gourmet coffee. The Diner kept its doors open for almost 30 years until it closed in the 1990s. In 2008, the former location of the bus station and The Diner is the site of Thomas Keller's Ad Hoc Restaurant. (Courtesy of Barbara and Bud Dulinsky.)

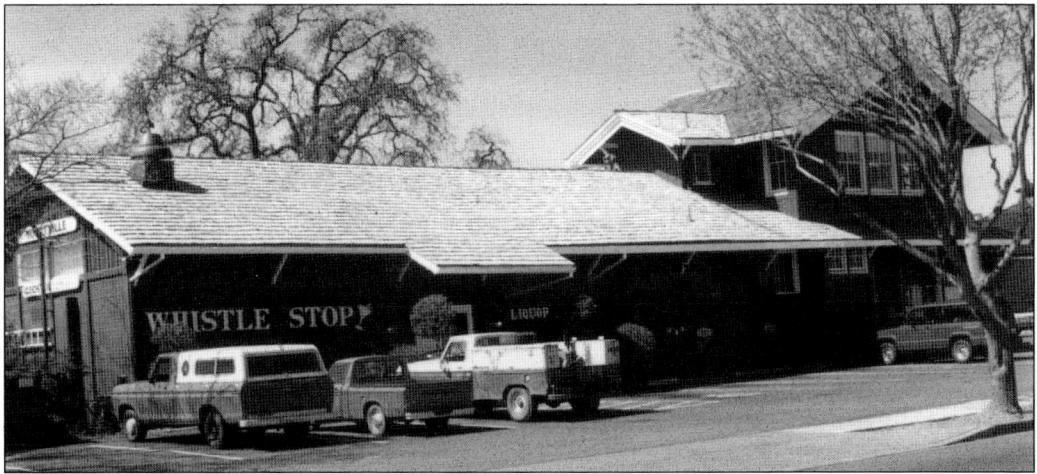

Another favorite Yountville local hangout was located on an annex to the Southern Pacific Depot building on Washington Street. Pictured around 1984, the Whistle Stop offered residents a bar and grill menu in a beautifully restored interior featuring red leather bar stools and deep-set leather booths. The Whistle Stop is now doing business as a high-end retail clothing business. (Photograph by Chuck Wharff, courtesy of the Town of Yountville.)

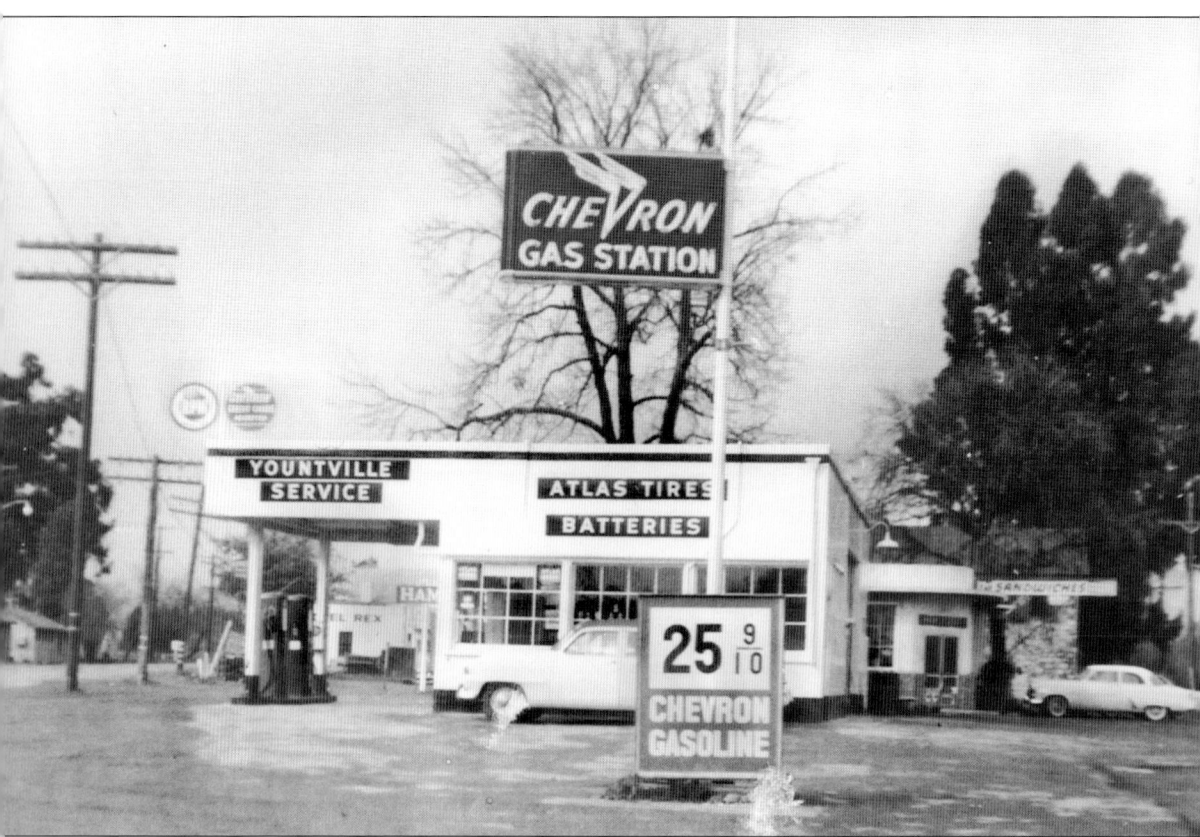

This Chevron station, pictured around the mid-1950s, was once operated by Ray Caravantes and occupied what is now the site of the outstanding Hurley's Restaurant and Bar at the "Y" intersection of Yount and Washington Streets. To the left is the Hotel Rex, the present-day location of the Bouchon Bakery, and on the right is the Magnolia Hotel, the current site of Maison Fleurie. (Courtesy of Barbara and Bud Dulinsky.)

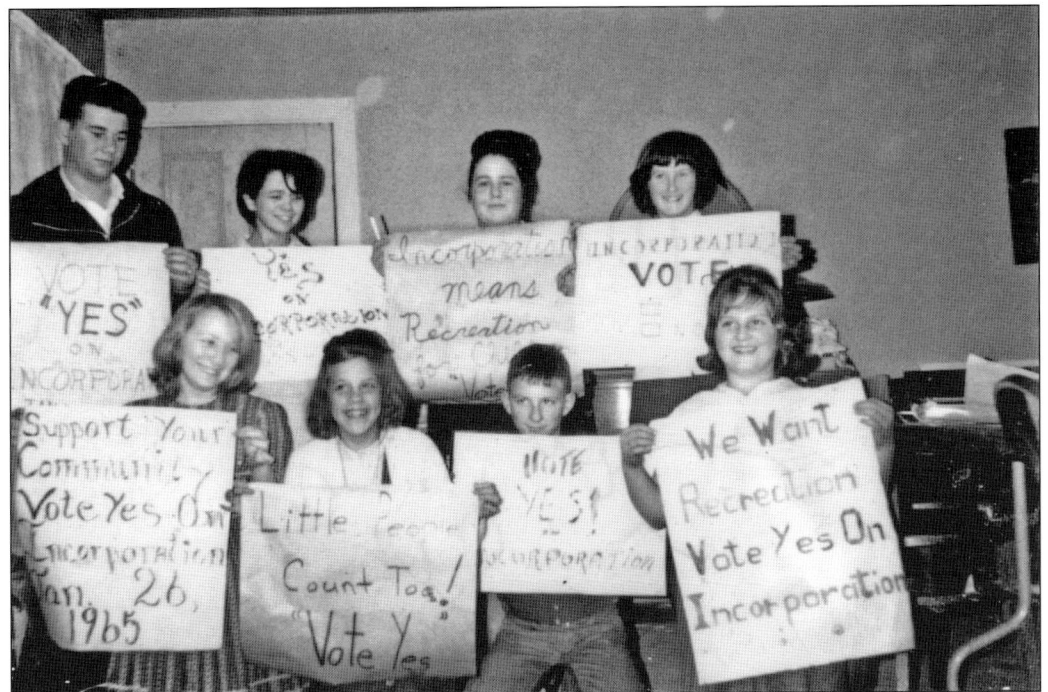

In the early 1960s, residents began to plan for the future expansion and growth of Yountville. In a special election held on January 26, 1965, voters approved a mandate of incorporation. On May 4, 1965, the town of Yountville was officially incorporated. A group of local children made posters for a parade in support of incorporation. Pictured from left to right are (first row) Nancy Burnside, ? Miller, George Dulinsky, and Bea Dulinsky; (second row) Robert Detmar, Edith Burnside, Sandra Detmar, and Lucy Smith. (Courtesy of Barbara and Bud Dulinsky.)

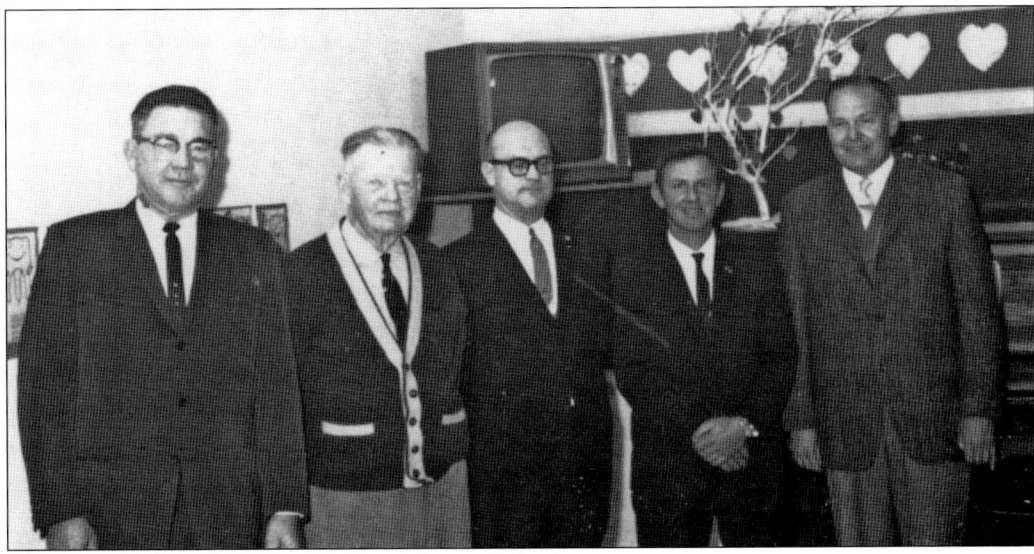

The first Yountville City Council meeting took place in the St. Joan of Arc Church meeting hall. This photograph shows the mayor and city council in 1965. From left to right are John Lloyd, Cleve Borman, Osmond O. Capito, George "Bud" Dulinsky, and Dr. E. C. Johnson. (Courtesy of Barbara and Bud Dulinsky.)

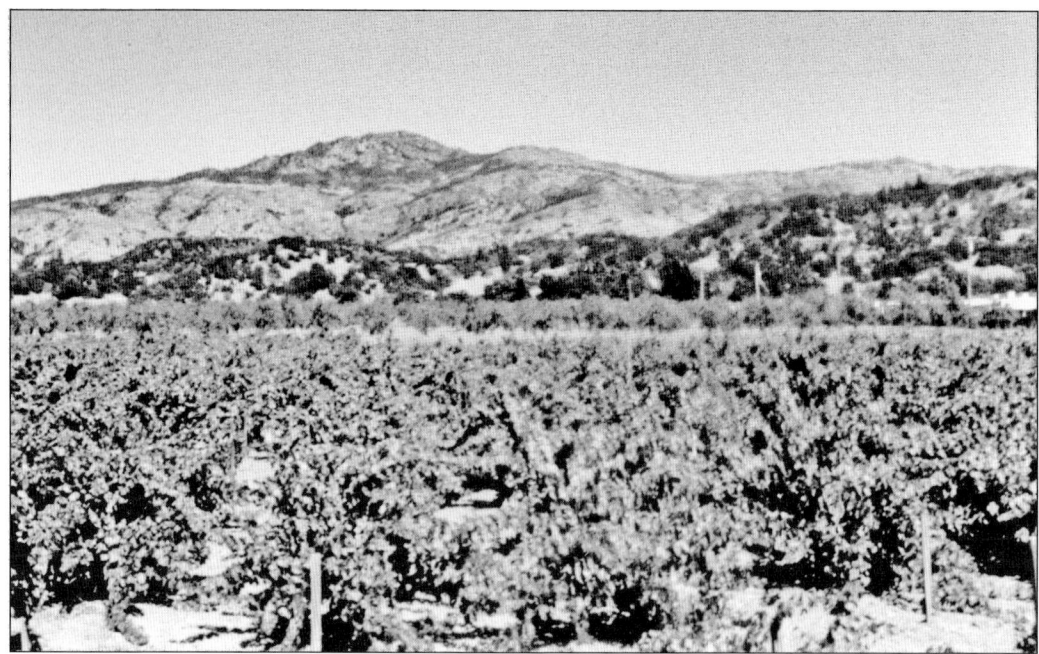

The Rancho De Napa mobile home park was constructed on property once owned by the DeHaven family. Prior to the development of the park, this entire area was planted with 15 acres of prune and pear orchards, along with 20 acres of vineyards and pastures. The DeHavens had their fruit picked and processed in a dehydrator that was built in 1935. This was the view in the summer of 1968, a few months before the land was cleared for development. The photograph was taken from the present-day location of the intersection of Mission and San Antonio Streets. (Courtesy of Dr. Jim Atwood.)

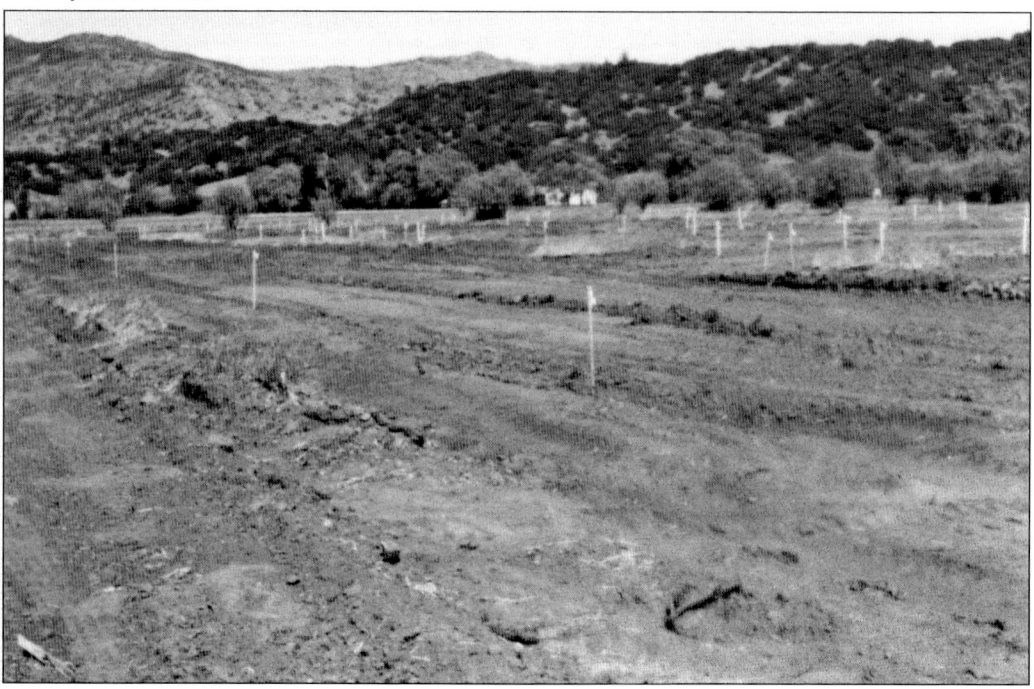

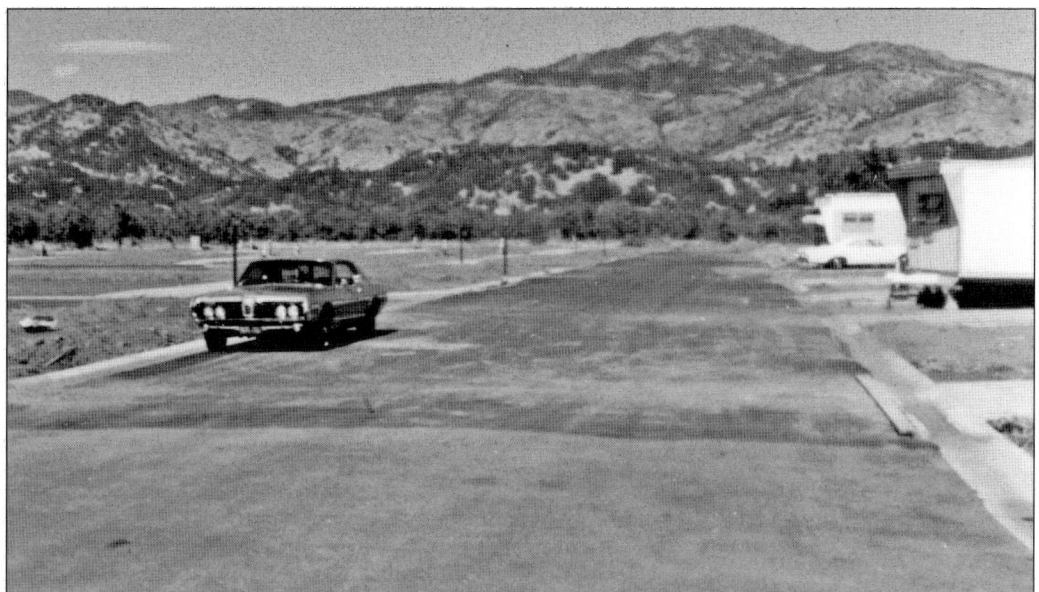

Typical of most major construction projects, the development of the Rancho De Napa mobile home park took place in stages. In the first phase of development, the land was cleared and surveyed, which was followed by the paving of roads. The picture above, taken in the summer of 1970 looking east from Antonio Street, shows the park at 25 percent completion. The photograph below, taken from the Highway 29 overpass in 1973, shows the completed development of Rancho De Napa. Notice pristine Atlas Peak before development and the absence of the bank to the left of the Rancho De Napa entrance. (Both photographs courtesy of Dr. Jim Atwood.)

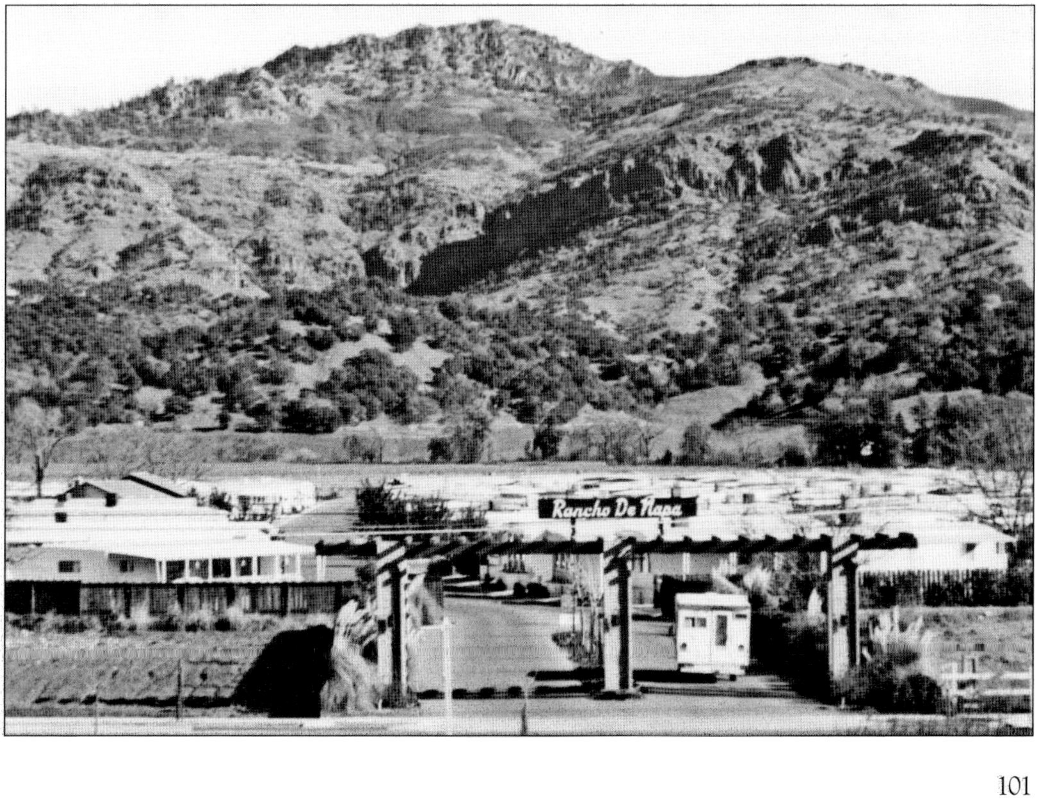

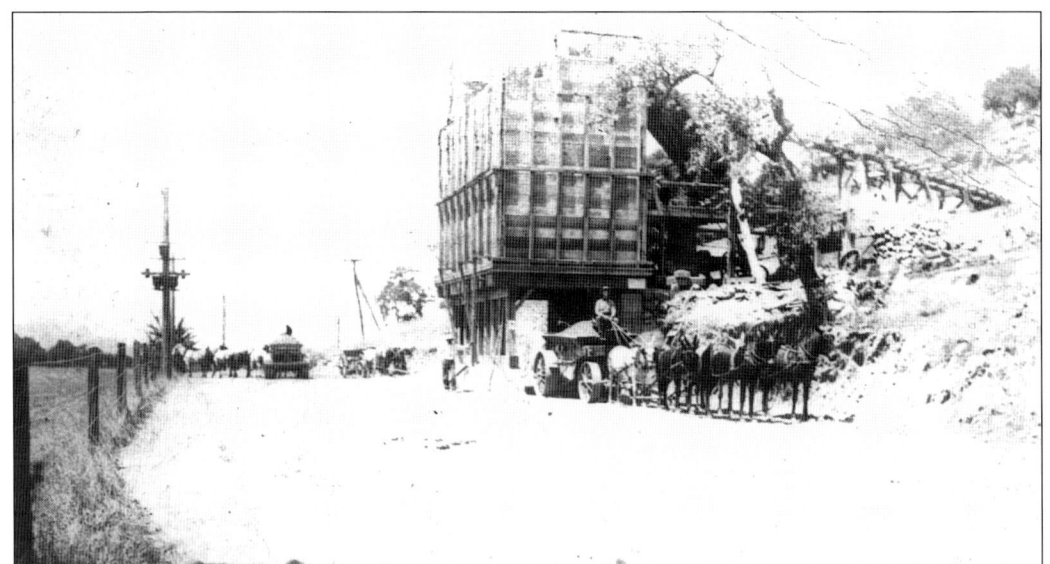

Pictured above around 1913, the original Rock Villa was an actual rock quarry located approximately a quarter mile north of the Yountville Cemetery. The Rock Villa Quarry supplied the quarried rock needed to construct the three historic stone buildings in Yountville: the Charles Rovegno stone house, the French Laundry, and the Magnolia Hotel. Later on, the Rock Villa building (below) became the Rock Villa Bar. Many Yountville and Veterans Home residents were patrons of the Rock Villa Bar due to a law originally enacted in 1872 that stated, "Every person who, within two miles of the land belonging to this state upon which a state prison is situated, keeps, gives away, or offers for sale any vinous, malt, or spirituous liquors, is guilty of a misdemeanor." In 1915, the law was amended to include the Veterans Home at Yountville and also to designate the limit from two to one and a half miles. (Above photograph courtesy of Lee Hart; below photograph courtesy of Phyllis Vallerga.)

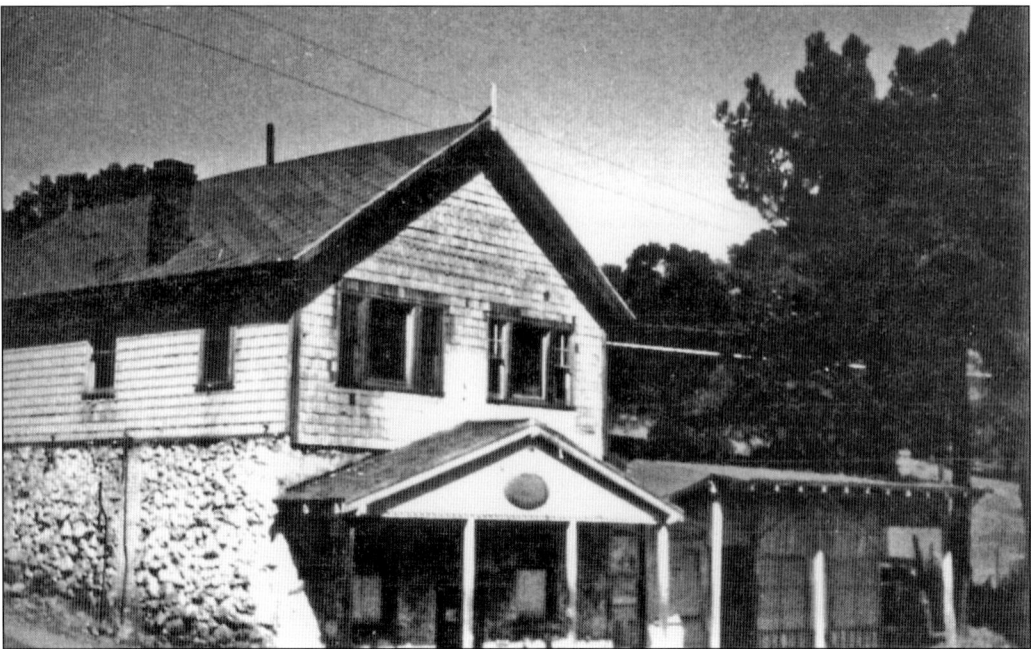

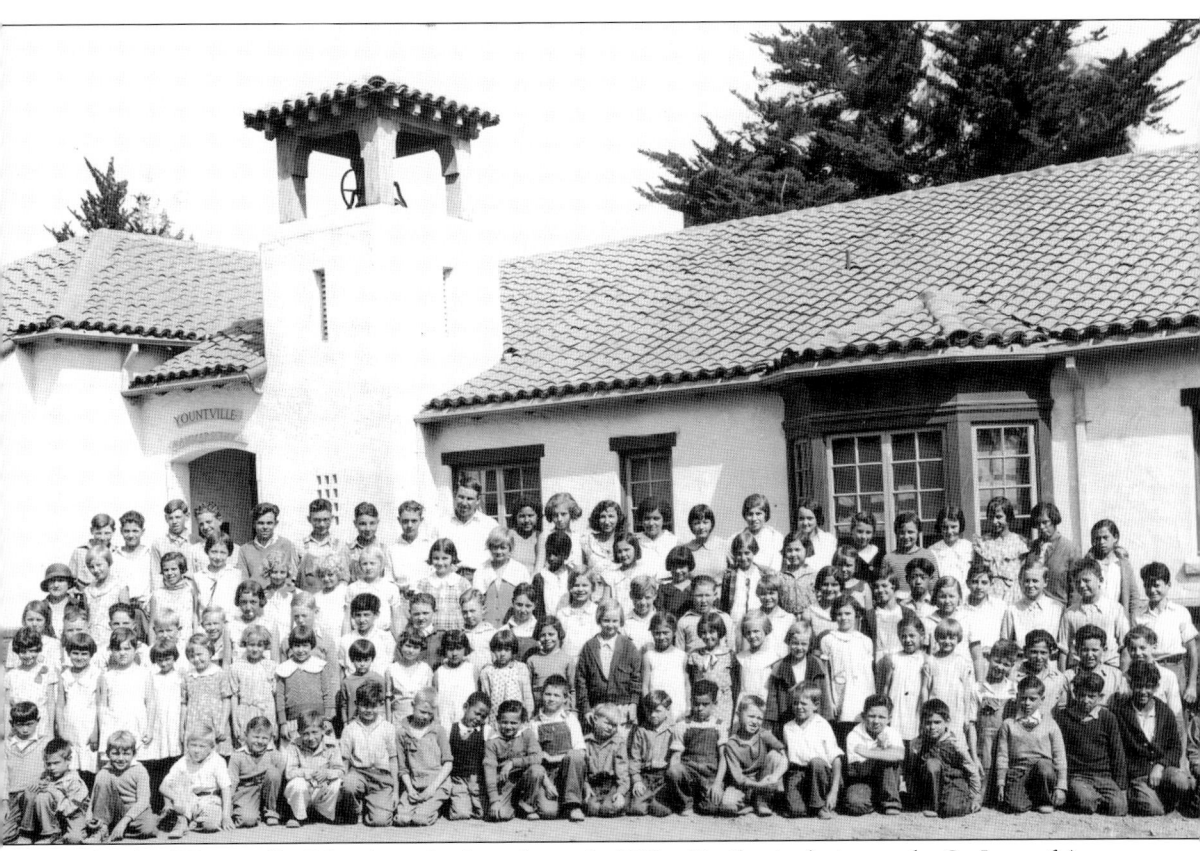

The third Yountville School was built in the early 1920s. Similar in design to the St. Joan of Arc Church, this architecture is representative of the Mission Revival style. The bell tower and bell were taken from the original Yountville Grammar School. (Courtesy of Barbara and Bud Dulinsky.)

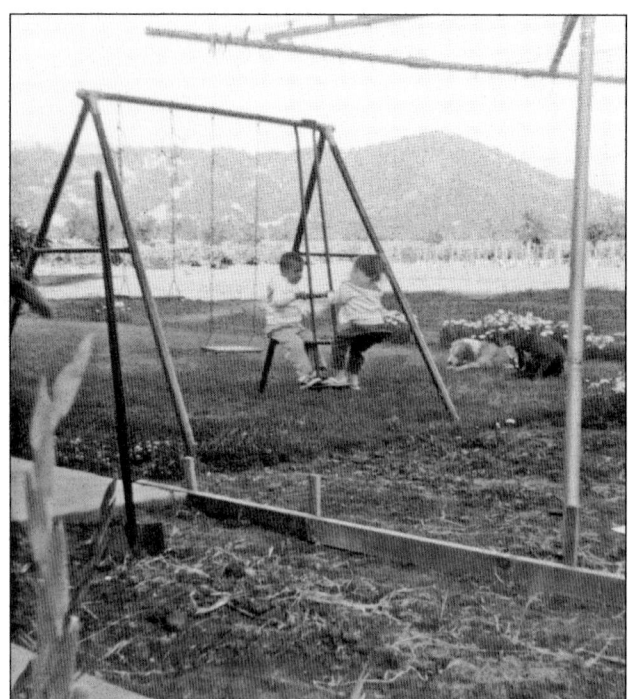

The Bardessono family has lived in Yountville for over 70 years. Both Pete Bardessono and his brother Steve attended the Yountville Grammar School. Pete Bardessono was hired to direct the Yountville Department of Public Works and continued to serve the community for over 30 years until he retired in 1989. Pete and his wife, Maxine, raised their three children in the small-town community of rural Yountville. This photograph of the Bardessono children (left), taken in the late 1950s, shows the backyard view of the Bardessono residence. The vineyard in the background shows the future development of the Toyon Terrace housing subdivision. (Courtesy of Maxine Bardessono.)

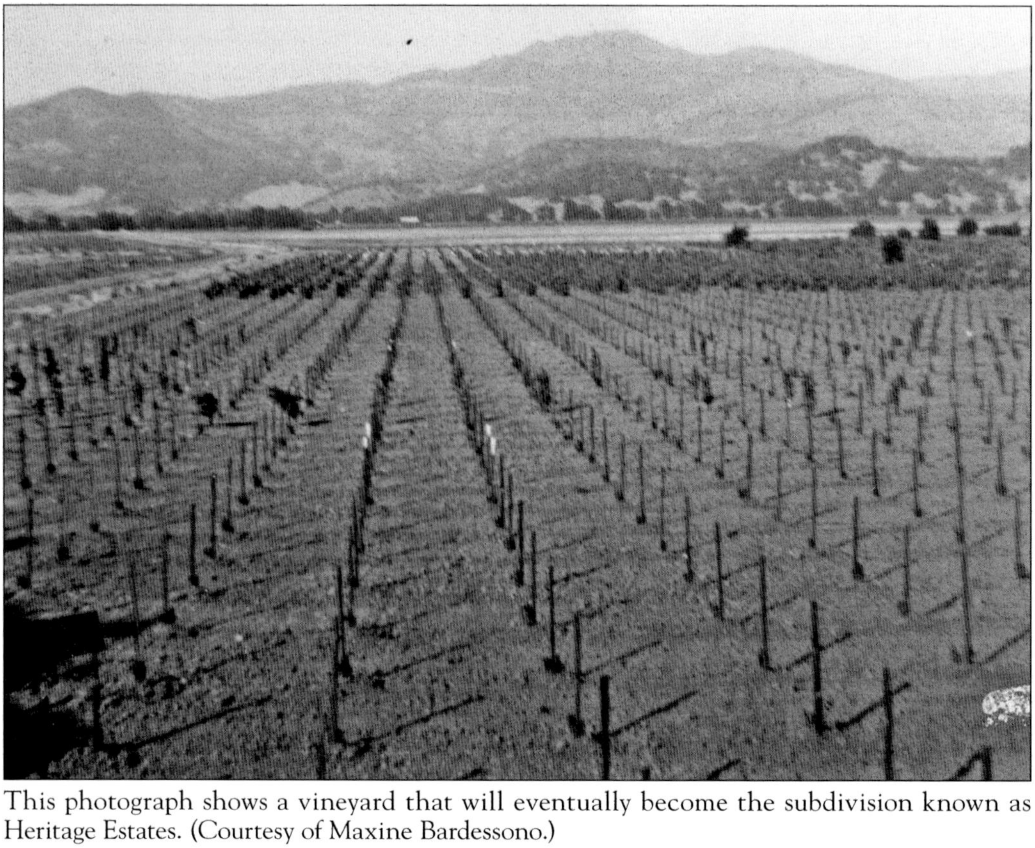

This photograph shows a vineyard that will eventually become the subdivision known as Heritage Estates. (Courtesy of Maxine Bardessono.)

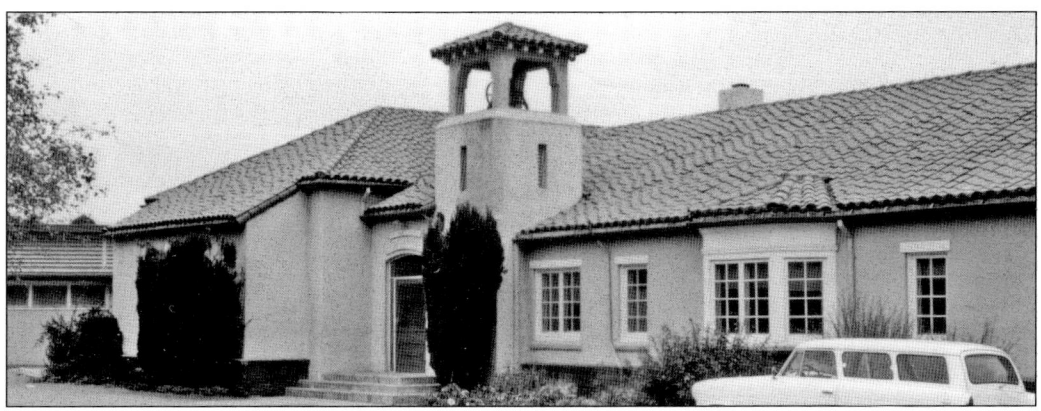

The Yountville School building shown above was constructed in the mid-1920s and was actually the third location of the school. Several generations of Yountville's children passed through its doors until a fourth school was constructed in the mid-1980s. At the completion of the fourth Yountville Elementary School, the Town of Yountville's civic offices moved into this historic structure, pictured below in 2008. (Both photographs courtesy of Stuart Alexander.)

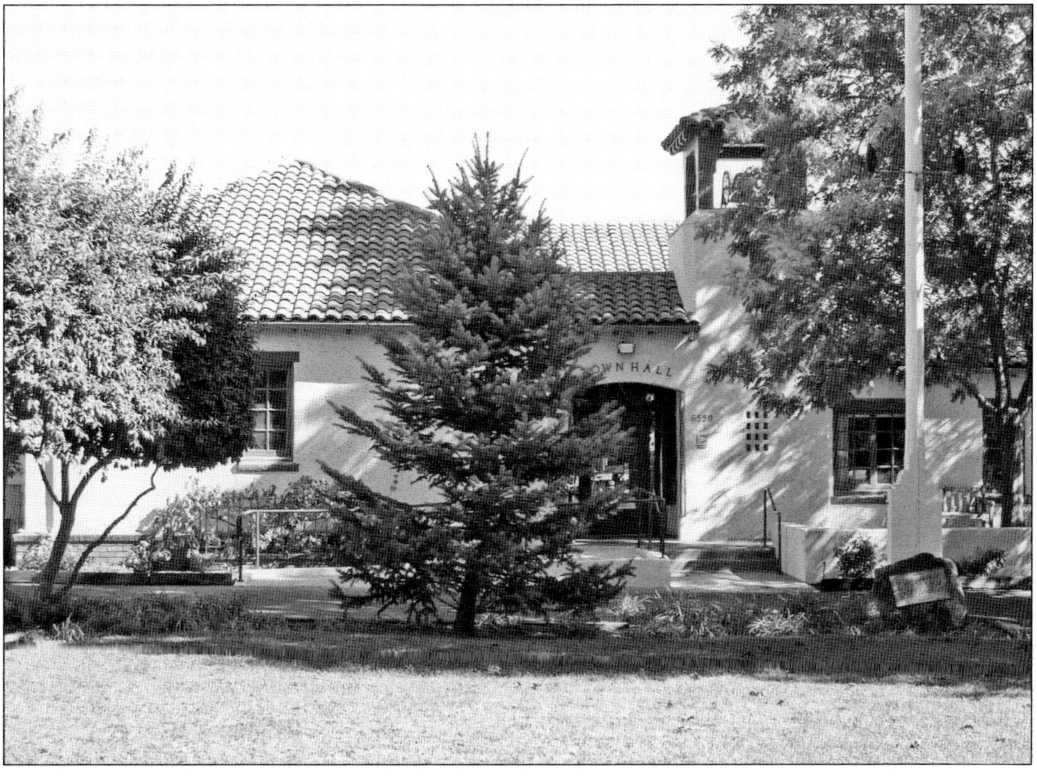

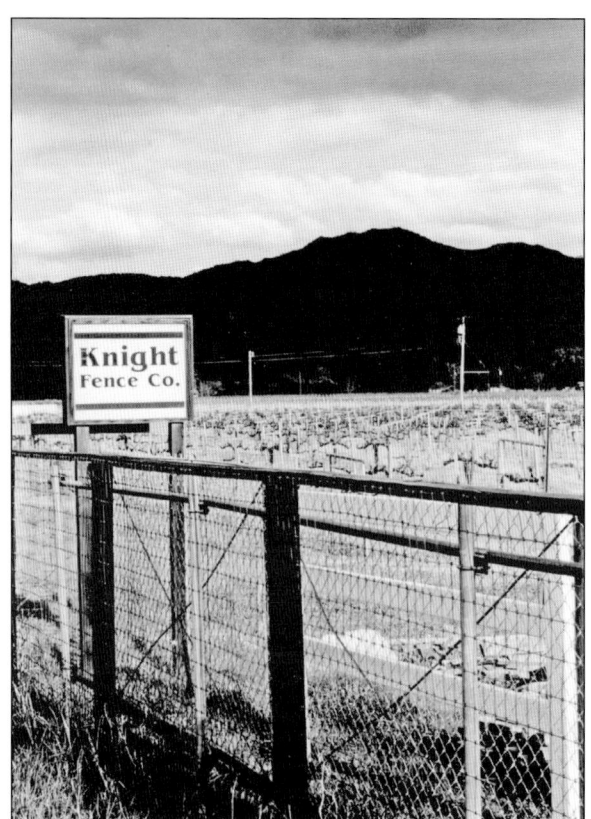

George Knight was a longtime Yountville resident who owned several commercial and residential properties in the town. The original Knights Lumber and True Value Hardware operated in Yountville for 43 years. Prior to the lumberyard, this was the location of a chicken ranch. The property looks out on the eastern ridge of Atlas Peak. (Courtesy of Eric Knight.)

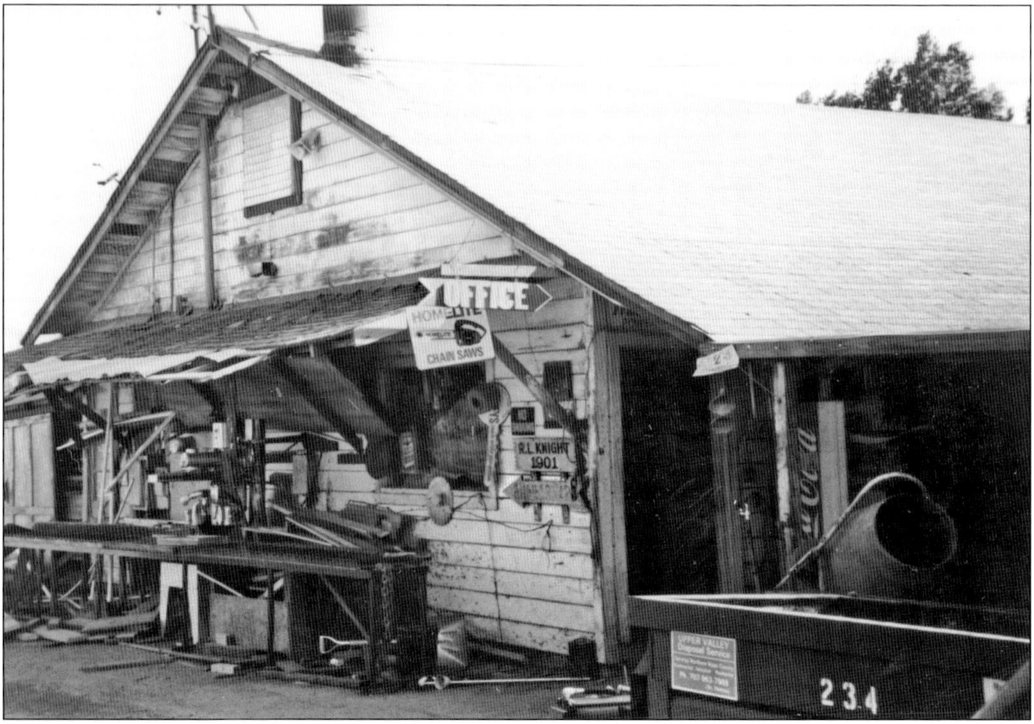

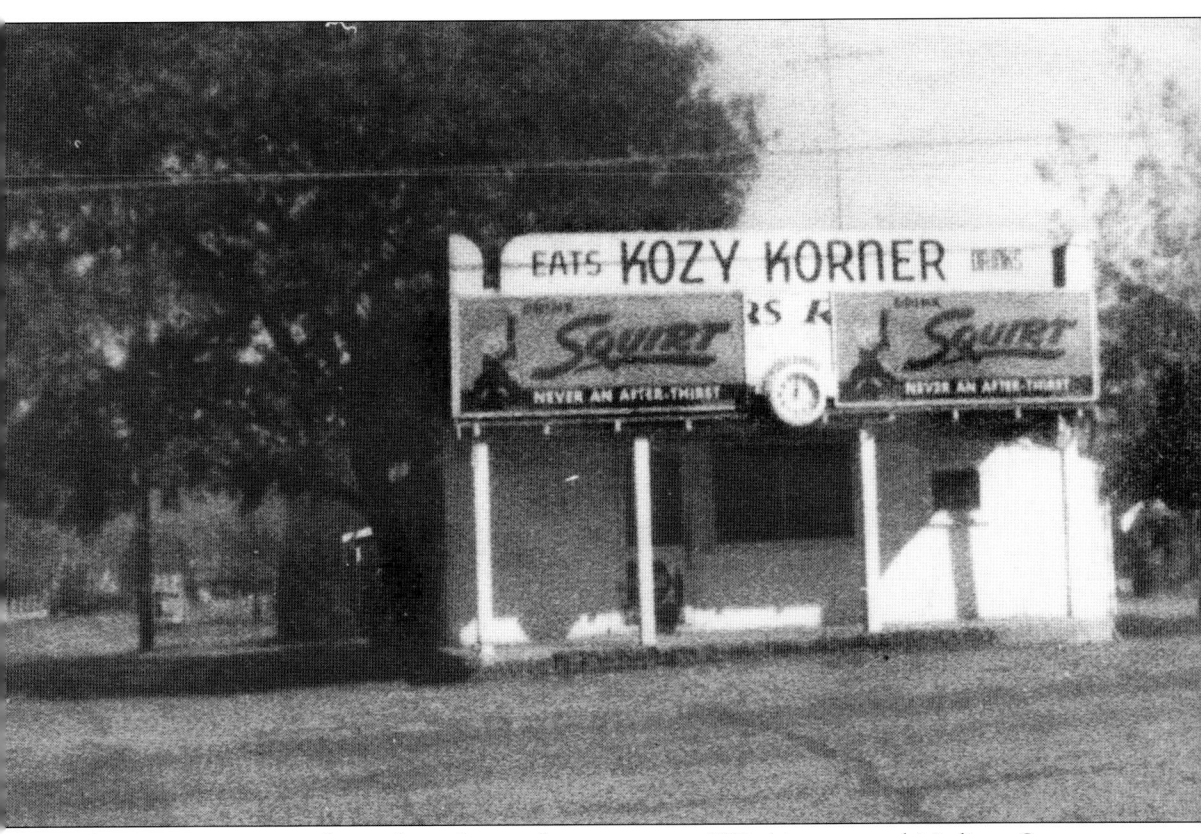

The Kozy Korner was located on the southeast corner of Washington and Madison Streets. Believed to have been constructed in the late 1920s, the building served as a small bar and grill and, later on, as a storage building for the Tonascia Market, which was located to the right of the right edge of this *c.* 1950 photograph. (Courtesy of Barbara and Bud Dulinsky.)

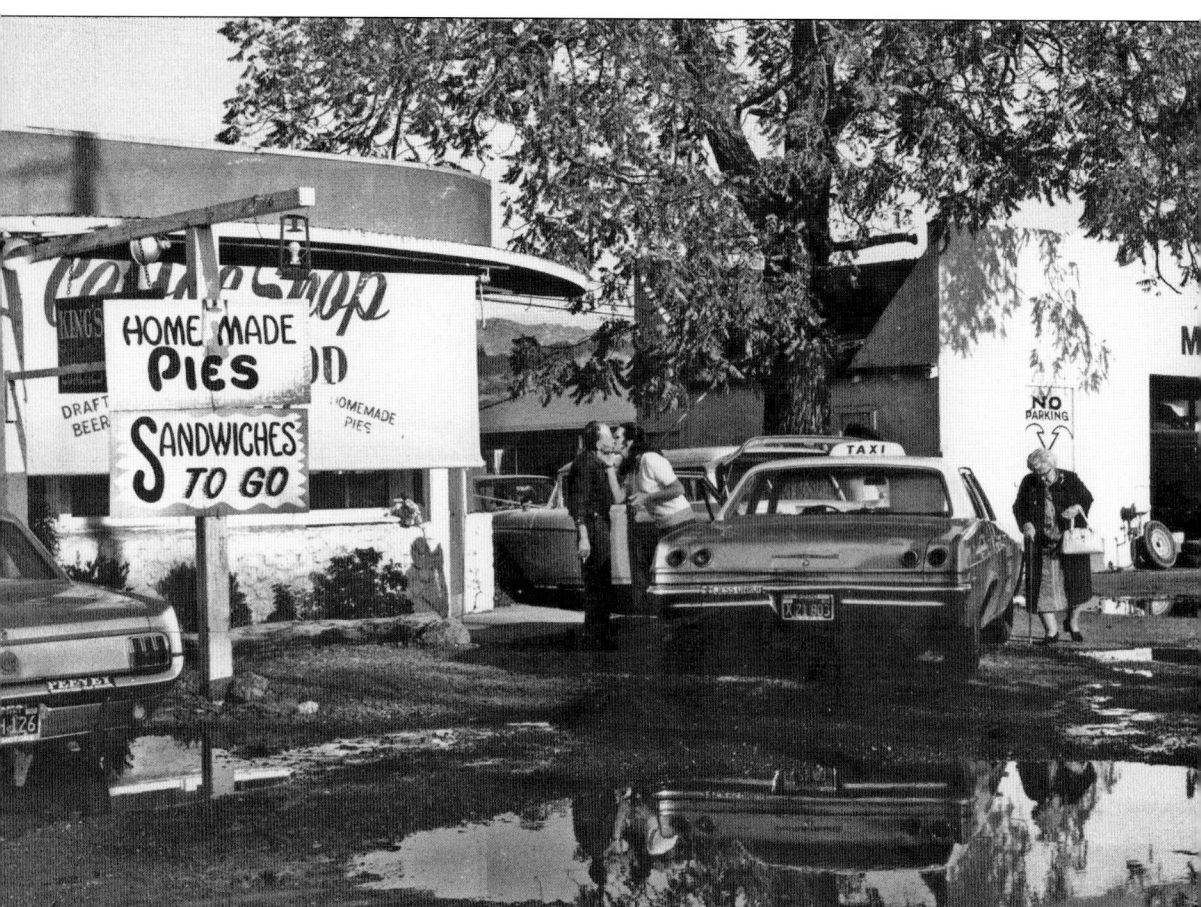

The "Y" intersection of Yount and Washington Streets dates to 1870. When Gottlieb Groezinger decided to add the "Groezinger Addition" to Yountville, his property line had to conform to the right-of-way from the preexisting railroad tracks. As Washington Street was surveyed in a southerly direction, the road had to deflect 24 degrees southeast until the merge with Yount Street. The "Y" Intersection building site has been the home of many Yountville businesses. This photograph shows the intersection as it looked in the early 1970s. The coffee shop on the left is the present-day location of Hurley's Restaurant. While the two people in the center of the image are unidentified, the older woman on the right is Mae Fugandus, a longtime Yountville resident also known as Missy Mae. (Courtesy of Curtis Van Carter.)

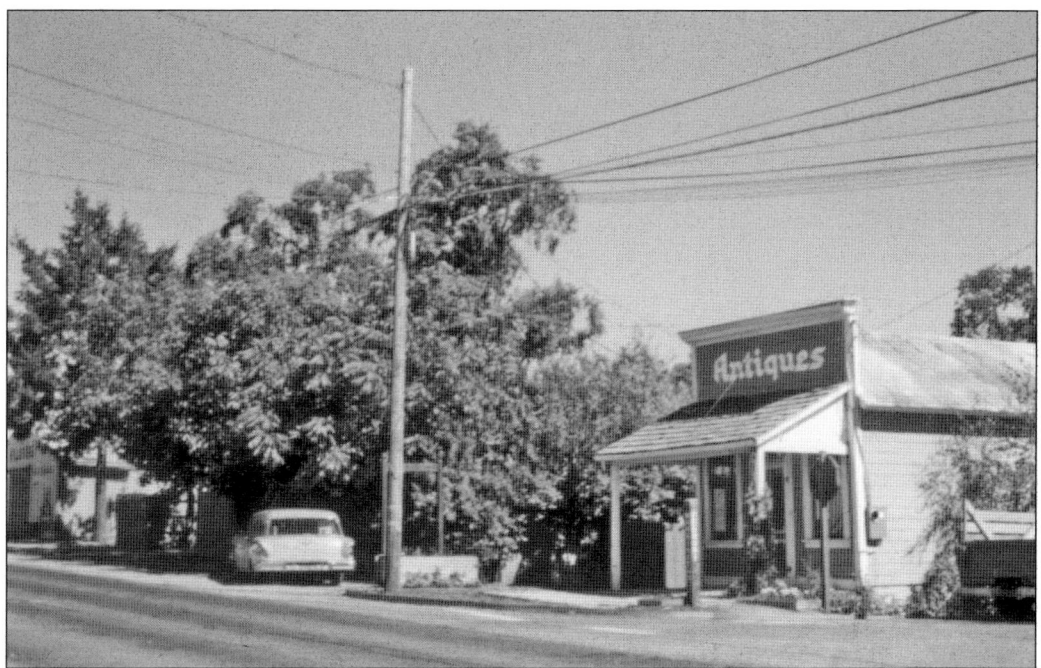

This small building has changed very little in 100 years. Like several other historic Yountville buildings, this structure has a false-front exterior with large sash windows. Originally built in the early 1900s, the building operated as a small dry-goods store. In the mid-1960s, the property housed an antique store. For the past 30 years, this building has been a private residence. This photograph dates to around 1970. (Courtesy of Mindy Jordan.)

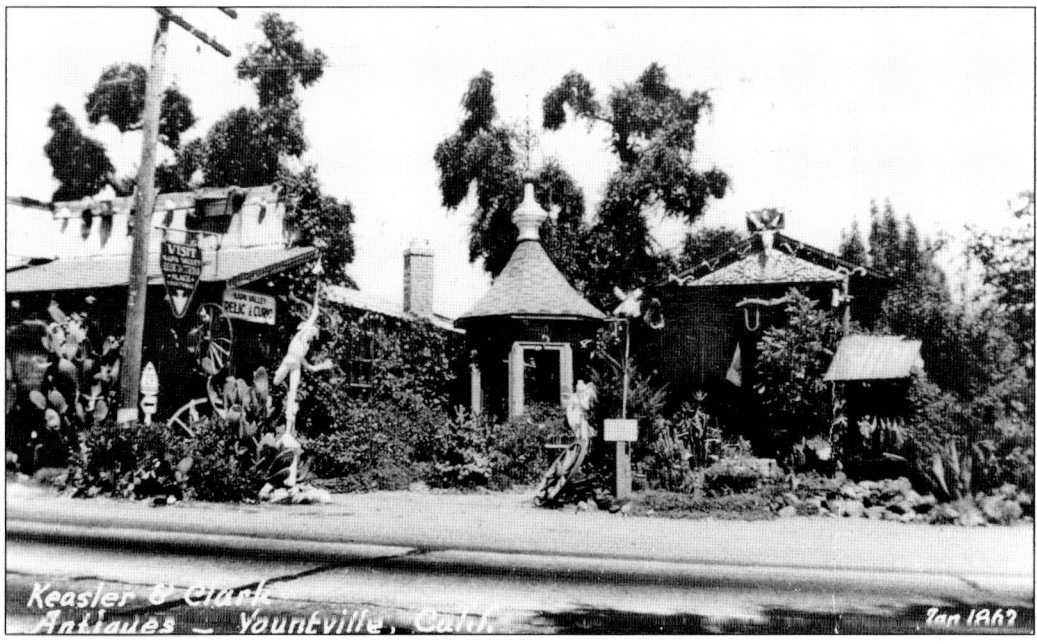

The Kessler and Clark Antiques store, pictured around 1970, was a local favorite for residents and visitors alike. The store was closed in 1989, and the gazebo was moved to its current location at the V Marketplace. (Courtesy of Barbara and Bud Dulinsky.)

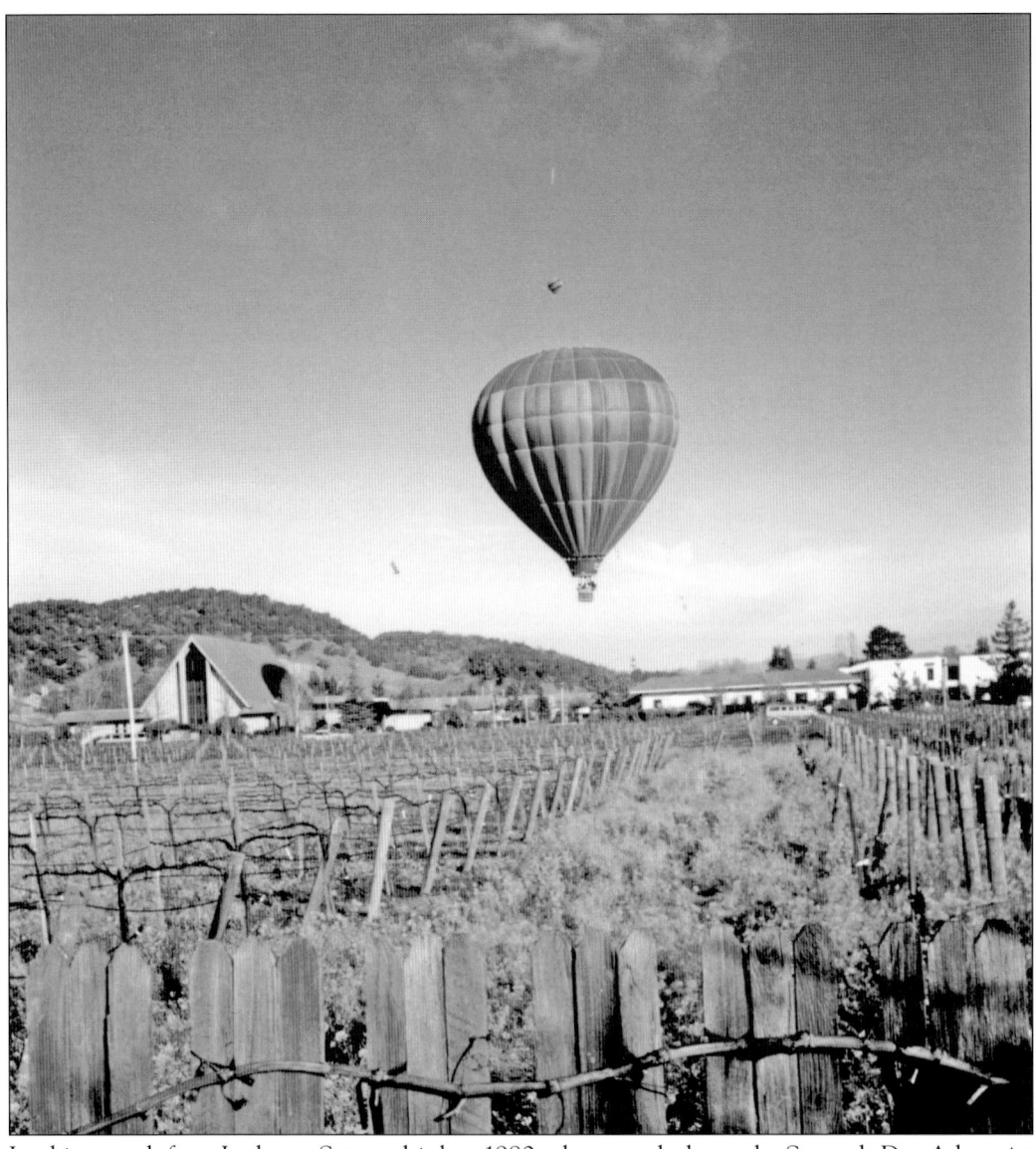
Looking north from Larkspur Street, this late-1980s photograph shows the Seventh-Day Adventist Church on Finnell Street. The land and vineyards, owned by the Bardessono family, would later be the site of the housing development known as Heritage Estates. (Courtesy of Denise Jackson.)

In 1978, the Town of Yountville, local nonprofit service clubs, and town residents decided to commemorate Yountville's rich historic past. Celebrated each year on October 5, the anniversary of George Yount's death is the annual Yountville Days and Parade Festival. The parade begins on the grounds of the Veterans Home and makes its way down California Drive, through town on Washington Street, and ends in the Yountville Park next to the Yountville Pioneer Cemetery. This 1985 photograph shows a tethered hot air balloon at the festival. (Photograph courtesy of Town of Yountville.)

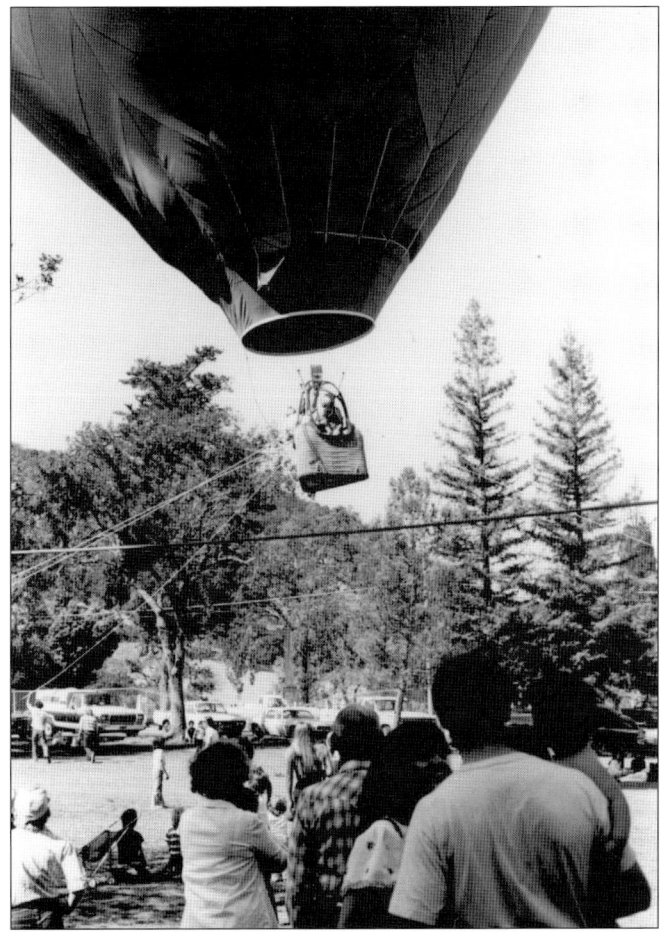

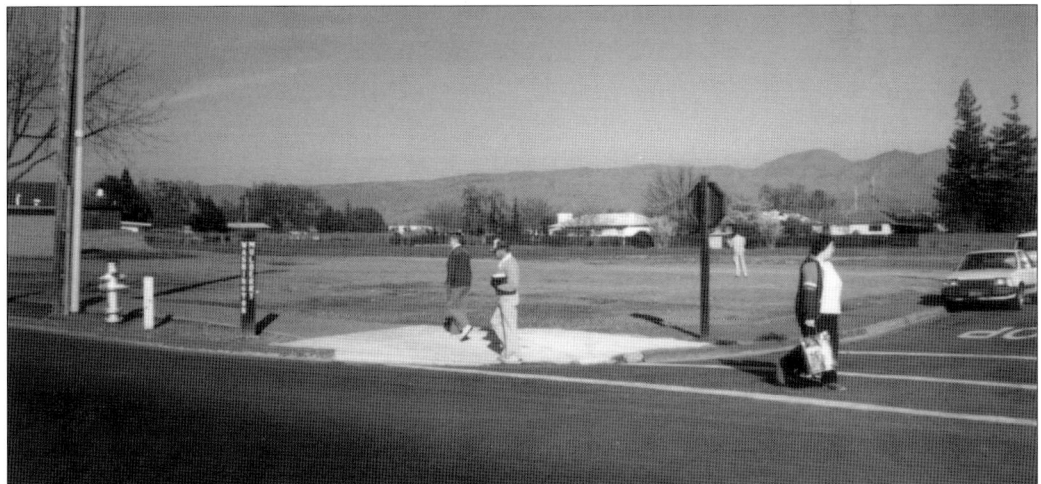

Over the years, the location of the Yountville Post Office has changed several times. In the late 1980s, plans were drawn for the construction of a new postal facility. This picture shows the site of the future post office to be located on the corner of Washington and Mulberry Streets. (Courtesy of the Town of Yountville.)

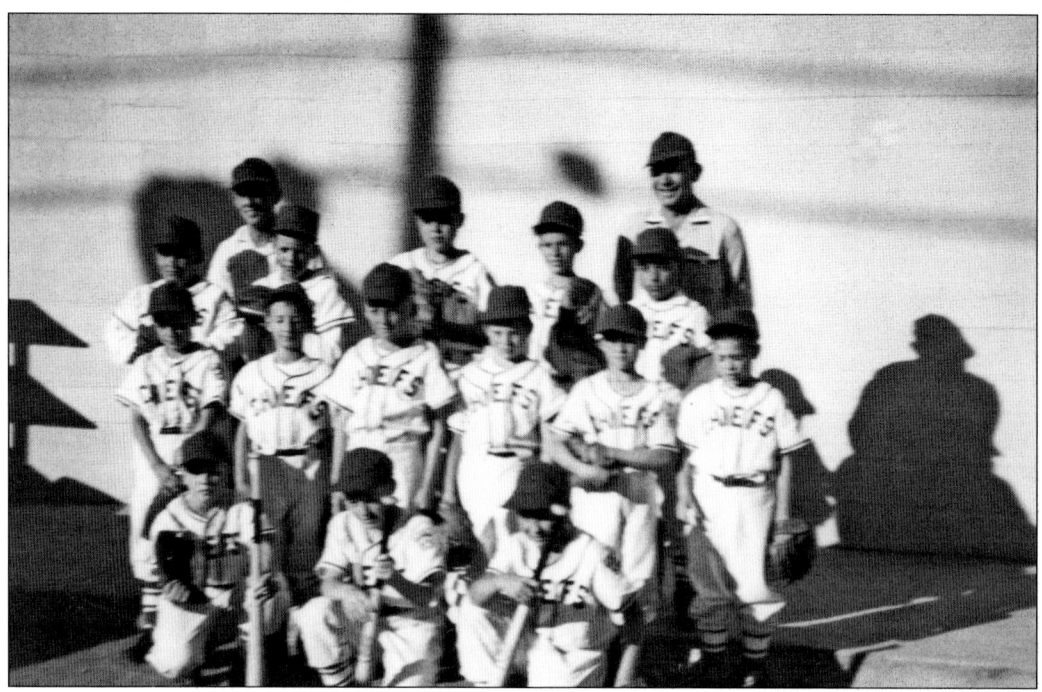

Baseball has been a popular pastime in Yountville for over 80 years. The baseball field, located in the back of the elementary school, was named Kaneshiro Field in honor of well-loved Yountville resident and baseball coach Richard Kaneshiro. Kaneshiro and his wife, Jan, were instrumental in coaching several generations of Yountville Little League youth. Richard and Jan's daughter, Jennifer Carvalho, continues the same tradition of caring for Yountville's children and currently serves as the supervisor of the Yountville Recreation Department. The first two established teams to wear Little League uniforms were the Yountville Chiefs (above) and the Yountville Giants. These photographs were both taken around 1970. (Both photographs courtesy of Barbara and Bud Dulinsky and Maxine Bardessono.)

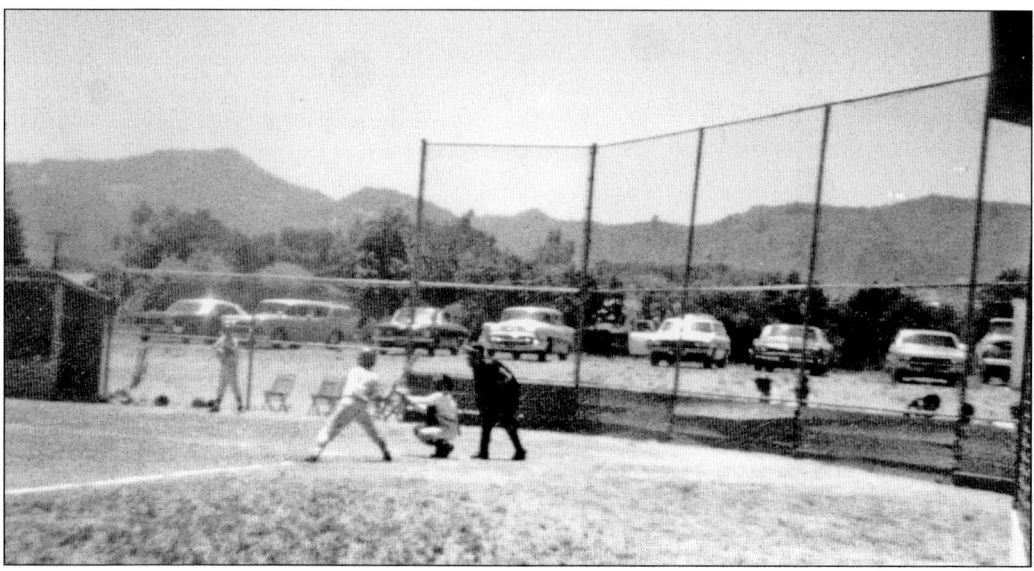

Six
Yountville Today

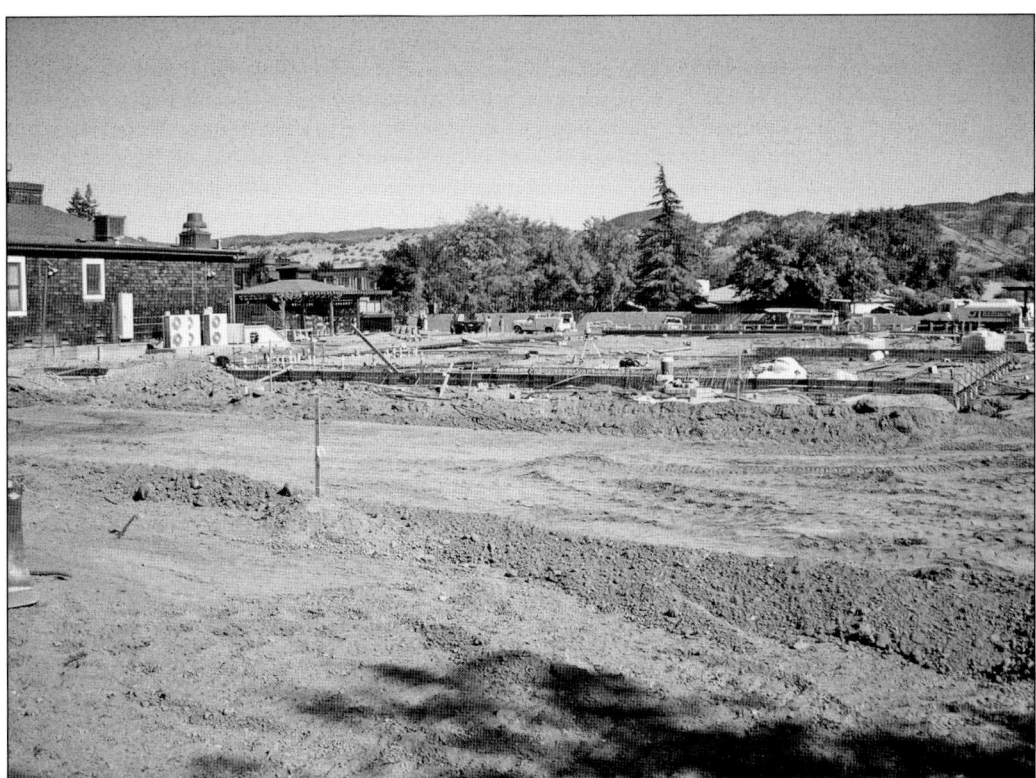

In 2008, ground was broken for the addition of a new Yountville Community Center. Located between the current location of the community hall and the post office on Washington Street, this center will house a new library, sheriff's office, and large community recreation center. (Courtesy of Beau Alexander.)

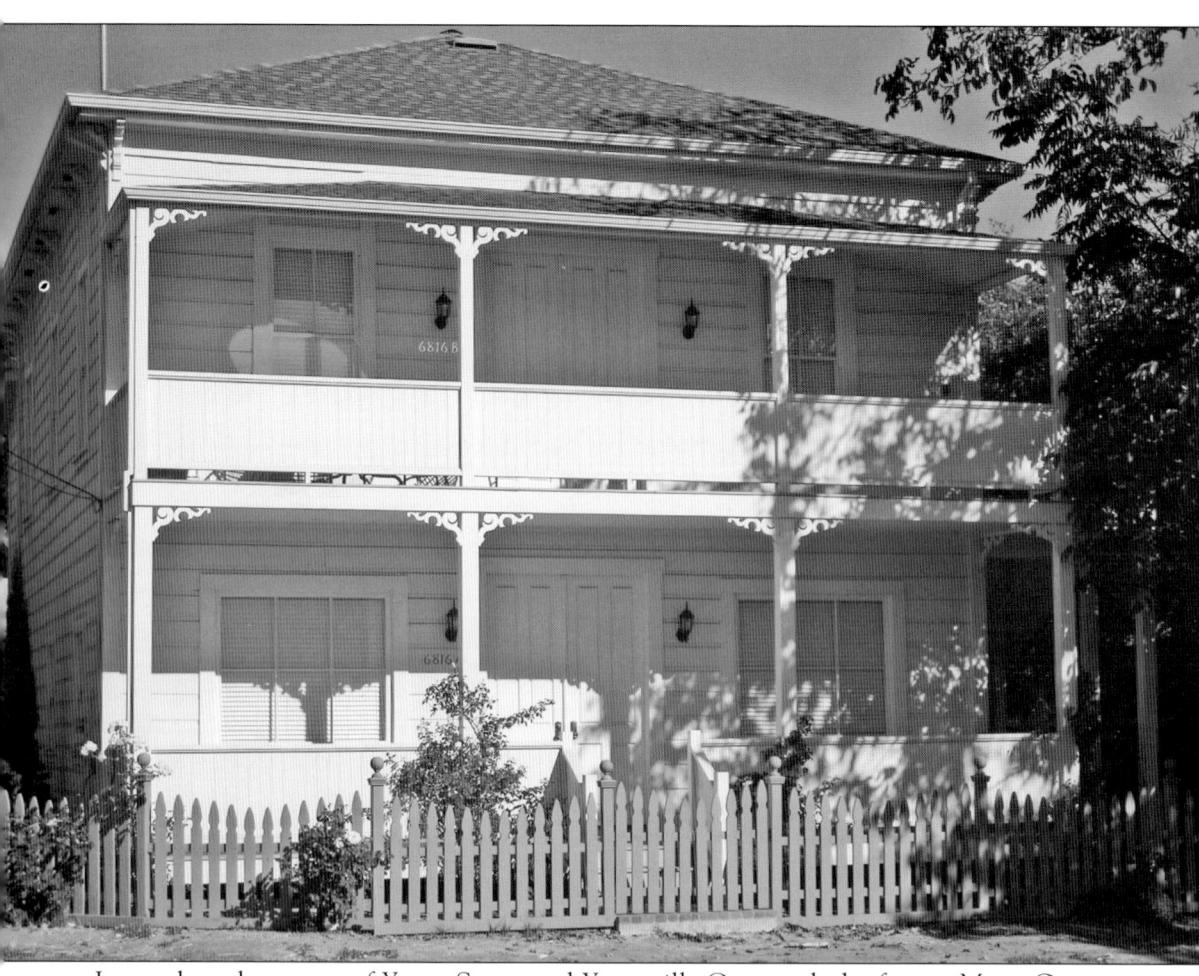

Located on the corner of Yount Street and Yountville Crossroad, the former Myers Grocery Company (see page 33) is now a remodeled building housing two families. This photograph was taken in 2008. (Courtesy of Stuart Alexander.)

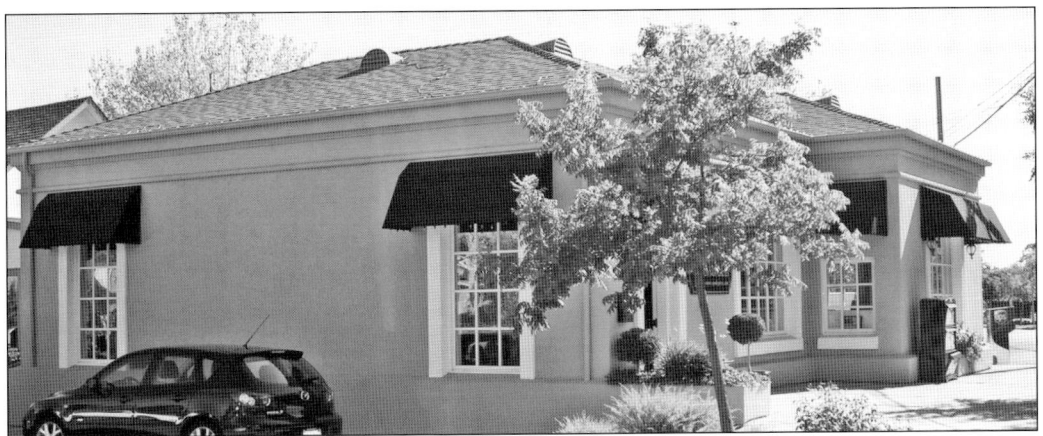

The old post office (see page 49) has seen many changes throughout the years. Pictured in 2008, it is now a real estate office. (Courtesy of Stuart Alexander.)

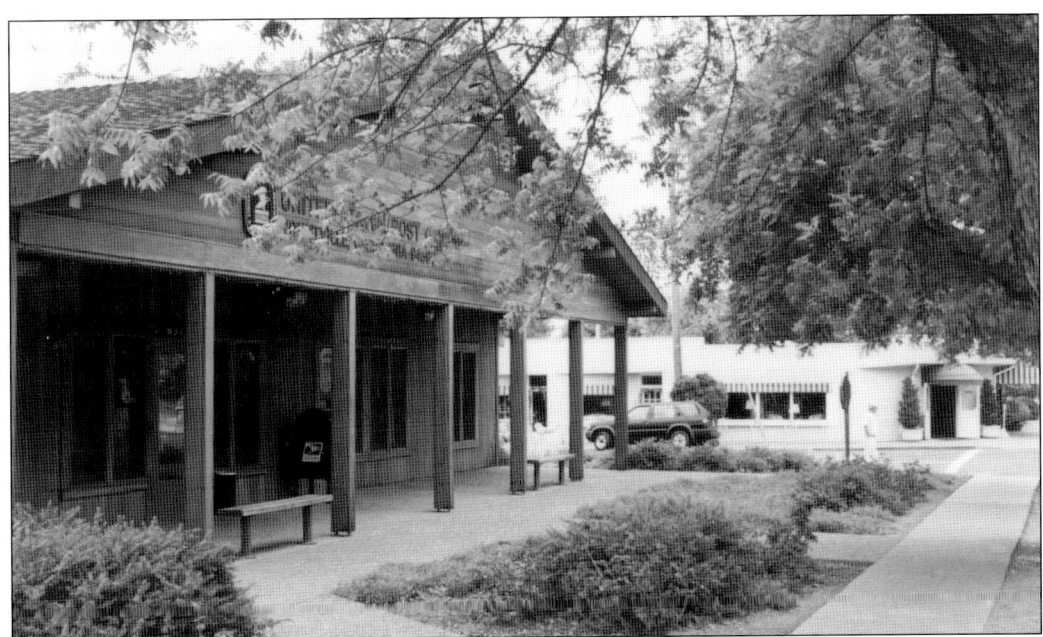

This 2008 photoraph shows the post office location on the corner of Washington and Mulberry Streets. (Courteys of Beau Alexander.)

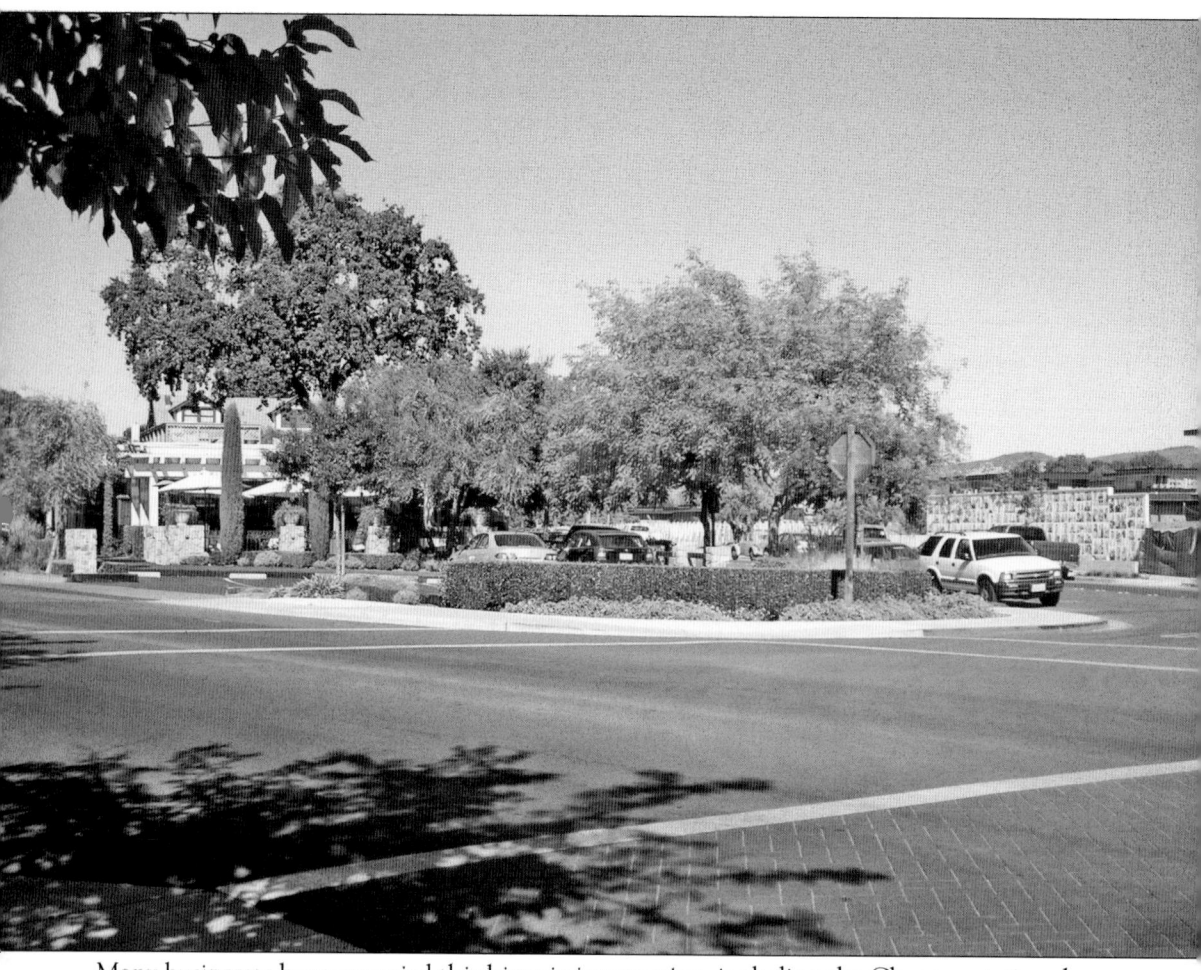

Many businesses have occupied this historic intersection, including the Chevron station shown on page 98. Pictured in 2008, the restaurant currently operating at this location belongs to famous chef Bob Hurley of Hurley's Restaurant and Bar. (Courtesy of Stuart Alexander.)

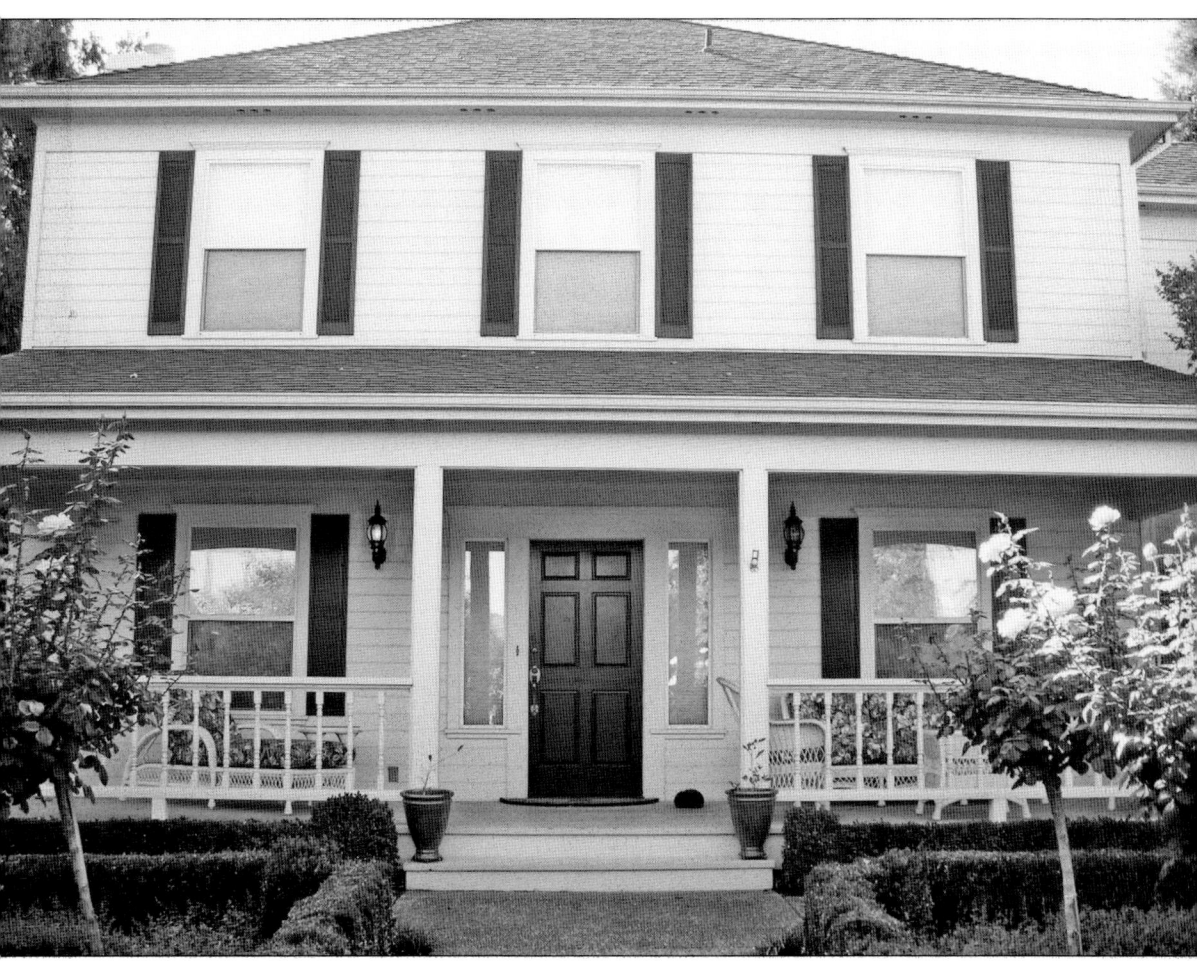

The Casaday house, shown early in its life on page 47, has changed little over the past 90 years and still maintains the charming Yountville character of days gone by. It is pictured here in 2008. (Courtesy of Stuart Alexander.)

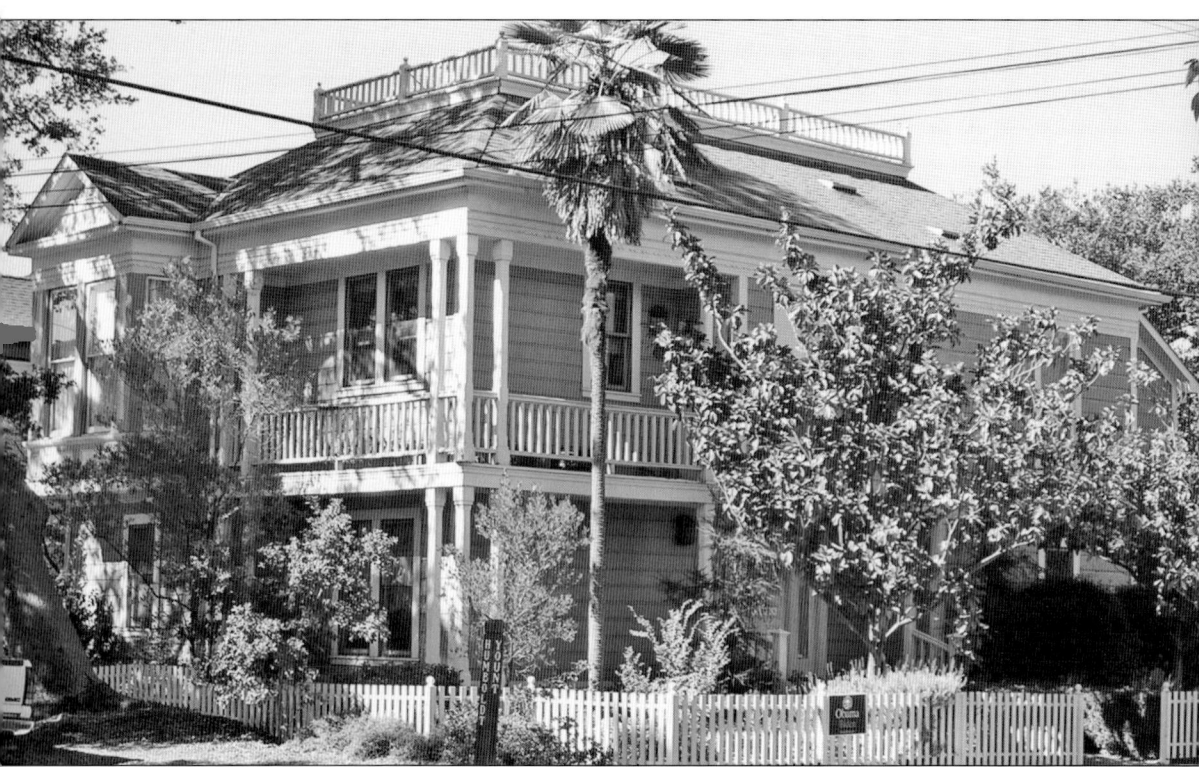

The Whitten house in 2008 looks very different from how it looked in the early 1900s (see page 46). These changes came about through extensive restoration and remodeling, including the addition of a second story. (Courtesy of Stuart Alexander.)

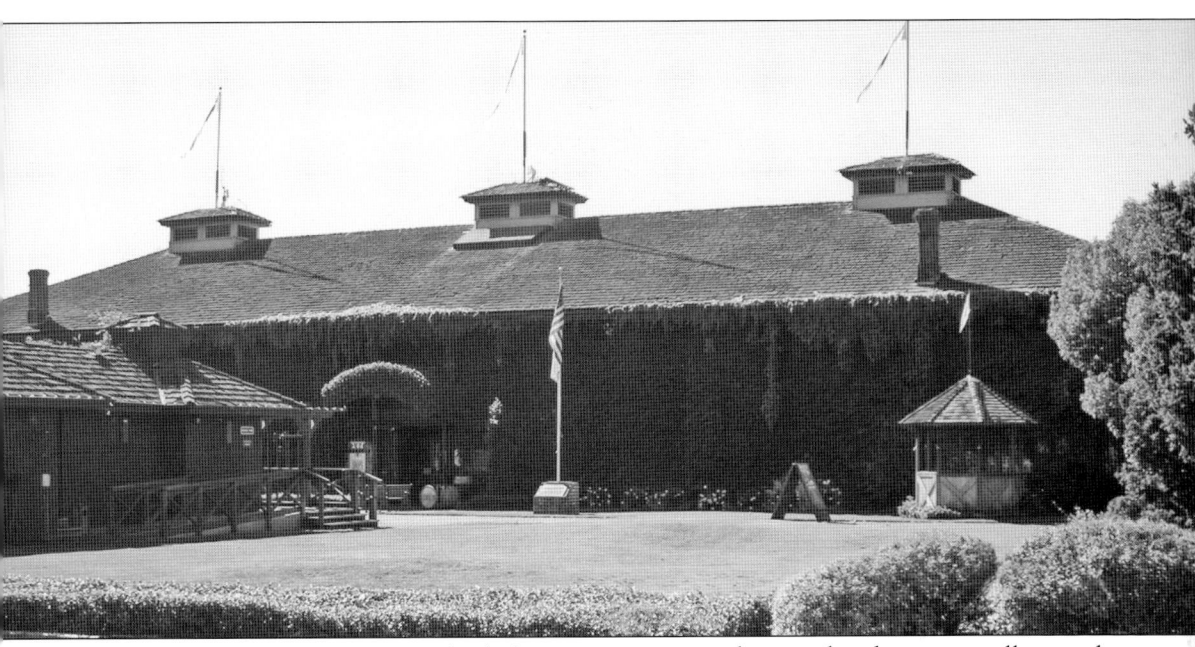

The former Groezinger Winery, which for many years was the popular shopping mall named Vintage 1870, continues to serve Yountville residents and tourists as V Marketplace. Pictured here in 2008, the winery is shown in its original form on page 26. (Courtesy of Stuart Alexander.)

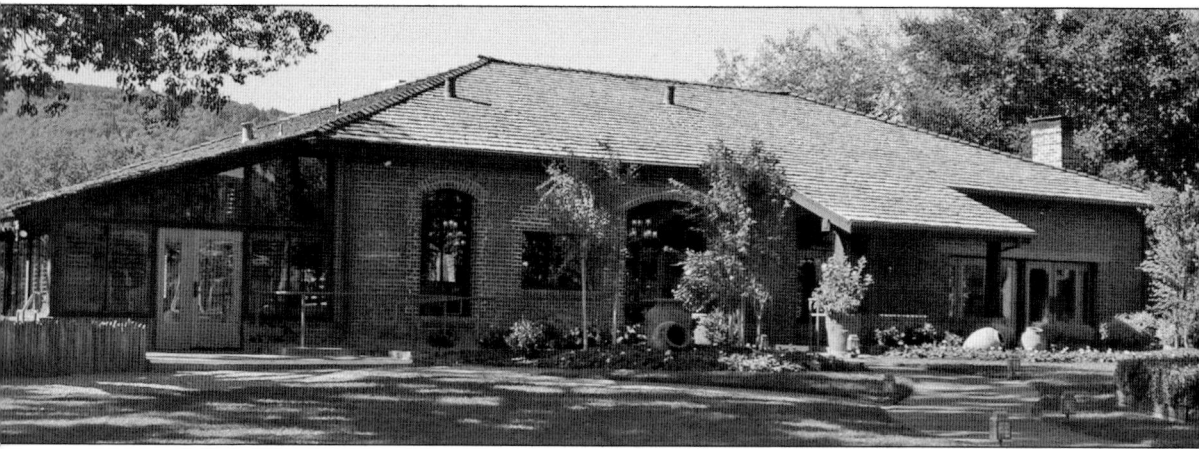

This historic structure was rebuilt from the bricks of the Groezinger Mansion. Later on, it was the site of the popular Yountville Restaurant, Compadres Mexican Bar and Grill. Pictured in 2008, the site is used today as a banquet hall for the service needs of V Marketplace. (Courtesy of Stuart Alexander.)

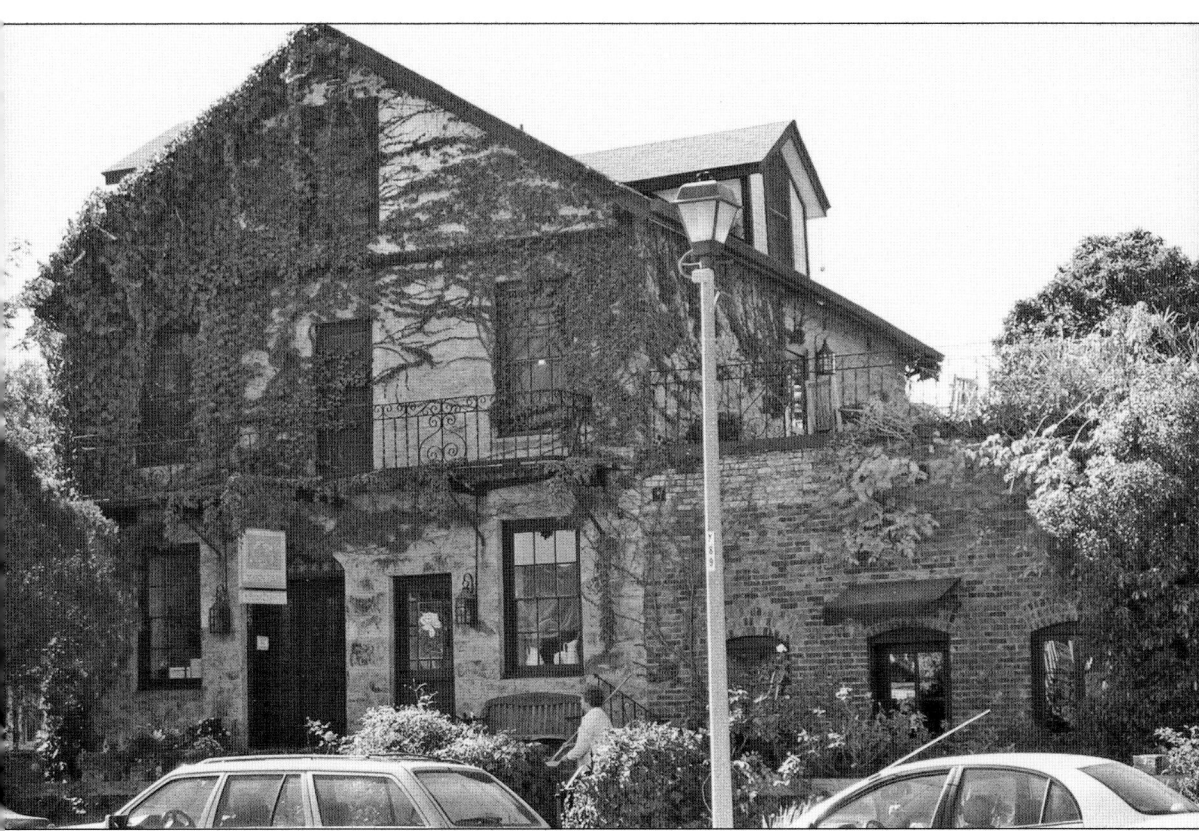

Pictured here in 2008, the Magnolia Hotel has remained one of Yountville's original historic pioneer structures for 138 years. Since its remodel in the early 1980s, the hotel has been providing charming accommodations for both residents and visitors of Yountville. (Courtesy of Stuart Alexander.)

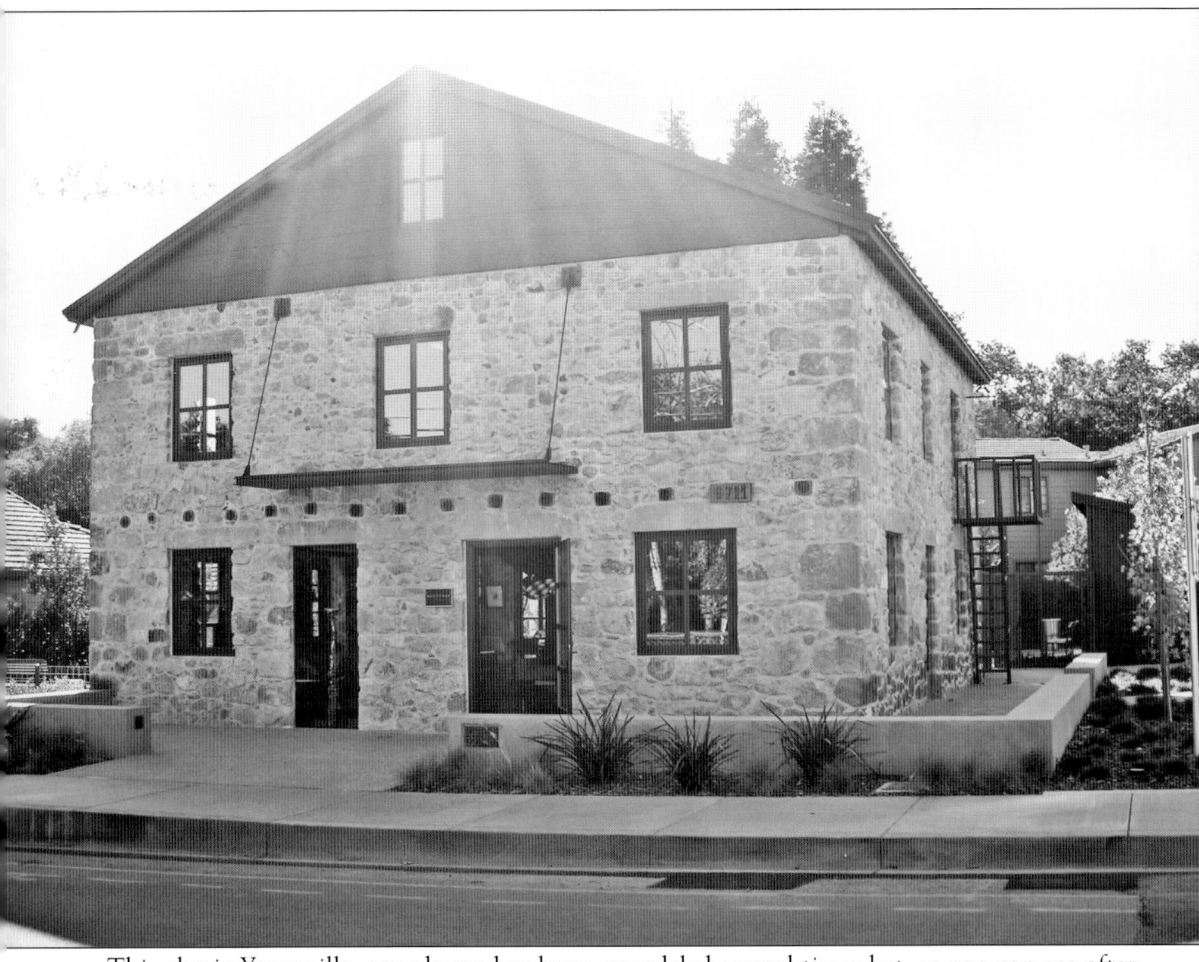

This classic Yountville stone home has been remodeled several times but, as one can see after comparing the images on page 37, retains its original architecture. The historic Charles Rovegno house was completely restored in 2008 and now serves both Yountville visitors and residents as a wine and art gallery. (Courtesy of Stuart Alexander.)

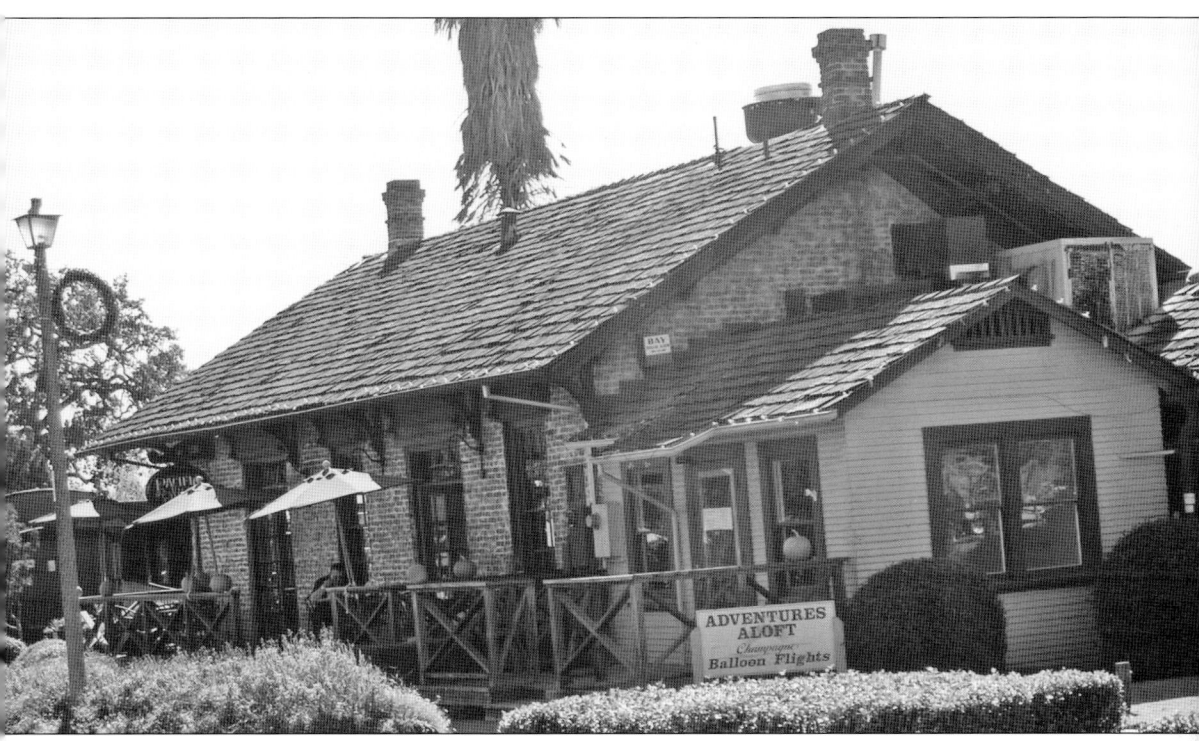

Shown on page 40 during the time of its original purpose as a railroad depot, this structure now hosts the popular Pacific Blues Café. This café, pictured in 2008, is well known by locals and tourists alike for great breakfasts and live music on weekends. (Courtesy of Stuart Alexander.)

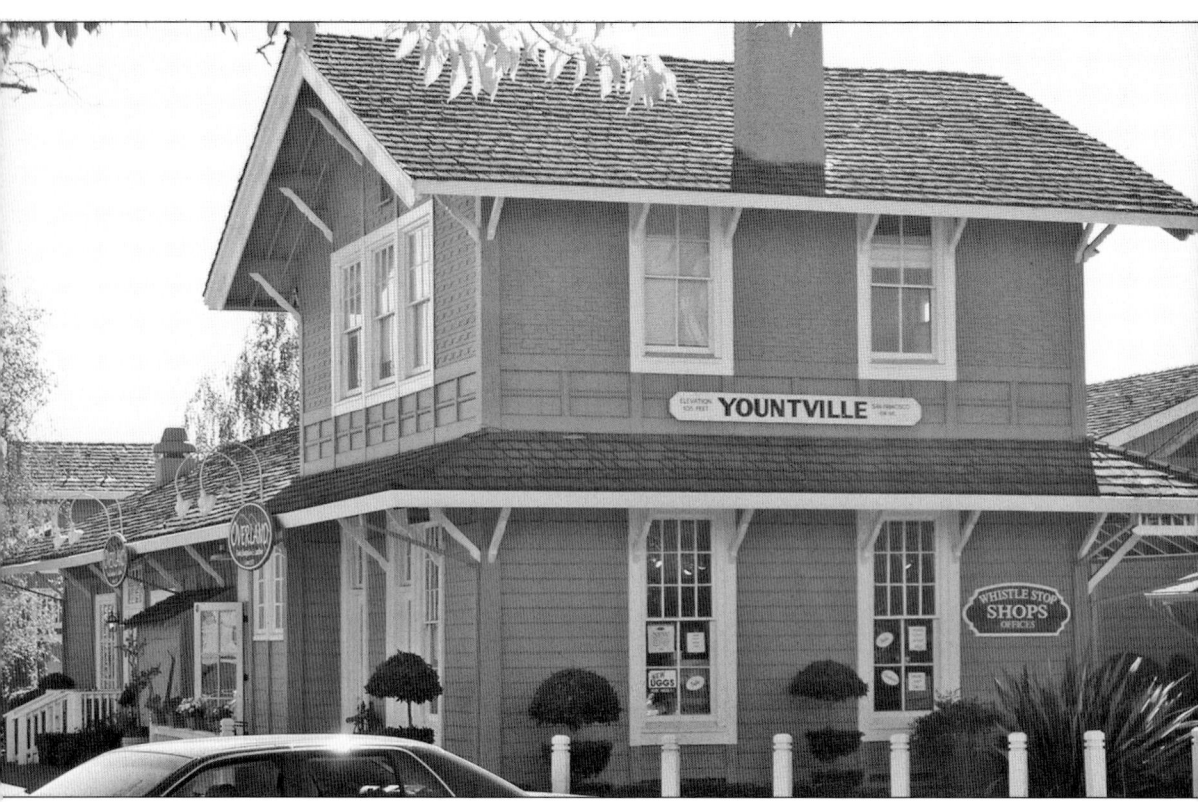

Now home to a modern specialty clothing and accessory store, this former railroad depot still looks as it did over 100 years ago (see page 41). (Courtesy of Stuart Alexander.)

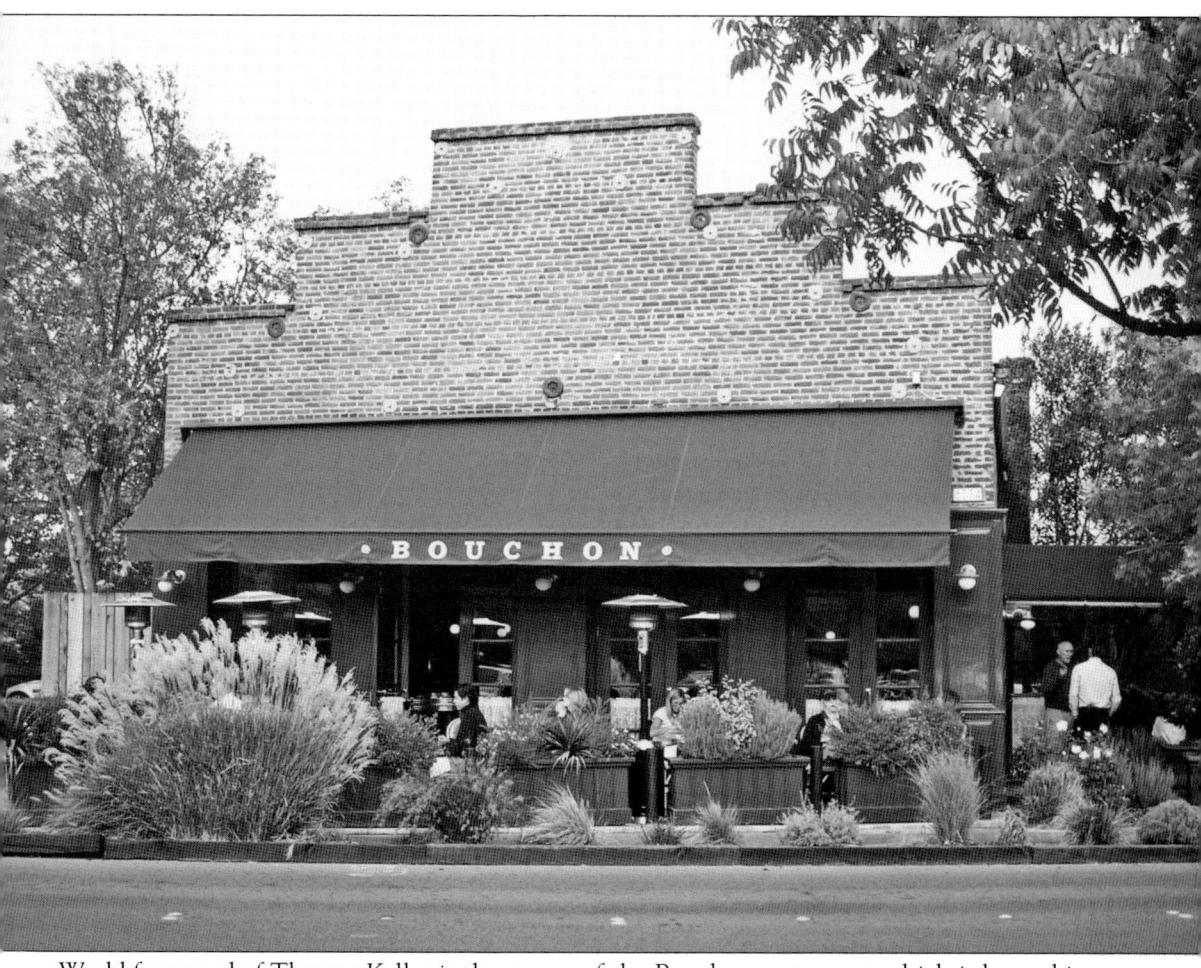

World-famous chef Thomas Keller is the owner of the Bouchon restaurant, which is housed in what was originally known as the Gibbs Building. (Courtesy of Aren Alexander.)

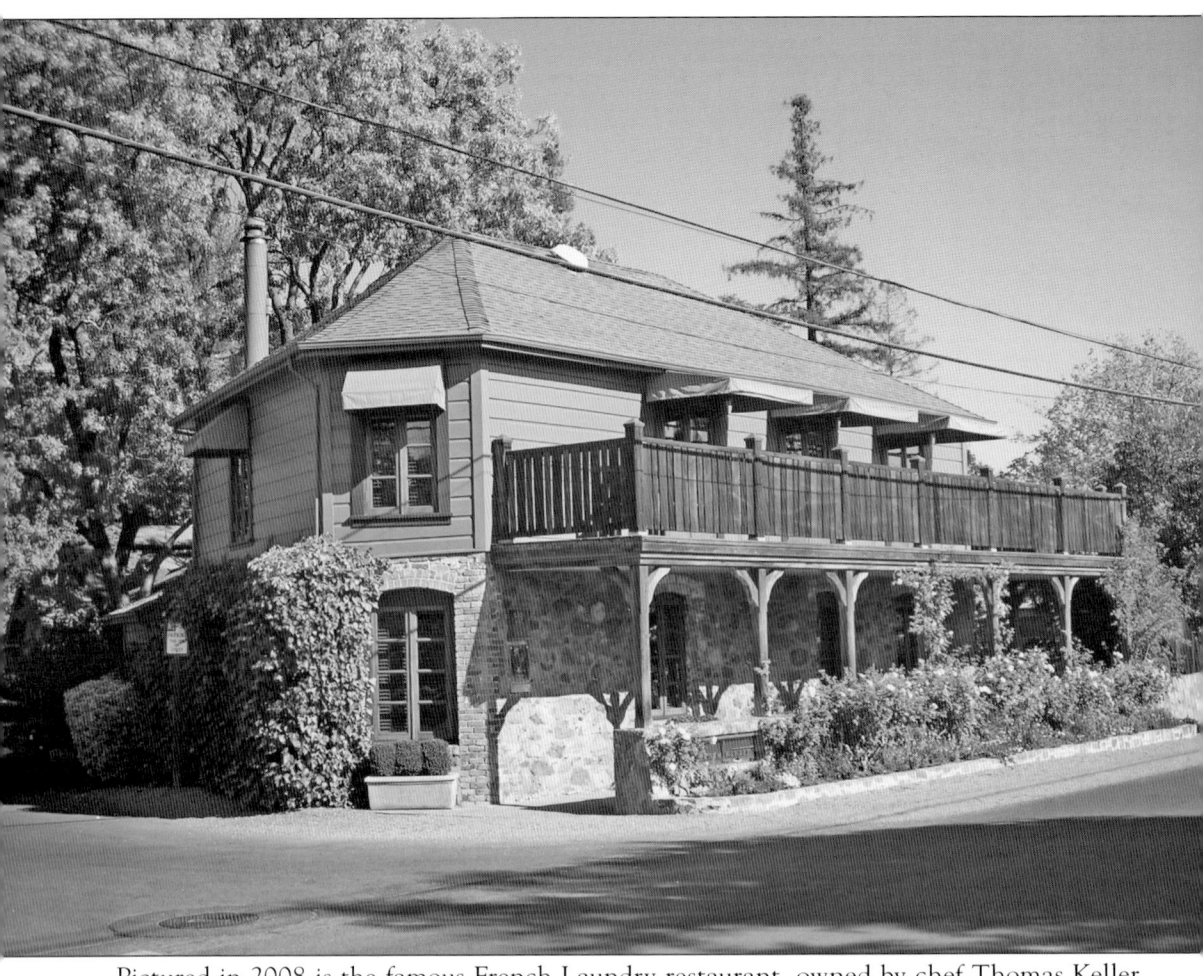

Pictured in 2008 is the famous French Laundry restaurant, owned by chef Thomas Keller. The building once housed a French-style steam laundry service (see page 29). (Courtesy of Alora Alexander.)

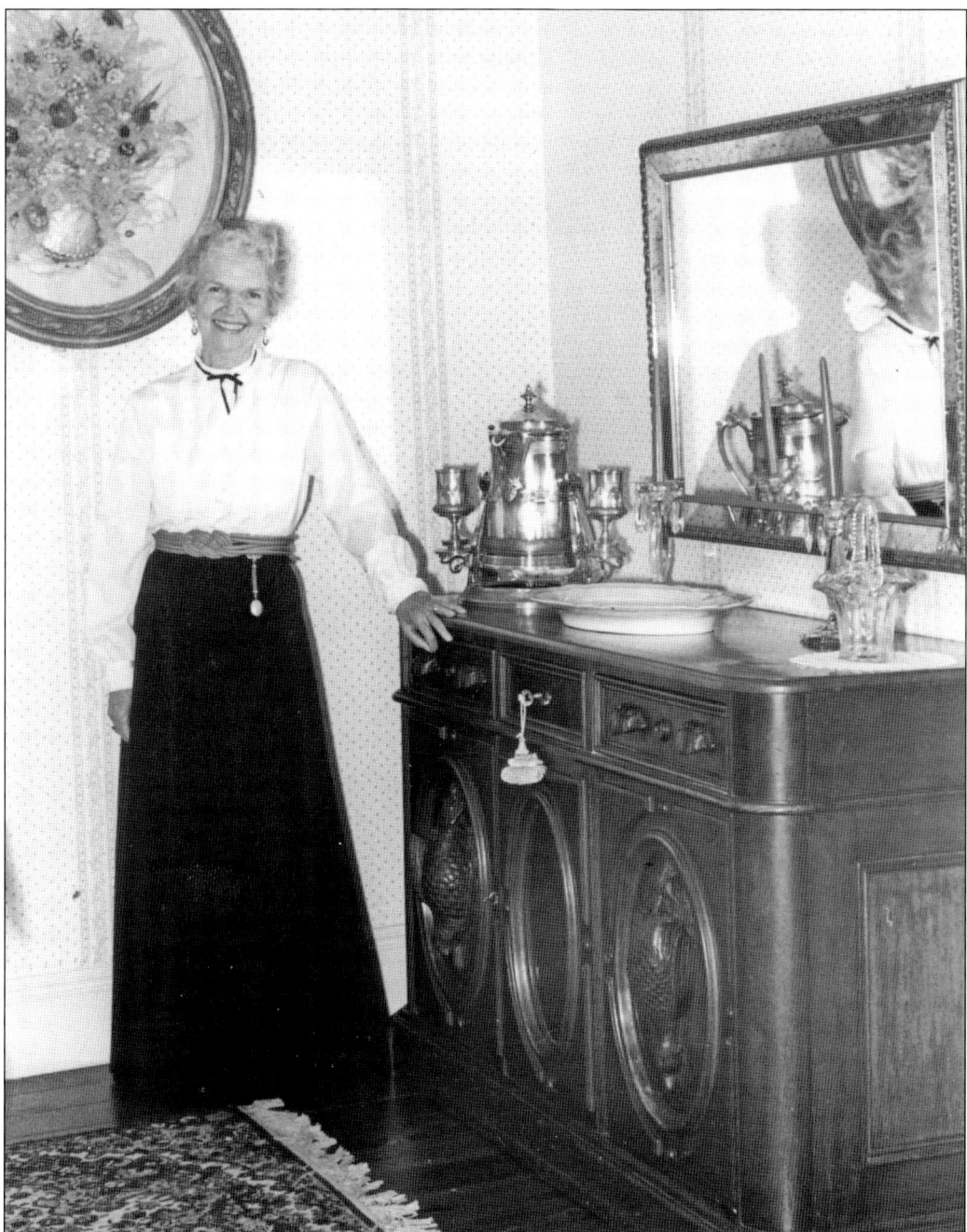

Meredie "Toni" Porterfield is an active researcher and biographer of her great-great-great-grandfather, George Yount. Toni has volunteered research information for both the Sharpsteen Museum in Calistoga and the Napa Historical Society in Napa, California. In 1993, Toni donated the dining room furniture belonging to her famous pioneer ancestor to the Sharpsteen Museum. In this 1993 photograph, Toni stands next to the sideboard that served five generations of George Yount descendants. (Courtesy of Meredie Porterfield.)

Across America, People are Discovering Something Wonderful. Their Heritage.

Arcadia Publishing is the leading local history publisher in the United States. With more than 5,000 titles in print and hundreds of new titles released every year, Arcadia has extensive specialized experience chronicling the history of communities and celebrating America's hidden stories, bringing to life the people, places, and events from the past. To discover the history of other communities across the nation, please visit:

www.arcadiapublishing.com

Customized search tools allow you to find regional history books about the town where you grew up, the cities where your friends and family live, the town where your parents met, or even that retirement spot you've been dreaming about.

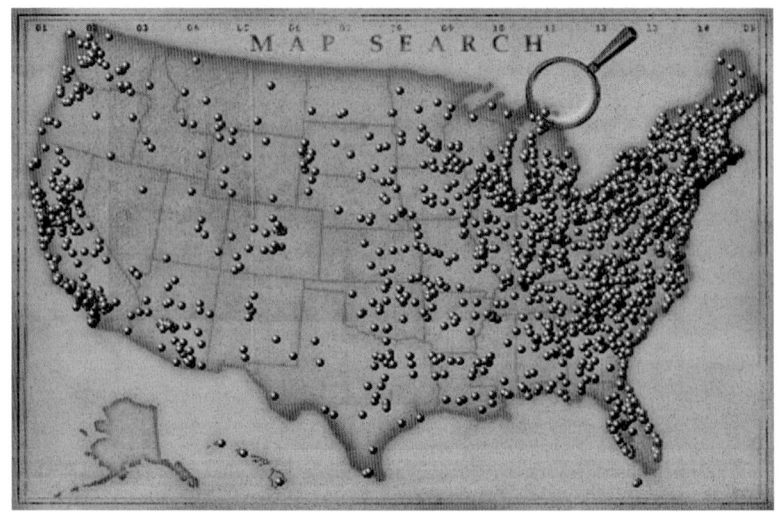